THE LESS TRAVELED ROAD

Other Books by Rev. M. Raymond, O.C.S.O.

Burnt Out Incense

Three Religious Rebels

The Family That Overtook Christ

The Man Who Got Even With God

God Goes to Murderer's Row

Trappists, the Reds, and You

A New Way of the Cross

THE ROAD NOT TAKEN*

Two roads diverged in a yellow wood,
And sorry I could not travel both
And be one traveler, long I stood
And looked down one as far as I could
To where it bent in the undergrowth;

Then took the other, oh, just as fair,
And having perhaps the better claim
Because it was grassy and wanted wear;
Though as for that the passing there
Had worn them really about the same,

And both that morning equally lay
In leaves no step had trodden black.
Oh, I kept the first for another day!
Yet knowing how way leads on to way,
I doubted if I should ever come back.

I shall be telling this with a sigh
Somewhere ages and ages hence:
Two roads diverged in a wood, and I —
I took the one less travelled by,
And that has made all the difference.

ROBERT FROST

DOM MARY FREDERIC DUNNE, o.c.s.o.,
at the time of his election as
Abbot of Gethsemani
February 6, 1935

THE
LESS TRAVELED
ROAD

A Memoir of
Dom Mary Frederic Dunne, o.c.s.o.
First American Trappist Abbot

By REV. M. RAYMOND, o.c.s.o.

THE BRUCE PUBLISHING COMPANY • MILWAUKEE

Nihil obstat:
    Fr. Maurice Mulloy, O.C.S.O.
    Fr. Paul Burne, O.C.S.O.

Imprimi potest:
    Most Rev. Abbot General, Dom M. Gabriel Sortais, O.C.S.O.

Nihil obstat:
    John A. Schulien, S.T.D., Censor librorum

Imprimatur:
    ✠ Roman R. Atkielski, D.D.
        Administrator Sede Vacante Archidioecesis Milwauchiensis

Die 24 Augusti, 1953

TO

REV. J. P. F., S.J.

   IN

LOVING FRATERNAL TRIBUTE
      FOR
YOUR SACERDOTAL SILVER JUBILEE

YOU HAVE WALKED THE LESS TRAVELED ROAD

FOR AND WITH

HIM

Contents

viii   *Contents*

The Less Traveled Road

The Facts of the Case

*A*MERICA is astonishing. . . ."

Thus cried one of the most heroic figures of World War II. It was wrung from him by — of all things — the cloistered contemplative life in America.

Early in the war, Father Raymond Bruckberger was a member of the fearless French commandos. When his country fell, he became Chaplain General of those greater fighters and more fearless men, the *Résistance* groups. In 1951 he came to our shores. He was with us only a few months when he became both enthusiastic and prophetic. For first he found a convent of cloistered contemplatives in — of all places — *Hollywood*. Then he learned it was frequented more and more by those whom he called "stars from a lower heaven." Next he was told that this was but one of more than ten such convents of cloistered Dominicans in America. Surprise mounted to astonishment and turned almost to consternation before changing into a determination to learn as much as possible about the cloistered contemplative life in our country. He was especially anxious to see if it was being cultivated by men as generously as it was by women. And when he discovered that America has more Trappist monks than any other country in the world he could not suppress his cry of astonishment nor keep from adding: "This flowering of the contemplative life seems to me as important here as atomic research."

To some of us it seems more important. That is why we pray

1

so earnestly for the fulfillment — and that soon! — of the prophecy this brave priest uttered when he said: "Some day the prayers of these children of God will burst on the world like the bomb of Bikini."

It is no wonder that this man grows exclamatory; for the fact is that in this land of crass materialism and multimillionaires, where seventy million people admit they have no Church affiliation whatsoever, Religion, and that in its highest flight and purest form, has suddenly assumed an ascendancy it seems to have lost in the so-called Catholic countries of the Old World. In a land where ninety-five million radios blare jazz and jungle music night and day, *Silence* is exerting such an attraction that youth is literally overcrowding cloisters. And where it is quite ordinary to have sixty and seventy thousand people throng a stadium to watch a major league ball game, and eighty-two thousand cheer themselves hoarse over capers on a single college gridiron, utter *Solitude* and deepest *Seclusion* are suddenly winning recruits in such numbers that, as Father Bruckberger puts it: "the Trappists each year have to send some to other orders, because they cannot keep them all."

He was stating fact; for Trappists are making many Americans God-conscious — and this God-consciousness is making many Americans Trappists.

In his very first book about us — *One Sky to Share* — the French Dominican wrote: "This aspiration to prayer of a whole section of American youth seems as meaningful to me as the élan of the whole people toward the defense of Korea. It is proof that America poses problems in all their dimensions and wishes to solve them on the levels on which they are presented."

To solve this problem of the Trappists, and solve it on its own level, is the purpose of this book. That level is higher than the "one sky we share"; it is up beyond the stars, for it is found in God the Holy Ghost and in the eternal, divine designs He has on America.

Here are the facts of the case. . . .

For almost a century the Trappist way of life, that of the cloistered contemplative, attracted no native-born Americans. A handful of Frenchmen fought for existence down at Gethsemani, Kentucky; a few Irishmen did the same out at Peosta, Iowa; while up at Valley Falls, Rhode Island, a group of French-Canadians engaged in the same fierce struggle. Extinction seemed ever imminent, and was staved off only by securing replacements from the mother houses in Europe and recruits from foreign lands.

But now, all that is changed. Lately, something marvelous has happened. The three monasteries, which for decades on decades have had about them the atmosphere of death and decay, suddenly stir with buoyant, vigorous life. Grizzled and bent monks still make their slow-paced way about the cloisters, but at every turn are met with youngsters simply abounding with energy; buildings which had merited the slur of Renan, because of their "vastness, emptiness, and lack of solidity," are suddenly found filled beyond capacity; communities which had had to plead the possibility of another French Revolution with its consequent expulsion as an excuse to continue their meager existence in this pagan land, suddenly find themselves faced with the necessity of making foundations of their own or allowing American vocations to go unanswered.

How explain this seemingly un-American phenomenon which suddenly has become an all-American fact?

Some point to the dust clearing away from Hiroshima and to the Iron Curtain creeping relentlessly over Europe and Asia; others to the blasting of our "brave new world" by the bombers of World War II; and still others to the cringing fear of the annihilating potentialities of atomic fission gripping our civilization.

But that these are merely contributing factors and not the real cause is evidenced by what is going on in the other five continents. They are far more cognizant of the ruin left by the late World

War than are we. And each has more reason to shudder because of the threat of annihilation slumbering in those implements which now lie ready for the next world war; for they well know who will feel the impact first. Yet, nowhere are cloisters being so crowded and the contemplative life so richly cultivated as in America. We, the most modern and progressive people in our very progressive and modern world, are startling that world by a return to the monasticism of the Middle Ages and the building of a second Thebaid. What is the explanation? What is drawing American youth to contemplative cloisters?

Surely, no one will say they are "being drawn by the cords of Adam." For they come from surroundings in which TV's are more common than V 8's; from a milieu in which hotels and even hospitals have radios in every room, and movie palaces rise on almost every city block. They go to a place where they will never even glimpse a baseball, football, basketball, or golf ball; to a place where they will never be allowed a single invigorating swim in the summer or a blood-stirring skate in the winter; to a place where the innocent enjoyment of a recreational walk in the woods or along the street is perpetually denied them, and where they will never be given the pleasure of anything like a companionable chat for the space of a single cigarette. They go from all the noise, news, attractions, and distractions of our bustling modern world to silence, solitude, and the simple manual labor of an ordinary dirt farmer. No, no sane man will ever say they are "being drawn by the cords of Adam" — at least not by those of the first Adam! What, then, is drawing them?

The ultimate answer, of course, is God. For He is the Seeker and the Sought; the Prime Mover and the Ultimate Rest; and it is He who has given that desire which is "natural to mankind, for the active repose of the soul, breathing what is eternal." Man wants God. Man has ever wanted Him. Man ever will. But that simplification of our problem only complicates it. For God, the

First Cause and Creator of us all, uses, as secondary causes, His creatures. And our question is focused on these. What or who is God using so to awaken American youth to their manhood, that they find it, in its deepest depths, to be a craving for a share in the Godhood?

Inscrutable indeed are the ways of God. He alone can plumb the final fathom of His own Divine Providence. But we do not err when we seek plausible explanations for palpable facts, and in secondary causes an elucidation of the work of the Primal. That our youth is not being pulled to Cistercian cloisters by the cords of Adam is practically self-evident, but that they are being held there by the cross of the Second Adam can be made manifest by drawing up a memoir to the man under whom this movement began and during whose short abbatial career it reached such startling heights.

It is not a philosophical fallacy we are about to commit; it is simply a refusal to blink an historical fact. We are not saying *"post hoc, ergo propter hoc";* we are merely stating that it was in 1935 the influx to Trappists cloisters really began; that by 1945 it had reached a puzzling high; and that by the summer of 1948 both Europe and America were amazed — and those are the years Frederic M. Dunne ruled Gethsemani. When his hand first closed over his crozier there were but 70 men in his community and only two other monasteries in these United States, with a combined personnel of less than 120 monks. As he lay in the crude black box which served as coffin, his crozier still in his hand, Gethsemani was housing 172 religious, had already made two foundations and completed plans for two more. He was not two years dead when those foundations had been made, the mother house was shattering a six-hundred-year-old record by holding more than 270 men within her stern gray walls, and the United States could boast of ten monasteries of Trappist monks, with a combined personnel of almost a thousand.

Countless, and varied indeed, were the instruments God used to bring these many recruits to Gethsemani: the chivalry of giving one's life to God attracted some; the challenge to be as Christlike as it is humanly possible attracted others; a salutary selfishness prompted the careful to lay hold on the surest means within reach for the salvation of their own immortal souls; while the altruism of living every moment of every day for the souls of others brought the generous. Practically every means under the sun, from success and failure to sanctity and sin, were used by God to bring these men here. But to keep them here He used men — and the man He used most was Frederic M. Dunne.

That statement is apodictic, for God wrote His signature in cleanest calligraphy over every year of this man's life, and put it in italics and even underscored it during every week of his short abbatial career. God's signature is the cross.

Because I believe in God I can borrow from an unbeliever. Mencius was to Confucianism what St. Paul is to Christianity. He once said: "Whenever Heaven wants to confer a great work on anyone, it first drenches his heart with bitterness, submits his nerves and his bones to weariness, delivers his members and his whole body to hunger, reduces him to the most extreme indigence, thwarts and upsets all his enterprises. By this means it wakens in him good sentiments, fortifies his patience, and communicates to him what had been lacking."

That is what I call insight into Divine Providence. It may not be even a dim prophecy of the life of Christ, but it most certainly is a very accurate outline of the life of one of Christ's close followers — Dom Frederic Mary Dunne. To the many who knew the man, and need not this memoir, I give the secret of his charm in an aphorism of this same Mencius. It runs: "The great man is one who has not lost the heart he had when a child."

To those who did not know him and who wish to learn the charming holiness of this childlike man I would say that Edwin

Arlington Robinson helps us understand this charm by telling us that "the world is not a prison house but a kind of spiritual kindergarten where millions of infants are trying to spell God with the wrong blocks." Dom Frederic Mary Dunne had the right ones, and spelled correctly.

One would be justified in saying he was always playing with those blocks and had them spelling only God; for though this man has been fittingly characterized as "cold steel sheathed in silk," it was the warm aura of charming childhood that he ever carried about him. And since it is the Trappist life which explains these opposites by fibering the heart of a man until it is that of a Viking, even as it recaptures and revitalizes the Faith which was vibrant in him as a child, this memoir may tell as much about that life as it does about the man who lived it. But what else could be expected from an author who is allowed to write only to tell of God?

I have found Him using the Trappist life to form Dom Frederic, and Dom Frederic to form the Trappist life. So I am going to try to give you a glimpse of the divine Smithy at work and to show how He hammers a soul on the anvil of time to shape it and temper it for eternity.

I begin on my knees; for I agree with Henri Ghéon when he says that no one should dare write the life of a saint, or of a saintly man, without reverence, respect, and much earnest prayer that he probe aright the inscrutable ways of God with a soul and show to the world something of the Divine Mind and the Omnipotent's Will. But since it is a mystery story I write — as is every story of a soul — I begin as so many mystery stories have begun — with death. But the mystery I reveal is that of life — and of Him who is the Source of all that lives. . . .

CHAPTER ONE

The Mystery

ON THE morning of August 4, 1948, the choir members of Gethsemani's community filed into their chapter room with a touch of languor. They had been up since 2 a.m., and though the sun had not yet burned its way through the mists and it still lacked a full ten minutes to six o'clock, they knew they were in for another scorching day. They sank into their backless seats and listened to the singing of the Martyrology and a chapter from the Rule. Every dawn brought this routine after hours of chanting in the dark. But now some of them straightened expectantly, for in the Abbot's absence, the Prior, Father Odilo, would have to address them, and he, with his comical gestures and heavily accented English, had often mixed wit with wisdom and given them a hearty laugh.

But this morning something was wrong. The Prior was squirming in his seat, and there was nothing of the actor or anything artificial about his evident uneasiness. "My Fathers and Brothers . . ." he began, then squirmed some more. Looking up he found almost a hundred pair of eyes intent upon his face. He looked down and hesitantly began again: "My Fathers and Brothers . . . I have some very sad news. . . . I don't know how to phrase it. . . ." The tension in that already tense room grew. Then with a twist of his heavy shoulders he straightened in his chair, lifted his huge head determinedly, and blurted out: "Gethsemani is an orphan. . . . Our Father Abbot died on the way south last night. . . ."

Stunned, the entire assembly sat staring at their Prior. Dom Frederic dead? How could that be? Had he not been with them just a few hours before? Had he not sprinkled each with holy water as they filed from the church last night? Now it was hardly morning, yet they were saying he was dead. Why yesterday he seemed more alive and energetic than usual as he finalized plans for the next ten days: he would hurry down to Georgia, make a speedy visitation of the monastery there, rush back to Gethsemani, welcome the Vicar-General of the Order, then the two of them would fly to Europe for the General Chapter of the Cistercians of the Strict Observance. His visa was even now on its way from Washington. No, it could not be that he was dead! But what was the Prior saying?

". . . He was found alone in the empty smoking compartment of a Pullman. . . ."

Alone . . . in an empty smoking compartment of a Pullman . . . my Abbot? What mystery is this? What is God doing? What meaning lies hid . . . ? Thus did the questions leap to my mind. For I had been one of the last to speak with the Abbot yesterday evening. It was with a start that I recalled we had discussed death. Was not that strange, I asked. Or was it? Could God have been using me as an instrument to alert him? Could He . . . ? We had agreed it was not death which men feared, but the subsequent judgment. He had startled me with the announcement that he himself feared that.

"You!" I had cried. "You — afraid of the judgment? Oh, Reverend Father!"

"Indeed I am," he had replied with emphasis. How well I heard that reply and that emphasis as I sat in the stunned and silent chapter room. And then he had added: "But let me tell you, Father, I would not change my Judge for all the world."

Those were the last words I had heard from his lips. Those were to be the last I would ever hear. For now he was dead. Already he had been judged. And by Jesus Christ. How sudden — strange — swift are the ways of God! What was He teaching by thus snatching our Abbot away?

I thought the announcement had stunned me that morning. I see now that under the seeming stupor my mind had taken fire. I was questioning God's strange ways with men and this strange man's ways with God. Unknown to myself I had plunged into mystery. . . .

The strangeness of it all filled my mind as I went about my work that day. Normally a Trappist dies in his monastery. Why was it that my Abbot, Dom Frederic, a man who had spent fifty-four years of his life in this monastery at Gethsemani, should be found dead in a Pullman car outside the city of Knoxville, Tennessee? Why? How insistent that "why" was that day! I knew I was probing the very Providence of God in my Abbot's regard. But why not: this was my Abbot, and He is my God! Further, I felt that down in the depths of this mystery was a message for me. So I moved about the monastery musing. Why was it that he who had closed the eyes of so many of his brethren in death, should be found sightless and staring? Why did he die alone — he who had so often said he would die as did the monks of old: lying on ashes strewn in the form of a cross, the community grouped around him praying, a priest bending to stigmatize his five senses with holy oil, then giving him the Eucharistic Christ as Companion for the way? How strange that there had been no one near. Stranger still that he who had so loved the black and white of the Cistercian habit, should be found half clad, should die with nothing but the ring on his finger to tell the initiate that he was a man of God — priest, prelate, and religious.

Around and around went my thoughts the whole day through. At twilight I went to bed with the mystery looming larger and

more mysterious. Shortly after midnight they wakened me. Out
into a night stilled with stars I went and saw a lonely hearse
come down a lane shaded and silent save for the light whisper
of leaves. In the hushed moonlight I helped carry the corpse
across the garden through which he had hurried only the night
before. An hour later we had him dressed: hands crossed on his
breast, abbatial ring glistening amid the folds of his white cowl,
pectoral cross sparkling brilliantly just above his stilled heart. After
straightening the miter on his head I stepped back to study those
familiar features in their utterly unfamiliar fixity of death. It was
then that I got an inkling of what had happened in that empty
smoking compartment of the idle Pullman. Death, the Conqueror,
had not conquered!

The majestic calm and imperial poise of every feature of that
face told me that while my Abbot may have known pain in his
last moments, he also knew peace. Face to face with what all men
fear, quite evidently he had been fearless. The sly smile lingering
at the corners of his lips testified that at the last he might well
have used the line I had so often heard him speak, and the walls
of that empty smoking compartment may have heard him open
his rendezvous with death saying: "Strong Death, I am thy Victor!
Dread Death, where is thy sting?"

As I stood looking down on the remains of the man who had
sired me to the Trappist life I suddenly realized that the mystery
surrounding his death was as nothing compared to the mystery
enshrouding his life — and that the solution of the former depended
upon the probe, and the successful probe, of the latter. If one
could get down to the secret which set his heart beating the way
it did, he would know why it stopped where it did.

A few days later more facts surrounding the death came my
way in the form of the statements made by the porter who found
Dom Frederic and the conductor of the train. But while these will
serve admirably for human records, they helped me not at all in

the search for the one record I wanted. Porter W. R. Anderson of Louisville had this to say:

> I was called at 3.45 A.M., just before arrival at Knoxville. I had two passengers detraining there. As the train was backing into the Station and I was taking out baggage I met this passenger going to the Men's Room. While I was receiving passengers, the occupant of Upper 6 came to the vestibule and told me there was a mighty sick man in the Smoking Compartment. I immediately went and found this passenger sitting on the long seat holding his chest. He appeared to be in great pain. I said: "Father, is there anything I can do?" In a very weak voice he replied: "Get a doctor." I immediately went to the Station and notified the Train Conductor and the Station Master. I then returned to my car. When I got to the Men's Room this passenger was very still and appeared to be dead. When the doctor arrived he pronounced him so. The Station Master checked the passenger's money and belongings in the Conductor's and my presence.

The conductor, H. A. Hanshue of Cincinnati, was briefer in his report, yet added another detail for the human records. He said:

> Reverend Dunne got up at about 4.00 A.M., went to the Men's Room and sat down on the sofa. Porter Anderson discovered him sitting there and not moving. He notified the Train Conductor, myself, and the L&N Station Master at Knoxville. Together we checked his money and belongings. A doctor was called and pronounced the passenger dead. The body was taken to Mann's Funeral Home. The Station Master and Night Dispatcher took full charge.

Then come names some of us will never forget: "Car *James Longstreet;* Train L & N # 17 *The Flamingo;* Lower 11, Car 21, 4:00 A.M., Aug. 4, 1948."

These men tell us quite accurately when his heart stopped and where; but they say nothing of why it stopped then and there — and that is our mystery.

My probe of it had begun all unknown to me the moment the Prior had announced the doctor's verdict that Dom Frederic had died from "natural causes — obviously a heart attack." It became official a few months later when Dom James Mary Fox, Abbot Dunne's successor, commissioned me to write the life of Gethsemani's fifth Lord.

Had my investigation remained private I might have limited myself to the Trappist life. Dom Frederic had lived that for fifty-four years; if his days and nights made no sense, neither would mine. Death, you see, always pulls us up short, and forces us to ask where we are going and what we are doing with life. This sudden death of my Abbot had me questioning not only his life and my own, but peering deep into the entire Cistercian regime. The roots of that regime I found not at Citeaux, as one might at first suspect, but going back into the Garden of Gethsemani and even to the rock of Golgotha. They go further still. Tracing them to their ultimate source I touched God.

Had not obedience set me ferreting out all I could about the seventy-four years Dom Frederic lived — fifty-four within the cloister, twenty without — I might never have plumbed to its furthest fathom this Cistercian mode of living, nor learned so much about the human soul and its Sculptor Divine, God the Holy Ghost. My searching has given me some idea of the place America holds in the plan of God and the place the plan of God should hold in America. More than political and economic leadership has been entrusted to this youngest country in the newest continent of the world. And the growth of the cloistered contemplative life proves it. God the Holy Ghost would sculpture the nation's soul through men who prove as pliable as Dom Frederic. On them, as on him, the divine Artist begins work early. One can hear His hammer blows and all but see the chipping of His chisel as one goes back into the life of this man who became a monk and even something of a mystic.

It has taken me more than three years to probe this mystery. Today, at the conclusion of my work, I find that the intuition I had in the chapter room the morning Dom Frederic's death was announced was true. My Abbot did not die alone . . . nor should it be said that he died from merely natural causes. His letters, diaries, sermons, conferences, and the archives of Gethsemani yielded many a clue, but the first, and perhaps the best, came when I looked into his heredity and early environment.

In the molding of His man God's work begins long before birth, and He uses everything from ancestry to seeming accidents. In Dom Frederic's case these furnished not only enlightenment but amusement.

CHAPTER TWO

Heredity Is a Fact

I T WAS at Ironton, Ohio, on April 25, 1874, that Frederic Arthur Dunne first saw the light of day. But that was about all he ever did see at Ironton or in Ohio. For at the age of two with his family he was floating down the Ohio River heading for the Mississippi and Mexico's Gulf. At New Orleans he changed boats and crossed the many leagues of sea to the Florida coast, debarking at a little town called Cedar Keys. That was a lot of travel for one so young; yet it was only the beginning. At Cedar Keys the family belongings were loaded on two small flat boats and the trip begun to Tampa Bay. The travelers were seeking the mouth of the Manatee River; for Captain Hugh Dunne, father of the family, had bought one hundred and sixty acres of land sight unseen near the small town of Manatee, which he hoped to turn into some sort of plantation.

They found that river, but it was only after the boat holding the household furniture had capsized. They even found the wharf which was to be their place of final debarkation. But when Captain Hugh and his wife, the former Mary Lois Stenger of Zanesville, Ohio, went to look at their purchase, they found they had become undisputed owners of a good-sized swamp. A certain Mr. Montgomery had not only taken the former Civil War Captain in, he had also taken out of the Captain most of his war and postwar savings! So what had begun amid the excited laughter of the

children ended now in the louder laughter of the parents as
Captain Hugh, with typical Irish wit, turned to his frowning wife
and said: "Honestly, Mary, this place was perfectly dry on
the map!"

That difference between the picture drawn by the salesman with
the aid of his map and the actuality found by the travel-weary
family accounts for the further fact that, before he was three years
old, young Frederic Dunne had traversed most of the southeastern
portion of the United States. For while Captain Hugh could make
his wife laugh at what was almost tragedy, and swallow his own
disappointment — even though the swallowing was hard — he was
also keenly conscious of his responsibility as husband and father.
He had five living children now — the sixth had died — and a loyal
wife. He must have work and have it immediately. So as soon
as he housed his dependents in what was then known as Braden
Castle — a large, roomy, snow-white house made of sea shells and
some kind of plaster which Dr. Braden had recently abandoned
and which gave the name to the present Bradentown — Captain
Hugh headed north on foot. For the only river craft that could
have taken him to the coast and the steamers of the Gulf, passed
Braden Castle and its wharf tooting its whistle in reply to what
were actually frantic signals of distress but which were taken as
friendly salutes and the waving of good wishes.

The nearest railroad station in those days was at Jacksonville,
three hundred miles across the country. Captain Hugh trudged
every inch of the way and bought a ticket for Atlanta, Georgia;
for the James P. Harriman Company had been pleading with him
for some time to come and take charge of their printery. The
following spring he had his family of five in one of the finest
residences of Atlanta. It was a house he designed himself and
helped build, with seven large rooms all on one floor; for Mrs.
Dunne had difficulty climbing stairs. That is the kind of man
Captain Hugh Dunne was: resilient, resourceful, courageous, and

of unconquerable determination, qualities he had inherited from
Irish ancestors who once proudly printed on their coat of arms
the somewhat defiant legend: *Collis Armatus* — and qualities he
handed on to his third son.

Because heredity is a fact and environment helps shape a soul,
much in the make-up of Frederic Mary Dunne is traceable not only
to the man who was Captain Hugh Dunne but to the woman
called by some Englishmen "Good Queen Bess." To many it will
seem more than strange that I account for characteristics in the
mind and heart of the third son of an Irish immigrant and an
Alsatian-American, born in the third quarter of the nineteenth
century, by speaking of heredity and environment in one breath
and of Henry VIII's charming child, Elizabeth, without taking
another breath. But you see, I believe in God, and would have
you stare at some hard facts.

In 1848 there was a potato famine in Ireland. That was the
year Edward J. Dunne, of Castle Brach, a tiny village near
Tullamore in Kings County, looked deep into the eyes of the
colleen who fifteen years before had been Catherine O'Byrne of
Queens County, but who was now his wife and the mother of
what he called "his little brood," and told her it was time they
were leaving the country.

Now that would satisfy the superficial and, as far as they are
concerned, would adequately account for the presence of Hugh
Dunne in Zanesville, Ohio, in 1860. But it in no way accounted for
the flaming faith in the soul of Hugh nor the steel in the character
of his third son, Frederic. For those we have to go back to the
frightful famine of the mid-nineteenth century and even beyond
that foul institution of the eighteenth century called "Landlordism." The historical fact is that if Henry and his offspring
called "Bess" had been less violent in their persecution of the
Catholics of Ireland in the seventeenth century, the grandfather
of Gethsemani's fifth abbot would have spent his childhood in the

shadows of the frowning battlements and defiant-looking towers of his ancestral castle and not amid the waste of rocks that were the ruins of that once "fortified hill" — the *Collis Armatus*. Then Landlordism and famine might have been met with different measures; but it is debatable whether Captain Hugh Dunne would have loved his Catholic Faith with the same fiery ardor or handed on to his third son that doggedness in the face of difficulty which some label stubbornness but which no one can deny is strength.

That *Collis Armatus* of the Dunne's armorial bearing is more than a description of the place they called home; it is something of a character sketch of the family that lived on "the fortified hill." For even the twentieth-century descendants of the Dunnes of Castle Brach — especially the man whose life we are investigating — show all the courageous self-reliance connoted in those two words. I can almost hear the Dunnes of Castle Brach swaggeringly say: "This hill is fortified; whom have we to fear?"

Of course it is true that the hill was not sufficiently fortified to withstand the onslaughts of the soldiery in the pay of Queen Elizabeth, but the point I want to make is that something went into the blood of the Dunnes from the fact that they once could say their hill was fortified, and more went into the souls of the Dunnes from the fact that their battlements tumbled down and their towers fell in war against foreigners who were attacking their Faith.

Dom Frederic once told me he had been brought up by a soldier. What he didn't tell me, but what my searchings revealed, is that he was descended from warriors who had battled for what is dearer to man than home or family — his Faith. It would be truer to say his God. At any rate, to the qualities listed as the legacy Hugh Dunne received from his Irish ancestors and handed on to his third American son must be added the one which proved the determining factor in most of Hugh Dunne's moves and played the dominant role in Frederic Dunne's life — faith: that dynamic belief that God brought us out of nothingness for a divinely wise purpose and that every passing moment is pregnant with eternal worth, even as it is brimmed with His invisible presence and flowing over with His paternal love.

But this God-consciousness was not derived solely from the Irish in his makeup; his mother was Alsatian descent, the daughter of a man who had been born and brought up in Buchsweiler, a village of northern Alsace, near Strasbourg. And what Catholicism is to the natives of Ireland, Protestantism is to the natives of Buchsweiler. Add the fact that Mary Lois' mother was Anna Ruckel of Hesse, another stronghold of Lutheranism, and you have the secret of the steely faith that was Dom Frederic's. But perhaps I am a bit cryptic, so let us go back to 1848.

This was the year God had designed for two discoveries which, a short century later, would give America the economic and spiritual leadership of the world. He first allowed a man named Marshall, a mechanic from New Jersey, working out at Sutter's Mill, near Sacramento, California, to turn over a spadeful of black earth literally spangled with gold. He next allowed a man named Paulinus, a monk from Melleray, canvassing the United States for a suitable site for contemplatives, to find, hidden behind a circle of undulating hills in the heart of Nelson County, Kentucky, a fifteen hundred-acre estate for sale.

It was these two discoveries, besides persecution and famine, that brought the Trappists from France and the Dunnes from Ireland. America was the land of the free where God and gold could be found. It is noteworthy that the two parties had very similar voyages.

It is rather well known now that Death rode the waves with the Trappists. Gethsemani's first bit of "burnt-out incense" was dropped into the chilly waves of a stormy North Atlantic after the soul of the aged Frater Benezet had gone to God. But it is thanks to Dom Frederic's only surviving sister, Mrs. Mary Wichers, that we know now that Death rode the waves with the Dunnes. She tells what she heard from her father's lips: how the ship on which they came from Ireland was slow and the sea was rough; how fruit and fresh vegetables were wanting and the water became rancid; how cholera broke out and raged so fiercely that the passenger list was more than decimated; how half the "little brood" of Dunnes was buried at sea.

That is why Edward J. Dunne and Catherine O'Byrne Dunne arrived in Cincinnati with only four children: Hugh, John, Mary, and Peter; and perhaps why they did not go farther west. The Gold Rush to California was on, but prudence and poverty kept them east of the Mississippi.

Hugh, the eldest, was immediately apprenticed to a bookbinder and printer. He learned the trade so well that less than ten years later he had opened his own publishing house in Zanesville, Ohio. What took him to that town no one seems to know; but what kept him there is no mere guess. He stayed at the Granger House, Jacob Stenger's hotel, and soon met the proprietor's lovely daughter, Mary Lois. Shortly after that, the young Irish printer was striving to make impressions on more than paper — and enjoying some success.

But it was not long until Hugh learned that the Alsatian Protestants could be as tenacious of their faith as are the Irish Catholics of theirs. That gave him pause. For quite some time he was hesitant about "popping the question." Years later he was to learn how much more hesitant the Stengers were about allowing Mary Lois to answer that question. But at last it was done. Perhaps war drums had much to do with wedding bells; for it was in the year that Sumter fell that Mary Lois Stenger became Mrs. Hugh Dunne, and Mr. Hugh Dunne became a member of the infantry outfit known as the 78th Ohio Volunteers.

That one fact influences the lives of father and son more perhaps than any other single occurrence in Hugh Dunne's existence —

for it led him to where Death plays no favorites and made him keenly conscious of the omnipotence of God. The 78th saw plenty of action and Hugh Dunne was made for action. Before half his term of three years had been served he was a first lieutenant. Ten months later he was wearing the double gold bar of a captain. His promotions were earned.

Eighty years after the events, his son recounted the happenings to me with so much vividness and vibrancy that it was easily seen what an impression they had made on him as he heard them from the lips of his father, and what an impression they had made on his father as he experienced them in battle. Dom Frederic would smile and say that he had almost never been born, then would recount how his father had almost been buried alive. Just where it happened I never learned, but after one of the battles during which the 78th was badly shot up, a burying party came upon a heap of dead and wounded. At the bottom of that pile they found the blood-covered body of Captain Hugh Dunne. An open grave yawned at his side. Already many of those who had lain on top of him had been dropped into it. With very little ceremony two of the men lifted the Captain's body and were just about to lower it into the grave when one of them cried: "He's breathing!"

They laid him on the ground, dashed water on his face, and soon saw he was alive. A frantic search for his wound was begun; for he was covered with blood. But though they went over him carefully from head to foot they found not so much as a scratch. When consciousness returned, the story came out. Hugh had been hit on the chest by a ball whose speed was all but spent. It felled him and completely stunned him. But now, except for the blood which had oozed down from the dead and wounded above him, and a very sore chest, he claimed to be in perfect condition.

But the story with the most history in it and one that gives insight into the heredity we are probing, was always precipitated by Captain Hugh's determined way of getting to the windward of anyone who was smoking. When questioned about this habit he would laugh and say: "Have you heard the song about 'Marching through Georgia'?" Of course his hearers always had. "Well," Hugh would go on, "I have always wondered where the man who wrote that was during the summer of 1864. I know where I was. I was in Georgia with the 78th Ohio Volunteers. We did a lot of marching. But it wasn't exactly *through* that State! It took us from May the fourth until September the second to get from Dalton to Atlanta — and they are not a hundred miles apart." Then would come a rapid account of the bitter battles from Resaca to Kennesaw Mountain, then on to Smyna, Chattahoochee, and Atlanta. "It was fierce," the Captain would say. "Many a time I feared my entire company would be wiped out. One day, when we seemed completely overwhelmed, I swore to God that if He got me and my men out of that mess I would never smoke another puff so long as I lived. He got me out. So I can't smoke. But I never promised God I would never smell it."

The Captain was mustered out before Sherman began his march to the sea; so his objection to the song "Marching through Georgia" was legitimate.

Less than two weeks after the capture of Atlanta, Captain Hugh was back in Zanesville, a private citizen and a printer with a very pretty and exceptionally happy wife. A year later their first child was born — a boy. They named him Jesse, but it was a name not received at the baptismal font. That is the fact which explains why Frederic Dunne was born in Ironton, Ohio; educated in Atlanta, Georgia; taught the trade of printer and bookbinder in Jacksonville, Florida; only to live his life in Gethsemani, Kentucky.

Some might dismiss it as mere "in-law trouble." But it goes deeper than that. Will Stenger, Mary Lois' younger brother, had become a Protestant minister — and was of the militant type. His sincerity is beyond all question and the depth of his faith is attested by the fact that his immediate descendants can be found today in India, China, and Japan as Protestant missionaries. But precisely because he was so deeply sincere, his opposition to Catholic Baptism was almost fierce.

For the sake of his wife, Captain Hugh temporized. But when the opposition showed no signs of waning after the birth of the next two children, Katherine and Mary, Hugh Dunne decided to move. In 1870 he set up his printing establishment in Ironton, and had his three children baptized there — with, it seems, no opposition from the children's mother. Shortly after their arrival a second son was born to them who was christened Edward Jacob — a subtle compliment to Grandfather Stenger. But when he saw that this in no way lessened the relative's opposition to Catholic Baptism, Hugh Dunne began to wonder if he were far enough away from Zanesville.

Edward Jacob died in infancy. But the sorrowing parents were soon comforted by the birth of the boy they named Frederic Arthur. Once again Captain temporized a bit, postponing the child's baptism from April until September. But when Frances was born two years later and the Stenger opposition proved just as bitter, Hugh Dunne was ready to listen to the suave Montgomery and even a bit eager to buy the one hundred and sixty acres he and his wife were to find under water just outside Manatee, Florida, in the year 1876.

Had these acres proved as habitable as they looked on the map, the Dunnes would have been as far from Zanesville as it was humanly possible to be while still remaining in the United States and staying east of the Mississippi. But just as too little water sent Hugh and his family south, too much water brought them north again.

Yet, once again the natural proves to be supernatural and the decisions of man the determinations of God. It was at Atlanta, Georgia, that Hugh Dunne came closest to death while battling for the sake of the Union. It would be at Atlanta that he would know the greatest joy of his life as the two Faiths, which had already been the cause of young Frederic's being carried over so much of the United States and which were his richest heritage, were merged into one.

But that, since it leads to what I call "spiritual heredity" demands another chapter. . . .

CHAPTER THREE

Environment and Spiritual Heredity

PHYSICAL heredity no one denies. Just what it is, no one knows; but that it is, no one questions. Scientists say it is a matter of genes in the parental chromosomes. Hence, they will be ready to admit that Mary Lois Stenger transmitted to her son Frederic Arthur her own sweetness of disposition by some miracle of biochemistry in that tiny cell which was he at the first moments of life. They will further concede that his unquenchable optimism and humor, his sparkling wit and winsomeness came from his Celtic father by the same miraculous process. But when I say the strong, deep, and dominant faith, which characterized the grown man, was an inheritance from both his father and his mother, some will accuse me of phantasy; others will charge me with heresy.

And why not? Is it not Catholic doctrine that God breathes an immortal soul into the child at the instant of conception — a soul that is a new and distinct creation, as unique as was the soul He breathed into the clay He Himself had fashioned for the body of Adam when life was young and the world not old? No Catholic can question the fact that God takes an utterly new mold, one He has never used before and which He will shatter immediately after the using, for the fashioning of each new human soul. Hence, in all creation there never was another soul, and there never will be another, just like the one the Omnipotent breathed forth in July, 1873, to be possessed inalienably by the person whom history would know as Frederic Arthur Dunne. Yet I predicate of it such a thing as a spiritual heredity.

When we find a son not only with the father's features but with that father's fight, does not the boy say to us that heredity goes deeper than the skin or even than the skeleton? The ancients used to claim that temperaments depended on the "humors" in the body. Moderns go no further when they say they depend on the hormones in the blood. But my theory goes beyond temperaments and even beyond talents. What I am saying is that children inherit tendencies that are purely spiritual; that an Augustine received much of his faith from his mother, Monica, and the Little Flower's genius for loving God came in some way from her loving parents.

It is absolutely sure that from our first parents we all inherited something purely spiritual — our tendency toward evil. Why, then, can we not inherit a tendency toward God from our immediate parents and call it spiritual heredity? At any rate, the undeniable fact before us is that Frederic Arthur Dunne had a faith like the faith of his parents — and in both that was vigorous.

With a father so militantly Catholic and a mother so stanchly Protestant, you might suspect Frederic Arthur would be some sort of a "spiritual schizophrenic." But no. There was to Mary Lois Stenger's faith something deeper than stanchness; there was sincerity. And because of this deeper depth, Frederic Dunne saw his mother received into the Catholic Church at Atlanta, Georgia; saw her make her First Holy Communion at the very rail at which he was soon to know the same transcendent marvel, and witnessed her Confirmation a few years before his own.

I used to wonder secretly at the surety with which Dom Frederic would correct his friends who claimed that they were Protestants.

"Oh, no you're not," he would say and his ever winning smile would light his every feature. "You may be non-Catholic, but you are not Protestant; for you do not really protest against anything." I suspect now that he learned this telling truth from his mother's conversion.

A Jesuit came to dinner is the whole story according to some. But while Father Joseph Desribes, S.J., may have been skilled in presenting God's truth and adept in dissolving Protestant prejudices, I do not believe he deserves all the credit for the conversion. I think most of that, under God, should go to Captain Hugh Dunne and the children.

People who know not how close Faith is to the heart's core have often wondered why the Holy Roman Catholic Church is so reluctant to bless "mixed marriages." These people know not how descriptive that adjective "mixed" is. Let the two involved be as circumspect as Circumspection itself; let them be as prudent as Prudence, the marriage will still be mixed. God, and faith in God, is closer to us than our thought or our thinking and is far larger than life. Hence, so long as there can be no full mutual sharing of belief, there is always something twisted and truncated about the marriage itself. Bodies have been married while souls remain single. They share everything but that which matters most — their minds, hearts, wills, and deepest beings. Hugh Dunne found this out long before he listened to Mr. Montgomery and his talk of real estate in Florida.

You can be sure there was discussion; probably even heated arguments. It was inevitable; for on the "red-letter days" of life, those occasions which some call milestones but which really are turning points — such momentous events as those of marriage, birth, death — there is distance between hearts that should be beating as one, distance between minds that should be thinking together, distance between souls that should be merged. Hugh and Mary Lois had some suspicion of these facts in Zanesville before they were married, but would not face them. At the birth of Jesse they had to face them, but they wrongly blamed them onto Will Stenger and his militant Protestantism. When Edward Jacob died, they faced them more fully and knew not then on whom to blame them. But when Hugh once realized that these momentous occasions are the ones in which God looms largest, suspicion of what was wrong with his marriage became conviction. His prayers increased; his discussion all but ceased; and he became a militant Catholic in the sharpest sense of the word.

While Captain of a company in the 78th Ohio Volunteers, Hugh Dunne had learned the advantage of enfilading. His direct attacks had failed. He now used indirection. He talked to his wife by talking to his children and brought about conversion while imparting instructions. In other words Captain Hugh catechized his children carefully — always managing to do it within earshot of his curious and slyly attentive wife. But while mindful of St. Paul's words that "Faith cometh by hearing," he was not unmindful of the fact that it is a gift given in answer to prayer. So he insisted, with military insistence, that the family Rosary be said every evening. After all this, and during all this, Fr. Desribes, S.J., came to dinner; shortly thereafter Mary Lois was baptized. Who should get the most credit?

That was in 1879. Little Frederic was only five. But the devotion that made many marvel at the aged Frederic Dunne began then. Mary Lois Stenger, like most Protestants, imagined that Catholics adore Mary of Nazareth. When she learned the truth, namely that we do not love a mother goddess but only the Mother of God who is also the Mother of men, she knew what had been missing to her religious life all the years that had passed and she turned to Mary as a love-hungry child turns to her late-found mother who is full of love. And the result was the childlike love in the man who was Dom Frederic Dunne.

Mary Immaculate, the little maid of Nazareth who became the

Mother of God, is hailed as "Mother" by every Catholic no matter what his or her age, nationality, or position. The pope, Christ's vicar, visible head of the Holy Roman Catholic Church, as well as the child just learning to bless himself, calls Mary "Mother." But Frederic M. Dunne had a way of using that title which caused every attentive listener to look up and listen more attentively. There was a warmth, a vibrancy, an overtone that gave a new nuance of meaning and deeper intimacy to the term. It may have puzzled many. No doubt there were those who attributed it to the fact that he was a Cistercian and hence a child of Mary in a very special fashion. For it was the Cistercians who first began to salute Mary as *Notre Dame*. But the truth of the matter is that Frederic Dunne knew Mary was his Mother long before he knew there were Cistercians or that they called our Lady *Notre Dame*. He learned it at what was the most sacred and impressive moment of his childhood — the moment of his earthly mother's death. He himself told me the story more than once — the last time just a few months before his own death.

With that flare he had for exact dates, he usually began by saying, "It was in February of 1881 — Washington's birthday to be exact — that my last brother was born. I was not quite seven years old, but I remember it more clearly than some things that happened yesterday. . . ." Then he would tell how the seventh child born to Mary and Hugh Dunne was baptized immediately and named Charles Joseph. The promptness with which this child was changed from a soul stained with original sin into a soul shining with Christ's sanctifying grace was due not to the fervor of Mary Lois' new-found faith, but to the fever which was racing in her veins and the delicate condition of the newly born. Puerperal fever had the mother pushing the coverlet from her perspiring body and moving restlessly in her bed. At the same time some respiratory difficulty set the newly baptized infant gasping. While the doctors worked, Hugh Dunne watched and prayed. Days passed and still the patients gasped and perspired. On the twenty-seventh the doctors gave up hope. Hugh Dunne summoned the entire family to the bedside for a last word, a last kiss. Jesse, Katherine, Mary, Frederic, and Frances knelt and answered the prayers their father was saying. Fright and a feeling of helplessness dominated the young hearts as the mother began plucking the coverlet as is the wont of the dying. Steadily came the "Aves" and the "Paters" from the Captain as Mary's beads slipped through his fingers and his eyes fixed on the pale face of the one who had become his other self. Suddenly, in the midst of an "Ave," he stopped. The children looked up. They found their mother's face suffused with a radiant smile, here eyes round with joy and riveted on something or someone just beyond her bed.

"What is it, Mary?" asked Captain Hugh in a whisper that was loud with anxiety and love.

"Don't you see her?" asked the dying woman in a voice that was filled with wonder. "Don't you see her?" came the joy-filled question a second time. Then — and here Dom Frederic's voice would grow soft — the dying woman said: "It is the Mother of God. . . . She has little Edward in her arms. . . . She has come to take me home."

A moment later she was dead. Little Edward, to whom the dying woman referred, was Edward Jacob who had died in infancy up at Ironton, Ohio. When Charles Joseph, the latest and last child, followed his mother in death, and was buried with her, Frederic, though not yet seven, knew he had two brothers as well as two mothers in heaven — and the other world became very real to this young child.

Was it the fevered fancy of a dying convert which peopled that room with the "Madonna" — the strange Madonna who held her own child instead of the Christ Child in her arms? Dom Frederic never claimed his mother had a vision. He simply stated the historical fact. He told what he saw and heard. What or who it was his mother saw — she alone could say. But it was from that moment that Frederic Dunne turned to Mary Immaculate with an utter confidence. And I believe it is that moment which explains those many other moments in later years when he would say to his community: "Think how wonderful it will be, at the hour of death, to look into the eyes of our Mother — and have her lead us to her Son!"

Since he lost his mother when he was almost seven, many will object and say that his devotedness to Mary Immaculate, if it came from his earthly mother at all, could only be called a legacy and not a part of his heredity. Perhaps the objection could be allowed and refuge taken in the broader meaning of the word heredity, namely "inheritance." But this thesis is too dear to me to allow such a dodge. I think that in the soul of Mary Lois Stenger was a seed which needed but the waters of Baptism to bring it to flower and that seed was love for Christ's and every Christian's Mother. I further believe she handed that on to Frederic Dunne, that it burst its bud when he was seven and kept on flowering until he was seventy-four.

In any event it is an undeniable fact that if a strong faith was not a spiritual inheritance with the Dunnes it most certainly was something that ran strongly in their blood. You will remember that the first trek of the family to Florida had been occasioned, if not actually caused, by Protestant opposition. The second trek to the same land was even more markedly so caused. It occurred one short year after the mother's death and brings into our history the figure of Honorable Edmund F. Dunne, Captain Hugh's cousin.

In 1875 Edmund F. Dunne was Chief Justice of what was then known as Arizona Territory. The reaction of the Indians to the government's efforts at organization gave the Chief Justice plenty to do. But he did not allow work in Arizona to blind him to what was going on in other parts of the United States. As has happened periodically in our history, a bigoted movement was set afoot under the deceptive name of "American." But Edmund Dunne was descended from men who once emblazoned *Collis Armatus* on their escutcheon. He was too keen to be deceived and too honest to remain silent while others were being deluded. He knew the "Native American Movement" was neither native nor American; and he saw through the efforts of the "American Protective Association" and their concentration on education. When they told the world that they were laboring to make the American Public School System "nondenominational," Chief Justice Dunne knew they really meant "secular." He grew concerned not only for his Church but for his country; for he recognized what may have escaped the promotors of the scheme. He knew that this would ultimately end by making our Constitution a basis of freedom *from* Religion rather than a bulwark of freedom *for* Religion.

When the Territorial Legislature of Arizona assembled in early 1875, Dunne came before those men and asked if our public schools were free for all Americans, or only for some. Many smiled complacently, others frowned in puzzlement at what sounded like an absurdity. But before any answer was given the Judge went on to prove three propositions which not only shook the complacency out of the members of that Legislature but stripped many a member of the A.P.A. of arrogant confidence. Judge Dunne had seen that behind this movement lurked a fear of the Catholics. The minds that framed this movement for the nondenominalization of our public schools argued that if Catholics were given equal rights in education they might grow too strong for the "Native Americans." They knew that in making the system "nondenominational" they were burdening their own Sunday schools, upon whom would fall now the full weight of "religious instruction." But that fitted in with the intent of the framers of the plan; for they felt their Churches could carry the burden, whereas the poorer Catholics, being unable to support their own schools, would be forced to watch their Church slowly dwindle and ultimately die.

It was a subtle move. But it was utterly un-American. Chief Justice Dunne saw this and argued first that the State has no right to teach religion. There were many nods of approval and murmurs of agreement. Yet when he went on to his second proposition and proved that the State has no right to teach irreligion, most of those heads stopped nodding and the murmurs changed from agreement to puzzlement. But when the speaker went on and showed that the state has no inherent right to teach at all, most of those men thought they were listening to some sort of heresy.

After that broadside, Edmund F. Dunne returned to the question of secularizing our public school system and showed that when religion is not taught positively, irreligion is taught by inference; hence, what they would have in actuality would be irreligious schools. He then turned on the A.P.A. and "Native Americans" and showed them that in a country such as ours, where each state guarantees religious liberty and equality of citizenship, there can be but one form of constitutional public school system — and that would be the application of the denominalization system.

The Chief Justice's conclusion was utterly logical and purely American. He said that since "most non-Catholics would be satisfied with secularistic schools, Catholics and the minority of non-Catholics and Jews, who believe vitally in religious education, should be given a *per capita* allowance to educate their children according to their own consciences."

That bit of sanity and irrefutable logic was considered so radical that Edmund F. Dunne, Chief Justice of the Territory of Arizona, was requested to tender his resignation from the bench of the Territory by no less a person than the President of the United States — General Ulysses S. Grant.

The Judge acceded to the President's request. But at the same time he resolved to found a colony somewhere in the United States of America where Catholics, and all others with them, could enjoy their constitutional rights, guarantees, and privileges.

Not many months later he wrote to Atlanta to his cousin, the recently bereaved Captain Hugh Dunne, telling him his plan. The ex-soldier unhesitatingly pointed to Florida. It was hardly a determination on the Captain's part to retrieve the losses sustained in the Montgomery transaction. It most likely was the memory of what he had seen as he trudged those many miles between Manatee and Jacksonville, after finding he had bought a swamp.

The rest of the story must be taken from one who well may be a prejudiced witness. Mrs. Mary Wichers, Dom Frederic's sole surviving sister, in an account of the founding of the town of San Antonio, Florida, which she drew up for me, says that the Judge accepted the Captain's suggestion immediately; for his brother, John, was attorney for the Disston Company which controlled almost endless stretches of land in that state and were only too anxious to have someone develop it for them. With something like genuine pleasure they granted the Judge the right not only to choose his own site but to take as much acreage as he deemed necessary for his enterprise. That is why the early spring of 1881 saw the Captain and the Judge walking down through the state seeking the most suitable location for their Catholic or "Freedom for Religion" colony.

When they came to the Withlacoochee River they took a ferry which allowed them to cross from what is now Hernando County into the rolling hills of Pasco County. The Captain was weary. Under his arm he was carrying a pair of slippers which he had used from time to time to ease the burning of his feet as they trudged the hot miles. With the sight of the hills and the refreshing green before him he threw his slippers down crying, "I take possession of this land in the name of my slippers." The Judge chuckled, bent over, and picked up the slippers, then led the tired Captain a few miles farther to where they found an enchanting lake. Pointing to a well-kept orange grove which stretched back from the shore, the Judge said: "This is the place."

"I like the looks of those hills," was the weary Captain's comment. "After my first experience in this state, I'll always like hills."

"And I," replied the Judge, "like the looks of that lake. I learned to love water when I was in Arizona!"

They went up to the house which stood in the center of a circle of palms and asked for the owner of the plantation. A man a bit beyond middle age came out and introduced himself as Benedict Mary Wichers. Soon the three men were in the cool of the large living room sipping chilled fruit juice and talking about the land. When Benedict Wichers told them how fertile the soil was, how well cattle fared in these parts, and how the few scattered settlers managed to reap a fair profit from their annual harvest of sugar cane, the two Dunnes felt that they had found their site. When Wichers went on and told them he was a Catholic and that he brought a priest from Tampa every month or so to say Mass for the scattered families who would gather in his house, they knew they had their location.

As the two men walked from Wichers to visit the other settlers the Captain kept pointing out the vast possibilities that stretched before them for laying out groves larger than Wichers' and thus enabling whoever would come to make a very comfortable living.

Within a few days the Dunnes had called on each of the settlers for miles around. When they found everyone echoing Ben Wichers' estimate of the soil's fertility and the possibilities that lay in the land, the two men set about staking off what was to be their own property. The Judge chose a site by the lake for his possession while the Captain preferred the high ground farther back. Thus it was that he had the distinction of building the first house on the site of what was to be the town of San Antonio.

The Judge was alive with the enthusiasm of a discoverer with his find or an artist with a new creation. He simply would not wait. When he learned that a little log house belonging to an old man called Uncle Johnny Howell was vacant, he hurried to find Uncle

Johnny and learn the terms for renting it. They were more than reasonable, so, widowed though he was, the Judge sent for his three girls and his two boys, and straightway the new settlement had its first family.

The Captain was more conservative. He decided soon enough that the thing for his household would be an orange grove, but he would not bring his children south until things were a bit less primitive. He hurried back to Atlanta and set his oldest boy's imagination afire with his descriptions of what was to be. . . . He pictured the hills shaggy with their growth of splendid timber, the lake lying in perpetual sunshine, and the rich soil. Jesse was soon seen drawing plans. Then one evening the Captain came home more eager than usual and announced that he had just purchased all that was necessary to set up a small sawmill and had even hired a man to go south with it and Jesse in the morning.

Less than a month later a letter from Florida told how enough lumber had been prepared for two houses, and how the Judge and his boys had already begun the construction of their future home. Jesse enclosed a ground plan of the house he wanted to build for the Dunnes who were still in Atlanta. It showed a large living room flanked on either side by smaller rooms designated as bedrooms, then in the rear was a large square representing the space for a commodious kitchen. The Captain liked the layout, and told Jesse to keep him posted on the progress of the work.

The summer had not reached its height when word came that the Judge had moved into his new home. The Captain immediately gave orders to the family to prepare for a long journey. Two weeks later they were housed in the log cabin Uncle Johnny Howell had originally rented to the Judge.

That summer was one of the most delightful in the Dunne's experience: the children loved bathing in the lake, playing in the sands of its shores, then idling in the shade of the woods; the men and older boys spent their days and many of the long evenings building the Captain's house and clearing ground for the groves. By early autumn the Captain and his family were ready to move from Uncle Johnny's log cabin to the house Jesse had designed and helped to build.

As the mild winter weather set in the Judge sat back in contentment. His ideal was becoming a reality. Three other families had come down from the north to form what he called the nucleus for his settlement. Friendly folk from around about, their harvesting done, would gather in his living room to discuss everything from their own crops and cattle to the nation's politics. When he found that the Captain's dining-room table had become the settlement's unofficial post office, he teased Jesse by asking if he had designed that room for his father and family or for the Postmaster General up in Washington.

When Ben Wichers and another of the original settlers drove their mule team to Tampa and brought back Father Peterman, who selected the Judge's house to be the place for Mass, the man who had so startled the Arizona Legislature that they called on the President of the United States for action knew a deep joy.

A year went by, during which more families came. A general store was built. The settlement gradually grew. More and more fields took on an orderly pattern as young orange groves were set out. But now of an evening the Captain and Judge could be seen bent toward one another in serious discussion. The education of their growing children had become a cause of deep concern. The Judge finally decided to send his children to boarding schools. They had an aunt in Canada, a nun attached to one of the leading educational establishments. The three girls would go there. His two boys were of college age. He would entrust them to the Benedictines who had flourishing schools in Pennsylvania, Indiana, New Jersey, and Kansas. He would let the boys make their own choice. The Captain shook his head. His children were too young for boarding school, he claimed; and put off his final decision.

In January of 1883 a tempting offer came from the Harrisons in Atlanta, asking the Captain once again to head their printery. He accepted and took his oldest daughter, Katherine, and his youngest boy, Frederic, back to Atlanta with him. Jesse said he was through with schooling, and Mary begged off with the plea that she was needed in San Antonio to take care of young Frances, the baby girl of the family, and to help the Judge keep house. None too willingly the Captain finally acquiesced.

* * *

Character specialists tell us that it is heredity plus environment and education that make the man. That is why such insistence has been put on "spiritual" heredity in this chapter. For I have learned so much of Frederic Dunne's early environment and education that I felt if I was ever to show that the man so many knew and loved was "fathered" by the hitherto unknown boy I had to speak long and earnestly of his spiritual inheritance. Let us look now at his education.

CHAPTER FOUR

School—But No Little Red Schoolhouse

NO ONE who chatted with Gethsemani's fifth Abbot for any length of time could doubt his possession of an exceptionally keen intellect and a real mastery in the art of conversation. The ease with which he discussed events and the skill with which he avoided any analysis of persons or personalities, the positive genius he displayed in bringing every conversation to bear on God or the things of God led practically everyone to conclude that he had been highly educated and had supernaturalized all his secular education.

I have heard him place phrases from Horace, Vergil, Cicero, Caesar, Tacitus, and Ovid aptly in conversation after conversation. Once when a discussion had almost developed into an argument, he turned the subject by quoting a line from Aristotle. Often he borrowed from Shakespeare. One day he read me one of Thomas Merton's poems — and as I have told my warm and ever understanding friend, Father Louis — he made that poem almost intelligible to me. The Abbot often told me of his vibrant love for poetry, and on more than one occasion manifested real appreciation of art, music, painting, and sculpture. How could I or anyone else escape the conviction that he had received a thorough training in what was known in the old days as a classical course?

Yet the plain truth is that while Dom Frederic Dunne was un-

doubtedly one of the most intelligent men ever to live at Gethsemani, nevertheless, among the choir religious, he was one of the
least educated in the sense of being schooled.

In 1883, when Captain Hugh brought his eldest daughter and
his youngest son up from the newly established town of San
Antonio, Florida, to live with him in Atlanta, Katherine Ellen was
not yet sixteen and Frederic Arthur was only eight. The Captain
would have them continue the education begun in this city before
the death of their mother and their smallest brother. In those days
Katherine Ellen had been enrolled with her sister, Mary Hastings,
in the Day School for Girls conducted by the Sisters of Mercy in
Atlanta. Young Frederic Arthur had to descend to the basement
of the Immaculate Conception Church where, along with others
of his age, he learned his A B C's, the multiplication tables, and
some reading and writing from the same good Sisters of Mercy,
who could not bear to see the young Catholic boys of the section
utterly neglected.

But Frederic Arthur Dunne's blessing of having his early instruction in charge of teaching Sisters lasted for all too brief a
period. He was under this expert care only until 1885. In that
short space of time, no matter how bright he was, the good Sisters
could not have brought him beyond the primary grades. Yet I like
to think that the chivalry Frederic Dunne ever showed toward
nuns in all his later years was nurtured by this all-too-short
schooling with the Sisters of Mercy in the basement of the Immaculate Conception Church.

But these were not the happiest years of life for the Captain
himself. For the family still lived in that one-story house he had
built for his beloved Mary Lois at the corner of Merritt Avenue
and West Peachtree Street, and he was too keenly conscious of her
absence. His own loneliness was increased by his insight into the
loneliness of his little ones. He knew they needed a mother; needed
direction and sympathy and affection only a mother can give. He

experimented with this housekeeper and that, even weighed the advisability of a second marriage. In the end he wisely allowed young Katherine to assume the role of the lady of the house, a decision he never had to regret.

Frederic told me about the family Rosary every night, and his sister, Mary, now substantiates him in a letter glowing with memories of these years in Atlanta. She pictures herself, Fred, and Frances going off to school every day (for the Captain had brought all but Jesse up from Florida in 1884); shows them side by side at the Communion rail every second Sunday of the month; tells of parties in the home at which Fred and Fannie entertained with songs and recitations.

Mary's letter is one which might well set any aging man or woman dreaming of childhood days and wondering what happened to mar the evident happiness and destroy the obvious peace of such a home. It was Dom Frederic himself who revealed that to me. He put it very pithily. "My father," he said, "had sent a sawmill down to San Antonio and with it a man who was supposed to go into partnership with Jesse. Since the settlers wanted lumber and this was the only sawmill for miles around, they did a thriving business. But after three years of hustling Jesse had nothing more to show for his labors than a mighty mound of sawdust. The partner took the profits, Jesse received the bills." At this point in his story, Dom Frederic's bushy white eyebrows went up and a quick turn of his head accompanied the side remark: "Nice kind of partnership, wasn't it — for one partner!"

Then he went on to tell how his father resigned from the Harrison Company, sold his property in Atlanta, arranged for the family to follow him, and hurried down to San Antonio and the sawmill. Before the children arrived the partnership had been dissolved and the mill itself sold. That was characteristic of Frederic Dunne's father — even as it was of himself. When a thing was to be done, they did it quickly.

The trip made by the children from Atlanta to San Antonio has been chronicled by the Captain's second oldest daughter, Mary, and that chronicle serves better than anything else would to give us a vivid picture of the environment Frederic Arthur Dunne knew in his childhood and adolescence. She begins by saying: "The ride from Atlanta was uneventful until we reached Callahan, Florida. Here we took the Plant System." That, I take to mean one of the earliest railroads in the state. "There was no schedule," she says. "We traveled on leisurely." But the leisure is much more evident than the travel in what immediately follows. "There were no passengers," Mary continues, "except our crowd — Katherine, myself, Fred and Frances — and a Vincent Acosta of Jacksonville. Once I admired some wild flowers along the track. The Conductor immediately stopped the train. We got out and picked all we desired, then clambered back on to go our leisurely way again."

"Later on," says the account, "the locomotive ran off the rails onto the cross ties. The train stopped. Some men came along and helped get the engine back on the tracks — and away we went again. The track ran right through the old Harris Grove. The Conductor again stopped the train so that he and Mr. Acosta might gather some fruit for us."

"Finally," says Mary, "we arrived at Wildwood, the end of the railroad. Here Jesse met us with a covered wagon drawn by two mules. With him was a Frank Bischoff, the son of one of our neighbors in San Antonio."

Most urban dwellers of today will conclude that civilization must have ended at Wildwood since the railroad terminus was there — and that conclusion will not be far from right. The travelers were still almost half a hundred miles from home and the train came to the end of the track at nightfall. Jesse told his sisters and younger brother that they were to stay in the rooming house which was called a hotel that night while he and Frank Bischoff slept in the covered wagon.

Early the next morning he and Frank kindled a fire under their animals to get them up and moving. Once under way he handed the reins over to fourteen-year-old Mary while he and Frank went back into the covered wagon to be with the rest of the family. It was a long ride and night was falling again before the flopping ears came to a halt near the little sawmill and the new house just beyond.

The Dunnes were home. And for the next six years — the most formative years in anyone's life, those between eleven and sixteen — Frederic Dunne was to be at home in San Antonio, forty-five miles from the nearest railroad — and that the Plant System.

If we believe in God, we have to believe that every event of life fits into a plan; that every so-called "accident" is part of Divine Providence — permissive, if not actually directive; that every single moment has a meaning all its own. Believing all this, it is easy to see how a selfish sawmill partner can fit into God's plan. Frederic Dunne could have been brought up in Atlanta, Georgia, or Ironton, Ohio. He was brought up in neither; for while neither was what we might call a metropolis in those days, they most certainly were populous when compared to the wilderness of Pasco County and the west coast of Florida. It is according to God's ruling that the grown tree show how the twig was bent. It was according to God's plan that his future silent monk should know some solitude when a very young man.

If the comparative silence and solitude of San Antonio were not God's prime purpose in allowing Jesse to gather sawdust from his labors, surely the hardships inescapable from any sort of pioneering were meant to prepare Frederic for the grueling regime he was to find at Gethsemani in his early years as a Trappist. Some may even think God was preparing him for his future meatless diet when they learn how he and the Dunne family first learned about skinning a rabbit.

Tired of the continuous round of fish that had been served at table of late, Jesse shouldered his gun one day in early 1886 and went looking for game. He was the man of the house at the moment; for Captain Hugh was up in Jacksonville negotiating with the H. and W. B. Drew Company, Stationers and Printers, about becoming supervisor of their shop. Jesse returned with a rabbit. He handed it to Katherine — who had become "mother" of the family — with the proud words: "Now we can have meat for a change." When he saw a cloud of perplexity gather on his sister's brow he asked: "What's the matter? Don't you know how to cook it?"

Katherine held the cottontail in her hands for some time before answering Jesse's question with one of her own. "How do you prepare it?" she asked.

Jesse laughed that short laugh which tells of a superiority that will condescend. "Uncle Johnny Howell says when it's cooked right it tastes just like chicken. So I suppose you get it ready just as you would a hen. Heat some water while I clean my gun and I'll help you fix it."

Twenty minutes later Uncle Johnny Howell happened along, and in true southern style looked into the Dunnes' kitchen. His roar of laughter could be heard perhaps to the opposite shore of the lake, which Judge Dunne had rechristened "Jovita." "Children! Children," he cried, "give me that there animal. You skin a rabbit; you don't pluck him." And there, in the heat of the kitchen, Jesse and Katherine learned how to prepare what will taste like chicken but will never allow itself to be plucked like one.

It was from incidents such as this, and from anecdotes told now and then, that I got my picture of the environment Freddie Dunne knew as a boy. His only living sister, Mary, and the Judge's only living son, Eugene, have sharpened many a detail in the picture by their generous letters filled with reminiscences of the early days in San Antonio.

Wildwood, the name given the place at the end of the railroad track, quite aptly described what lay around and beyond that station. Almost fifty miles due south of what is now known as Clear Lake, but which Judge Dunne insisted on calling "Lake Jovita" lay in the Florida sunshine — and just beyond it stood the tiny settlement of San Antonio. The few families, most of whom had come from the northeast expecting to set out an orange grove almost overnight and have it yielding a comfortable living within a very few years, soon learned that all the pioneering in America was not to be done in what was called the "Wild West." These people had to open up what was practically virgin territory even though it occupied what was some of the earliest discovered land in America.

Pioneering always means privations. It requires daring, initiative, resourcefulness, adventure, and conquest. It also means loneliness and suffering. What scenes leap to life from this crowded portion of a letter Mary Dunne Wichers sent me: "During the early days of the Colony, supplies of all kinds had to be hauled from Wildwood or the then small town of Tampa by wagon. It took at least two full days to make the trip to Tampa. And if any shopping had to be done, a week was consumed by the round trip. Range cattle furnished our beef. A cow could be bought for eight or ten dollars. Once every week a man came around with beef for sale. A large soup bone, with plenty of meat on it, cost only ten cents; while fifty cents would buy a roast large enough to serve a small family like ours for three whole days. Of course we had our troubles. Wild cattle and hogs caused plenty. The new settlers introduced fences to the country. We all joined them in gathering logs, splitting them, and setting up rail fences. Each family had its own garden and potato patch, but the big work and the big hope lay in the orange groves. As winter came on, it was customary with some of the settlers to fatten a few hogs, then invite everyone to a hog-killing and syrup-making, or, as they called it, 'to the cane-grinding.' We were a hard-working, but very happy people."

In such a situation there was opportunity for real education; but what chance was there for schooling? And that explains Dom Frederic's omission of all reference to "his school" or to things that happened "in the classroom." The truth is he did not refer to school or classroom because he could not. He had no school, and his classroom was a kitchen. But that fact holds many revelations. The first being that of his teacher, a certain Mrs. Morse.

I would give much to know more of Mrs. Morse's background; for I believe it would reveal to us what is best in the American character and manifest what has contributed most to our culture and our country. But all I know is that she came to San Antonio from Charleston, South Carolina, a widow, it seems, with her six young children. Like most newcomers her hopes were fixed on oranges. Now whether the Judge had been advertising his "Freedom for Religion Colony" or the Disston Company had been seeking people to develop their land, I have been unable to find out. But there is one line in a letter that lay among Dom Frederic's papers which gives some insight into the woman's deeper purpose for coming south. It runs: "She liked the Judge's idea of true American Freedom."

Mrs. Morse had not been in the new town long when she came on the Judge one day clearing a site with the help of Captain Hugh's two eldest: Jesse and Katherine.

"New house?" queried Mrs. Morse.

"House of God," replied the Judge without ceasing to shovel.

"Hmmm," was the woman's only comment. But the Judge caught all that was meant by the mumble.

"My house is no place to say Mass," offered the perspiring Judge as explanation.

"I'd love that," mused the motherly Mrs. Morse. "To have God under my own roof. . . ."

"*Non sum dignus*," grunted the Judge as he lifted an extra heavy shovelful onto the donkey cart. He then paused to wipe his brow.

"Have you thought of a schoolhouse?" asked the woman as Katherine and Jesse paused to follow the Judge's example.

"Too soon to think of that," came the answer accompanied by a shake of the head that bespoke more finality than his words or tone. "We've got to get more settlers and become more settled."

"The minds of the children now here won't wait for the settlers, Judge, before they grow. We ought to see that they grow right."

Judge Dunne leaned on his shovel, squinted at the mounting sun, then in a dreamy, faraway fashion said: "There was once a Chief Justice of Arizona who held that the right and duty of education devolves on the parents. . . ."

Mrs. Morse's laugh made music in the morning sunshine. "You'll never cease being a judge, will you? But now be a justice — and tell me what little Fannie and young Frederic Dunne are going to do when their father is off in Jacksonville and their mother up in heaven. Will you assume the responsibility of parent and the role of teacher?"

The ex-Chief Justice smiled. "Why couldn't you, who have the responsibility for a brood of your own, take these two chicks in with you. . . ."

And so it was done. But Mrs. Wichers tells me that not only Fred and Fannie Dunne joined the Morses, but the three Malones and the two O'Neills invaded the kitchen that was a school.

If we apply the Gospel test of "by their fruits . . ." we can only marvel; for in the man, Dom Mary Frederic Dunne, we can see that surprising and surpassingly efficient educator, Mrs. Morse.

Frederic Dunne is an animated argument for "education" as against "schooling." Too long and too often the two things have been identified in the minds of men, and it has been this confusion that has led to much that is confounding. Thousands believe that because children go to school and are taught how to read and write, they are being educated. Nothing could be further from the truth. That very process of schooling may erect the greatest possible barrier to these same children's ever being educated; for, as Frank Sheed once pointed out, reading in itself is scarcely an intellectual activity at all: "The power to take words off a page," he says, "is little more than an extra sense. By hearing, for example, what is said reaches the brain through the ear; by reading, what is said reaches the brain through the eye. The whole question is what happens to it when it reaches the brain. And," he adds, "literacy statistics cannot tell you that."

Carlyle said the aim of all education was to teach men to read. But by that he never meant the national pastime that has seized our country and so many of our countrymen — the game played by the eye accustomed to alphabets, spelling books, and ink on a page; the widespread game of devouring type. Frank Sheed has very rightly said that this kind of reading "becomes a craving like smoking," then pertinently adds, "and its intellectual value is about the same." But what Carlyle meant when he said the aim of all education is to teach a man to read, is exemplified in Mrs. Morse's product, Frederic Dunne. He assimilated, made part of himself and his personality, the ideas he found in print. More, I think he can also be pointed to as proof of that other pertinent remark by Frank Sheed; namely, that *what* a man reads is a much surer measure of his education than any number of degrees.

Mrs. Morse had the growing boy in her kitchen along with the other children of the settlement, for about four years. In that time she did not cram the child's memory with information, but labored to give the boy's intellect a real formation. That she succeeded is proved by the man. He may not have known as many facts as some of our modern college students, but he knew what to do with the facts he had.

What has been said of reading is equally applicable to writing. The question whose answer distinguishes literacy from scholarship, and this again from education, is not: "*Can* they write?" but: "*What* can they write?" And again Mrs. Morse appears as an educator.

Frederic Dunne was not a scholar in the sense that he possessed great learning. How could he be when he had only two years and a half in the basement of the Immaculate Conception Church in Atlanta, and four years in Mrs. Morse's kitchen? But he was educated. He had a mind; and he knew what to do with it. He had a memory and a will; the first was retentive of things worth retaining, and the second was made strong by discipline. He had an imagination and emotions that had been brought under control and made properly functional by the disciplined will and the trained mind. In this faraway kitchen he matured and gradually grew to be a man. What credit must be given to Mrs. Morse, Katherine, and Captain Hugh Dunne!

The last two are linked with the teacher, for they contributed no less to the education of the boy into manhood than she by her "schooling without any school." Katherine, as Dom Frederic announced to the community at Gethsemani the day he received news of her death, became his "mother." And he was always proud to say: "I was raised by a soldier." In the grown man we see the result of that happiest of combinations — the home and the school. In him we also see proof that our "little red schoolhouses" may not be all we sentimentally think them to be. Perhaps we need a few more kitchens like Mrs. Morse's; undoubtedly we need more homes like that of the Dunnes.

CHAPTER FIVE

"The Thoughts of Youth Are Long, Long Thoughts"

BUT what was the Dunne home like? With the mother in heaven, as Mrs. Morse had said, and the father up in Jacksonville the greater part of the time, it would seem that the Dunne home was something of an orphanage and young Frederic something of an orphan. But that is only seeming. For, despite the fact that when a mother dies a family often breaks up, the Dunnes remained united because of Katherine's generous heart and Captain Hugh's dominance.

This later annihilated distance and had him spiritually present to his children despite the physical absence necessitated by business. I call it dominance rather than discipline, for in it there was a fatherly warmth that called forth filial obedience and not the cold compliance discipline can command. A mere disciplinarian may be admired, he is never loved and made the hero Captain Dunne was made by his children, and especially by his youngest son, Frederic.

Katherine's eight-year seniority aided her in the assumption of her mother's place, but it was her tact in handling the growing children and her womanly intuition which enabled her to divine when to be unyielding and when to cajole — all of which sprang from her great sisterly heart — which made her to Fred and Fannie very nearly their mother.

30713   51

Of course no one, no matter how loving and understanding, can fully replace a mother. God seems to have given mothers something of His own great mind and heart. And since they cocreate with Him, they alone can win what He alone can claim as due — that love which is utterly pure and unselfish, and those acts which spring from such loving devotedness.

It is also true that, despite Captain Dunne's dominance, the children did suffer from his prolonged absences. Jesse became the man of the house and Katherine played the role of mother, but there is always a difference between those who are directly commissioned by God and share His authority, and those who are merely delegated. Further, it is incontestably true that physical presence allows for subtle psychic interchange and the unconscious assimilation by the children of the very spirit of their parents. All this was denied the Dunnes. It had its effects.

There was a loneliness and a certain lovelessness in the lives of these children due to the death of their mother and the absences of their father. Yet this irreplaceable love and inescapable loneliness knitted this little family more closely to one another and so entwined the hearts of the two youngest that Fred and Fannie grew up as one. It was that rarest of rare friendships in which the boy accepts the girl as both real companion and object of his budding chivalry, and the girl takes her brother as understanding as any girl and as wonderful as any lover.

Fred and Fannie roamed the woods above the lake and learned much of nature. Close contact with birds and flowers, with the land and livestock does something to the soul. To see new life spring up where old life molders away; to find unfledged mouths opening to the whir of the mother bird's wing; to watch instinct guide the unintelligent surer than any human genius, makes one conscious of a Power that is unseen yet all-pervasive. These two children wandering in the woods and playing on the shore of the lake fell in love with the wonders of Nature and all unconsciously

came in close contact with God. It was here at San Antonio that
a tenderness for all forms of life, even the lowest, grew in the
mind and heart of Frederic Dunne and was manifest in the aged
Abbot who would plead with his monks not to molest the few
bats that flew about Gethsemani's cloisters. To him they were
not only harmless animals, they were wonders of God's careful
devising.

But Mrs. Morse showed the youngsters more ways than one
to satisfy the curiosity of the mind that will hunger for truth
until it at last possesses Him who is Truth. She taught Fred —
and he taught Fannie — that literature is to portray life; that by
wise reading one can learn much about people and grasp some
important principles; that character can be formed by studying
characters. It is not strange then to find Fred and Fannie in one
of the "castles" Jesse had built on the shore of Lake Jovita reading
while the rain pours down. But what is enlightening is to scan the
contents of what Fred called his "library" and contrast it with the
mass of print Jesse had accumulated through the years. Katherine's
daughter, Mary, sent me the mementos her mother had saved
of Fred. One page reads: "List of Books from the library of Fred
A. Dunne." It makes an interesting study.

For the imagination there was Jules Verne with his *Around
the World in Eighty Days, The Desert of Ice,* and *At the North
Pole.* Other fascinating fiction and imagination developers were
Ragnarok and *Atlantis* by Ignatius Donnelly, and *A. D. 2000* by
Lieutenant Alvarado Fuller of the United States Army. It is not
surprising that the young Fred Dunne, the son of a Civil War
veteran, should have such books as *Incidents and Anecdotes of
the Civil War* by Admiral Porter; *Ohio in the War, Camp Life in
Florida* by Charles Hallock; and *Four Years — A Scout and a Spy*
by E. C. Downs. With such books it was easy to spend a rainy
day in one of the "castles" and have Fannie as avid for the next
page as he was himself. But as the boy matured he looked into

Guizet's *History of France* and the *Sermons, Lectures, and Speeches of Cardinal Wiseman as He Toured Ireland in 1858.* From the first, a four-volume set, he learned much about his mother's people; the second told him of his Irish ancestors.

No doubt Fannie was not taken by these more serious books, but Fred had the poetical works of Tennyson, Whittier, and Thomas Moore to recapture her attention. As they matured he read to her from Shakespeare and John Ruskin.

It is a revealing library. It shows the bent of the growing mind and the deepening of the maturing soul.

Jesse's hoard was a great stack of *Scientific Americans.* But even these intrigued both Fred and Fannie; for interest in the practical and the mechanical seems to have been a family trait. When over seventy and burdened with the countless cares of growing monasteries, Frederic Dunne would become as curious as a schoolboy whenever he came upon a machine or an invention that was new to him.

Being the first born, and consequently burdened with some responsibility for each of his younger sisters and brothers, Jesse had matured early. He was not more serious than Fred — no one could be. But he lacked Fred's vivacity, his keen, but ever subtle and sly humor. Circumstances really made Jesse a man before he had ever been a boy. The shifting from one abode to another, the early death of Mrs. Dunne, and the Captain's preoccupation with business made Jesse the responsible party for things down in San Antonio.

His experience with the sharp practice of his partner in the sawmill made him a very wary and shrewd man of business thereafter. He saw to it that the family got a deed for its property; that the forty acres he planted with trees had been surveyed and marked. He, with the Judge, became advisors to all new arrivals and insisted that everything be done in legal fashion. In many ways he was a mature man without ever having been a boy.

Frederic Dunne as a scholastic (top center)
about 1898

Prior Frederic Dunne (1st row, second from left) about 1914

Prodesse Magis Quam Praeesse
("I will be their minister more than their master")

Abbot Dunne at the time of his election

Abbot Dunne in his work clothes (1946)

All this, plus the almost ten years which separated Jesse and Fred, made their relationship more nearly that of father and son than two brothers. I remember how Dom Frederic at his golden jubilee celebration introduced Jesse to the community by saying: "There is one in our midst who used to boss me as a boy and exercised quite an ascendancy over me in the years that are gone. But I really think those days are dead." Would that I could catch all the lights and rippling overtones that carried those words to us. Then you would see what I saw; that between these two was a love that glowed.

But in the early days Jesse looked on Fred as too young to be his helper and too old to be a nuisance, so he commanded him to keep hands off his many inventions, hobbies, and works. He did allow his kid brother to help build the two little houses on the shore of the lake which he named Castle Thunder I and Castle Thunder II. He planned to sell these to settlers. Until purchasers arrived he used them as storeroom and laboratories for some of his electrical and chemical experiments, and as a library for his magazines.

Jesse was always making things in order to make money. At one time Fred would watch him fashioning boats to sell to those who would fish in the lake. At another he would accompany him as he peddled the fish he himself had caught in that lake. And always he could see his older brother tending the orange grove that was to be the source of the Dunne fortune. Jesse allowed Fred to be company, but his preoccupations never allowed him to make him his companion. Fred was practically forced to take Fannie as his bosom pal. Yet this was almost inevitable for she was nearest to him in age and most like him in temperament. She was warm, generous, sociable, and vivacious. The greatest tribute Fred could pay her was his inviting her to accompany him when he hunted, fished, or simply tramped the woods.

It was after one such tramp when Fred was about fourteen that the brother and sister found themselves in Jesse's Castle Thunder II. It had been a sultry afternoon and the two were sitting idly, resting after their walk, when Fannie pointed to a statue of our Lady which Jesse had placed high on a shelf and asked: "Is that what Mama saw before she died?"

The question was so sudden and utterly unexpected that Fred gasped. Soon, however, he recovered and answered with feeling, "No. No, Fannie. It was no statue Mama saw; it was the very Mother of God herself. And Mama said she had our little brother Eddie in her arms."

"Well, Jesse told me that statue came from Atlanta, so I thought . . ."

"It did. But as far as I can remember that wasn't even in Mama's room."

"Mary said —"

"Don't mind Mary. You ask Katherine. Mary doesn't remember any more than I do, even if I was only six going on seven."

"Mary says you're too independent."

"I know it. But one of these days I'm going to tell Mary that Lincoln freed the slaves. She's worse than Simon Legree. . . ."

"Where does he live — up at Wildwood?"

Fred laughed. "Sometimes I think he lives here in San Antonio under the same roof as you and I. And sometimes I think he is a girl by the name of Mary."

"Mary's all right," said Fannie as she moved over toward a bench and picked up a bit of nickel-plated pipe. She knew Freddie thought Mary too young to boss him and was on the verge of pouting now as she remembered she had absorbed some of Fred's resentment and failed to respond quickly to one of Mary's commands.

Sensing that his little sister was upset Fred looked for a diversion. Seeing the nickel-plated pipe in her hand he quickly called: "Hold that, Fannie, and close your eyes and I'll give you something to make you wise." Thereupon he snapped on the switch of the tiny battery Jesse had made.

A trifling electric shock passed up Fannie's hands and arms. She jumped and gave an excited squeal of fright.

Fred immediately turned off the switch and asked with a grin: "Are you wise?"

"Mary's right," came the pout from a chagrined little sister. "You *are* too independent."

"Glad you found out for yourself, Fannie," said Fred as he started for the door, "for very soon I intend to show Mary and everybody else just how independent I am."

"What do you mean, Freddie," cried the eager-eyed youngster as she caught up to her brother.

"Just wait and see," was all the satisfaction she got that day.

But one year later, when Freddie was fifteen, he announced to all that he was through being a little boy who went with other little boys and girls to learn reading, 'riting, and 'rithmatic from Mrs. Morse in her kitchen. He was now a man who was going to work and help support the family.

Mary laughed. Jesse looked questioningly and a trifle pityingly toward his younger brother. But Katherine, who knew the mettle of the boy, frowned. Later she took him aside and talked to him. But she could not persuade him that he was too young to think of going to work.

"Father's over fifty," he said in that incisive way of his. "Jesse has been working since he was fifteen. It's time for me to help. I can earn money enough for my own clothes and for some of your groceries."

"But what can you do, Fred?"

"I can go to work tomorrow as a carpenter on the monastery they are building."

Monasticism came into the life of Frederic Dunne before he was out of his teens. San Antonio did not grow quickly. But about

1886 the first railroad came through the town and the large, sprawling county called Hernando was divided into Citrus, Pasco, and Hernando Counties — a sure sign that authorities expected developments. Judge Dunne welcomed the activity. For with O'Neills, McCabes, Mullans, and Flanagans about him he knew he had Catholic settlers, but he was still wondering if he had a Catholic settlement. He had reason to wonder; for as stated above, it was only when Ben Wichers and Old Man Sultenfuss would drive to Tampa in their two-mule team that a priest ever came back to San Antonio — and that was only once a month. Father Peterman offered the Holy Sacrifice in the Judge's own front room those first few years. Then, when the little church was built, Father O'Boyle came as a resident priest. Still the Judge was apprehensive. The community was not large. He feared the Rt. Rev. More, Bishop of St. Augustine, might have scruples about leaving a priest there permanently. His fears were not absolutely groundless, for soon Father O'Boyle left the town and the county. But then God's hand is seen in the coming of a Benedictine named Father Gerard.

When this good priest got acclimated and found the atmosphere so saturated with Catholicity he appealed to Belmont Abbey to make a foundation in the section. In 1889 Father Charles Mohr with a few other priests and some Brothers came to found St. Leo Abbey. The Judge donated his home to these Benedictine pioneers. Years later he rejoiced to see the permanent building of the abbey rise on the site of his home, and to hear how daily Calvary was re-enacted over the very spot where it had been renewed for the first time in the settlement of San Antonio — his front room.

With the coming of the monks, permanence to the settlement was assured, at least to the Catholicity of the settlement. For the boys would be taught by the priests of the abbey, and with daily Mass a certainty, Benedictine nuns soon came to establish an academy for girls — and allow Mrs. Morse to use her kitchen for the purpose it was made and the children to go to a real school.

Before either school was built, however, Frederic Dunne was old enough, as he thought, to help support the family. Jesse had reason to look pityingly on his younger brother the night Fred first spoke of going to work, and Katherine had even more reason to marvel at his assurance that he could get employment as a carpenter; for while Fred was handy enough with tools, Jesse had done all the work that called for any skill. Yet Fred went to work and as a carpenter. Help was not plentiful in that part of the country, and those who were building the wooden monastery for the Benedictines were only too glad to take Fred Dunne on as a carpenter despite his age and his inexperience.

For two full years he worked with hammer and saw and, because he was thrifty, proved to Jesse and Katherine that he could not only support himself and buy most of the groceries for the house, but even have some left over for an occasional present to his sister.

Of course next to none of this was known to us in the community until after his death. That is why some of us used to wonder if the Abbot had garnered all his practical wisdom merely from observation and some shrewd surmising. For instance, whenever we older monks had work to do on hazardous heights, such as the roof, the steeple, or towering trees, he would warn us with: "The amateur seldom gets injured; for beginners are always careful. It is the old hand that grows careless. So, watch your step!"

Little did we know that he had learned that truth firsthand. The story comes from Jesse's eldest daughter, Ida, who heard it from her father. It was during Fred's first year of work as a carpenter. He was on the partially completed roof of the wooden abbey. A fellow carpenter, a much older and much more experienced man, made a misstep and began to fall over the side. Fred grabbed him. They both began to slip over the edge. But quick-minded, nimble Fred locked his legs about a projecting beam and managed to hold on until a third carpenter came to rescue both. No doubt it was this memory that made him say: "It is the old hand that grows careless. So, watch your step!"

When Captain Hugh heard that his youngest boy was a wage earner he began to wonder if he were not an old man. But in the spring of 1891 when he learned that Mary was about to marry Anselm Wichers he hurried from Jacksonville wondering why he did not feel old enough to be almost a grandfather. He could hardly believe his eyes on the morning of June 15 when Mary walked down the aisle of the little church of St. Anthony of Padua, which the Judge and his children had built for the newly founded settlement. How the years had flown! It was difficult enough to try to realize that Mary was of marriageable age, without complicating the situation by having Fred as best man and Fannie as bridesmaid. But there they were.

The Captain suddenly realized he was losing his children before ever having enjoyed them. He did some thinking during that marriage ceremony, and before the Benedictine Father Kitchner had finished with his ritual, Hugh Dunne had made up his mind to take Katherine and Fred with him to Jacksonville, to teach the latter the trade of bookbinder and printer and have the former help him as she had done in Atlanta. Fannie presented a problem only until he thought of the fine academy the Sisters of the Holy Names had opened in Tampa. She should go there to complete her education, the Captain decided. Jesse could stay on at San Antonio and care for the estate.

This breaking up of the Dunne home in San Antonio robbed the settlement of more than a young carpenter. It took from it the young man who had served most of the Masses that had been offered in the little church almost from the beginning. It robbed it of the one who had taken upon himself the task of reminding the folk of the countryside three times a day that they had been redeemed by a God who so loved them that He became one of them, being born of a woman. The Angelus ringer was going north. It robbed that settlement of a sight which had puzzled many — that of a young boy walking the dusty lanes with one hand in his pocket and the other tipping his hat at rather regular intervals. Frederic Dunne loved his rosary and reverenced the holy names. It took from the town a youngster everyone admired and most people loved because of his kindly sociability and his infectious good nature.

San Antonio lost. But Jacksonville did not really gain; for up in that growing city Freddie Dunne buried himself in his work and in the recreation poets, artists, and philosophers love: communing with the sea while holding a rod to which is attached a line, a hook and a sinker. They call it fishing. But more often it is only formulating plans, some of which are as important as life.

Captain Hugh Dunne knew book printing and binding thoroughly. That is why the Trappist Abbot, Mary Frederic Dunne, so often displayed such expert knowledge of paper and print; of cutting, binding, and trimming; and of the covering of books. Ever an apt student, he was at his best under the tutelage of his father. He learned bookbinding and printing as few learn it today. He knew every step in the process and every stitch in the finished work. So when choir books at Gethsemani needed to be repaired or replaced, he knew what he was about. And whenever a choir monk handled those books roughly he soon learned what he had been about; for the Abbot would say: "Be careful! A book is only a bit of paper, some glue, and a tiny measure of thread."

Who would ever link a Catholic settlement in Florida, a bindery in Jacksonville, and the Trappist monastery at Gethsemani, Kentucky? They were linked — closely linked as all subsequent history shows. God's providence is seen in retrospect and found as described in Revelation: "Disposing all things sweetly." Because Freddie Dunne was to walk the white road to Bethlehem and the bloodstained road to Calvary when his hair was white, he had to know the loneliness and the lovelessness of San Antonio

without father or mother, the privation of pioneering, the lack of
formal schooling, the independence that made him a worker on
wood before he was fully grown, and the silence of the forests and
the sea. These would have prepared him to be a monk, but since
God wanted him as abbot, he had to spend three years under his
father as bookbinder and printer. The long arm of coincidence is
always seen to be the strong hand of God when one studies facts
in their fullness.

Abbot Dunne once said: "I wouldn't give the world for the
three years I spent with my father in business. They have helped
me more in the last two decades than any other three years of
my life." He was then seventy-two.

Was he talking about the knowledge and skill acquired about
printing and binding books? Not at all. Did he mean the ability
to transact business with foresight and dispatch? Perhaps. But even
more than that he meant the knowledge he gained of men — their
ambitions, drives, ideals, ideas; their selfishness and surprising un-
selfishness; their disgusting greed and their astonishing generosity.
The business world can be a revelation of all that is good and
great in man as well as an open confession of all that is small and
niggardly in him. Frederic saw both — and learned how to handle
men; even the one who was named Frederic Arthur Dunne. For
it was here, more than any place else, his independence learned
discipline and his energies, direction.

By the summer of 1893 he had not only mastered his trade,
but he had saved enough to take his first vacation. He decided to
travel. His choice of destination was typical. His ever active
mind and keen curiosity took him to the Columbian Exposition in
Chicago, where in a week he would learn more about people,
places, mechanical progress, and scientific advance than he could
by a year's reading and study; for the Exposition was truly a
world's fair.

A good idea of that experience can be gained from the description he gave to his close friend and onetime schoolmate of Mrs. Morse's kitchen, Will O'Neill. Fred had gone to visit Fannie, who was still at school in Tampa, and he was thrilled to learn that Will was in town.

It was a night of stars in late September, he told me, when he and his friend were seated on the edge of a wharf overlooking Tampa Bay. The only sound was that of the lapping waters as they set some of the piles gently swaying. Far out on the breast of the bay phosphorescent streaks broke the soft sapphire ripples. The sheer loveliness of the night struck a contrasting chord in his memory. He chuckled. When O'Neill asked him what the joke was he got the surprising answer, "I am." Then Freddie Dunne told him about his trip.

"I looked Chicago up on the map," he said, "and saw it was next to the Great Lakes. Beyond them I saw Hudson Bay. I had read Jules Verne and thought I knew something about the cold in that part of the world. So I prepared for my trip by purchasing a few suits of heavy woolen underwear and an overcoat big enough to keep out the strongest wind in the Windy City. When I got there, I found it hotter than Florida!"

Then for two hours he told of what he had seen at the Fair. Freddie Dunne had a gift for vivid description and rapid narration. When they arose, preparatory to going home, Will said: "How marvelous is the mind of man! Think of all those wonderful inventions and those marvelous machines."

Freddie Dunne startled him — and, as he confessed to me, startled himself — by replying: "It all made me think how wonderful God is and what His mind must be like."

When O'Neill grunted and said: "Fred Dunne, you get the strangest ideas! I often wonder why you don't become a priest. The girls don't seem to bother you. . . ."

"What's strange about the idea I just had, Will? I saw some wonderful sights in Chicago, as I've just been telling you; but there was nothing there to beat or even equal that" — and his hand went out toward the sapphire waters of the bay, then circled up toward skies that were spangled with silver. "You think the machines I described are marvelous. They are. But what could be more marvelous than the tides that come and go here in the bay; than the leaves that form every year and fall from the trees; than the fruits and vegetables that grow over the ground and under the ground year after year after year? Have you ever thought how wonderful your own eyes and ears are? No one can invent anything better — or as good!"

"And that's precisely why I say you get strange ideas," said O'Neill. "How many men would think of such things as marvelous?"

"But they are, aren't they?"

"Yes, they are."

"Then don't you see why Chicago with all its man-made marvels made me think of God? But now I'm going to tell you of a place more marvelous than Chicago, and I'm going to let you in on a secret no one else in the wide world knows. . . ."

Then, in the calm magnificence of that September night, standing on the deserted wharf, Fred Dunne told how his father had been up to Ohio for an encampment of the G.A.R. and on his way back had stopped at a place called Gethsemani, where some Trappist monks were spending their lives doing nothing but praising God. The young printer dwelt on that idea as long as he could, for he admitted that it not only intrigued him, it actually haunted him. He could not believe that men had been so wise as to devise a mode of living on earth that was, save for its limitations of time and place and the obscurity of faith, identical with the life lived in heaven. The more he had thought about it, the more he had been drawn to admire and envy with a holy envy those who were there, and finally to long to be one of them.

"I've thought a lot about it, Will," he concluded. "I'm not

good enough or educated enough to be a priest, but maybe I could become a lay brother."

O'Neill had been mesmerized by the talk. But when young Fred spoke of becoming one of these strange men he came out of the semitrance and objected. "Why think of the Trappists and Gethsemani when you have the Benedictines right in your own back yard?"

"If I go, I'll go far away from home."

"Well, why not think of the Jesuits? These monks sound strange to me."

Fred laughed and admitted he had thought of the Jesuits. "It was a Jesuit who converted my mother, you know. And Katherine tells me that one day when Father Desribes asked me what I was going to become — I was five at the time — I answered: 'I'm going to be a Jesuit priest.'"

"There you are!" exclaimed O'Neill.

"There I am not," was the reply. "I have not had half enough schooling to be a Jesuit. Furthermore the Trappists appeal to me because they earn their own living."

"Fred Dunne, you're the most independent cuss I ever met. How do these monks earn their living?"

"By hard work. Father says they have a large farm on which they work almost the whole year around. When not working on the farm, he says they work in the woods. I like the idea of earning my own bread and butter. . . ."

"I thought you said they didn't use butter."

"Oh, you know what I mean. I don't like to beg. . . ."

"Too proud?"

"Maybe. But let's go home. And remember all this is a secret. I haven't decided anything as yet. Nor have I spoken to anyone but you."

Seven months later Freddie Dunne was in Tampa again. But this time he was doing the listening. He was hearing his favorite

sister, who had summoned him, tell of a decision she had reached —
and, all unknown to her, that decision was to settle her brother's
doubts about his own life.

Fannie had been a boarder at the Academy of the Holy Names
since 1891. Her scholastic record had been consistently high
and she had more than one prize to show for her ability in
competition. Living in close contact with the Sisters day and
night, it was not unnatural that she should become attached to
them and to have mused more than once on their manner of
life. Fred admitted that as he listened, he learned how natural
the supernatural really is, and how normal that utterly sublime
thing — a vocation — can seem.

It was the spring of 1894 when Fannie finally said she felt that
God had given her a vocation to become a Sister of the Holy
Names. Fred was not exactly surprised, but he was curious. He
asked his sister how she had come to the conclusion that God
was calling her. When the baby of the Dunne family told him
that she simply felt an attraction to the life, thought that she could
be happy serving God as a teacher in that community, and that
both her confessor and the Sisters had said that this attraction,
along with sufficient health of body and mind to live the life, was
sign enough, Fred knew that he had a vocation to be a Trappist.

More than once he said to me: "Oh, Father, I can see the hand
of God in every event of my life. He even used my independence
and pride to make me a monk."

In July of 1894 Fannie went off to Canada to begin her
novitiate.

That event precipitated more major moves by the members of
the Dunne family than anything since Mary's marriage or the
mother's death; for before the end of that same month Fred
handed his sister Katherine a bulky envelope with the words:
"If I am not back in two weeks, open this and follow directions."

It was a strange statement. It frightened Katherine; for she had seen how Fred had grown more and more independent with the years — independent in thought and action. In tones shot through with anxiety she asked: "Where are you going, Fred?"

"Oh, heading north again on what may be another vacation."

"Where are you planning to take that vacation?"

"Haven't definitely decided yet. It may be up around St. Louis. There's some machinery there I'd like to see." When he saw worry trace its furrows across his sister's forehead he laughed and added: "Don't worry, Katherine, I'm not taking any woolen underwear this time."

Katherine laughed then. But just under two weeks later she was opening a letter with mounting curiosity. It bore Fred's handwriting, but was stamped with the stamp of a Kentucky post office. When she read the letter she did not know whether to laugh or cry. She did a bit of both, for now she knew that Fred and Fannie, the two she looked upon as her "children," were in religion.

She then opened the bulky envelope Fred had left with her ten days earlier. In it she found separate envelopes addressed to each in the family. She opened hers and read how Fred had decided to become a Trappist lay Brother, feeling that God was calling him to that life — and that, as far as he understood, this would be the last communication he would have with any of them this side of the grave. Then came a pouring out of his heart to Katherine in thanks for all she had done and been to him since the Blessed Virgin had come with their little brother Eddie in her arms to take their mother home. Katherine cried then — but joy was the cause of those tears more than sorrow, and every bit as much as were her loneliness and love.

That same evening she presented two letters to her father: one that was in an envelope that had been slit and which bore the Kentucky postmark; the other, unslit, had come from the bulky package Fred had left in her keeping.

Captain Hugh Dunne read both, then sat in stony silence, slowly shaking his head. When he finally did speak it was only to say: "No, I can't believe he should be a lay Brother." Turning to Katherine he suddenly asked: "Did Fred ever speak to you about this?"

"Never, Father. Never."

The Captain sighed, shook his head, and asked: "Didn't some poet once say: 'The thoughts of youth are long, long thoughts'?" Katherine was silent. "I wish he had told me what was on his mind."

"Would you have objected?"

"Not to his going, Katherine. But I can't believe God wants him for a lay Brother."

CHAPTER SIX

La Trappe in Kentucky

THE very thought which filled Captain Hugh's mind the night he read his son's two letters had been entertained by another earlier that week. This other's full name was Edward Chaix-Bourbon, but at the time he was thinking the Captain's thought he was called "Reverend Father" by his monks, "Father Abbot" by friends of Gethsemani, and "Abbot Chaix" by businessmen. As soon as he had identified the young postulant as the son of the Captain with whom he had been corresponding this past year, he shook his head and said: "No, I don't think we will accept you. . . ." When he saw a cloud of disappointment darken the countenance of the twenty-year-old boy before him he quickly added: ". . . as a lay Brother. I think you ought to become a choir monk and a priest."

"But I have so little schooling, Reverend Father," was the instantaneous objection. "Further, I am not worthy to be a priest."

The wise old Abbot smiled kindly. "Who could be worthy, son?" he asked. And Frederic Dunne heard overtones of wonder and sadness in the old monk's voice. Years later he understood the question and the overtones, but on August 2, 1894, he could only marvel. The Abbot then brightened and added: "As for schooling — there are places a man can be educated other than school. And I'd prefer intelligence to knowledge any day. A Trappist needs a will more than he needs a mind anyhow. Come in."

Frederic Dunne went in and found himself in a very strange world.

Only the afternoon before, while stranded in Louisville because no train would leave for Gethsemani until the following morning, he had known hours of real anguish. They began when he suddenly asked himself how he had ever come to think himself worthy of a Trappist vocation. That led him to wonder what rashness it was that took him from home before he had looked more deeply into the life of a monk and measured his own assets to ascertain whether he could meet the demand of the monastic regimen. "Am I good enough?" "Am I strong enough?" "Have I got the necessary will power?" "Will I be able to stand the silence Dad talked about? — and the fasts?" Question after question mounted in his mind until, as he later admitted, he found himself very definitely scared. He settled it all by saying to himself: "Well, at least I can give it a man's try."

When he detrained at the tiny station next morning, he saw that Wildwood, Florida, was a metropolis by comparison. He and a tiny sack of mail dropped off the train. That was all. The engine snorted immediately and went whistling away. Fred looked around. He saw a little man in a funny brown dress which was tucked up at his knees squinting at him from behind bushy white whiskers. There was an air of friendliness about the little man, so Fred mustered up enough courage to ask: "Are you the Abbot?"

Bushy white whiskers shook and blue eyes twinkled, but the only answer came from an arm that swung in a wide arc and a hand that pointed to the north. Then the funny brown dress moved off toward a horse and buggy, beckoning young Dunne to follow him.

Actually it was only a mile to the monastery, and the horse covered that distance in less than fifteen minutes. But the silence of the white-whiskered driver cast such an eeriness over the trip that Fred thought the drive endless. Some of the thoughts he had dismissed yesterday afternoon in Louisville came back. Then a new idea came into his mind! Even if he could stand the life, he began to wonder if he would like it.

The wait at the gate before the Abbot arrived did not help the situation. Freddie saw bearded men in black and white and bearded men in brown glide silently across the garth or just as silently come down from what he recognized as a school building on the opposite hill. It all seemed a bit weird to the young man fresh from the clang of the printing presses and the noise of the growing city of Jacksonville. When the Abbot arrived and proved to be a short, rotund man who was full of questions about name, age, address, employment, health, and reasons for applying — especially without having written previously — all asked in an English that spoke of French birth and upbringing, Freddie Dunne wondered some more. But once the Abbot walked him across to the main building, things happened so fast and were so contrary to expectations that the postulant had no time to wonder.

First came the definite reversal of status. He had come to be a lay Brother. People always spoke of the lay Brothers as "humble," and Freddie Dunne had known for years — and had been told by his sisters, brother, and father — that he was proud. Now the Abbot insisted that he be a priest, and surely the Abbot ought to know if he had the qualifications. Next came the revelation that he could write to his family. Dom Edward had insisted that he immediately sit down and write home, telling of his arrival and acceptance. The Abbot had not liked the idea of leaving as he did — without telling his destination or determination — and he wanted him to have definite word to them before Katherine opened that bulky envelope Fred had left with her.

But the monastery itself . . . mammoth was all Fred could call it as he viewed the length and height of the church and saw its silver steeple yearning into the sky. It seemed to him that St. Leo's Abbey, which he had thought quite large, would fit into the open quadrangle formed by the Gethsemani buildings. But when he attended his first choir service he was actually frightened to find that there were only six choir monks on each side of the church with two novices in front of each short row. Sixteen men to fill that apse with song! It seemed a pitiable sight and the postulant knew a real scare.

That same night he saw the entire community assembled for *Salve* — the Trappists' "Good night" to Mary Immaculate, their Queen and Mother. Fred was impressed by the setting: a lone statue of the Virgin flooded with light and every gaze riveted on it while the haunting melody of the song rose and fell in the dusk that was not yet damson. But the boy counted only forty-six heads. Could that be all there were in this mammoth monastery? It was a disturbed young American who slept his first sleep in Gethsemani that sultry August night. But he had fallen asleep telling himself he'd make a man's effort to lead the life.

Next morning he was taken along the bare wooden cloister and led to the novitiate where he was introduced to Father Henry Zumbush, who was to be his Master of Novices. In a very few moments Freddie had learned that the man who was to be his Master had come to Gethsemani in 1877, but had lasted only six months. He was back again, however, before the year was out. Then for twelve full years he had remained in the monastery as an oblate. It was only at Christmas in 1890 that he had become a novice. Young Dunne liked the man immediately and listened avidly to the tales he told of his home in Westphalia, his experiences as a secular priest, and finally of his years as a Trappist. Later in the morning he took the new arrival into the tiny room that was to serve as his novitiate and allowed him to bow his head to four men whom he introduced as: "Frater Bruno from Upper Rhine in Germany"; "Frater Mauritius from Bavaria — he is a priest"; "Frater Odilo from Württemberg"; and "Frater Nicholas from Prussia — also a priest."

When they were alone again Freddie smiled at the Master and asked: "Shall I learn the sign language in German?"

"No," replied Father Henry genially enough, "but you had better learn some French without signs. That is the language of this house. In Chapter that is all you will ever hear. In the refectory we read from French authors, and practically all the books you will use as a novice are in that tongue. Have you any knowledge of it?"

"None whatsoever."

"Well, don't be frightened. You'll catch on soon enough. Discouragement is the devil's handiest tool. Don't let him use it on you. But you don't look like one who would lose courage quickly. Here's a book you might like. It's in English." And the Master handed him Frederick William Faber's *Creator and Creature.*

Frederic Dunne read very little that day, for his mind could not do two things at once; it could not analyze the strange world he found himself in and reason along with the closely reasoning Father Faber. And Freddie Dunne wanted to analyze his new world.

The monastery was massive, but it was also austere and extremely poor. The wooden cloister around the inner garth showed rotted beams and leaks in the roof. Its wooden floor creaked under his foot and the damp odor of decay was all about it. The Church had beautiful arches and a few towering Gothic windows — but these had only plain, glaring glass. The altar looked small in the great yawn of the sanctuary, and the gigantic, crude wooden cross with its oversized dead Christ appeared repellent to the new postulant.

What little he had seen of the farm made him suspect the truth of the reports he had heard about the monks being expert agriculturists, and had him much more ready to accept the slur literature had cast upon them as "lazy." For the rail fences seemed slovenly built, and the fields themselves looked unkempt. Freddie was soon telling himself that the entire establishment gave the impression of being both unfinished and not very efficiently cared for. In the little room that was the novitiate the floor was of cruder cut than anything he had seen at San Antonio even in the earliest days. Then the monks . . .

The Abbot was a bit over sixty. His Prior, Father Benedict, was seventy-three. Father William, the Subprior, was just sixty. Father Henry, his Master, was fifty-eight. Father Leonard, Professor of Theology and of almost everything else in the monastery, was fifty-four. The only other professed priest in the community, Father Stanislaus, was fifty-six.

Last April Frederic Dunne had entered the year which would mark his majority — and he had felt quite a man. But now, as he looked around at the aged, bearded men, he felt like a child among ancients.

What he had found among the choir monks was accentuated by the lay Brothers. Two of these, Brothers Theodore and Antoninus, were survivors from the pioneer group which had left Melleray in France almost a half century earlier. But they were not the only old men in the group of nineteen lay Brothers. Brother Daniel was seventy-seven. Brother Alberic, seventy-three; Brother Lawrence was sixty-three, and Brother Dominic just turning sixty.

Frederic Dunne felt, and actually was, a mere boy in a small community of old men — and most of them Europeans. He, an American with a limited command of the English language, found himself among men who could converse with ease only in French. He wondered what had ever caused him to think he had been called to such a place and such a life.

From what he had seen and heard, it was clear that Gethsemani was living the life detailed in the form letter he had found on his desk the day of arrival. It said: "Our life is austere." Fred shook his head in agreement. He then went over the regime as outlined there. "We rise at two every workday, at one on Sundays, and at midnight for the solemn feasts." That did not phase him;

for the Master had told him they retired at seven o'clock in the winter season and at eight in the summer, but made up the hour by a siesta at noon. He could stand that easily enough, he thought. Then the seven or eight hours of Office in the church seemed formidable only when you looked at the figures. Freddie Dunne looked at the fact. He would be praising God all that time. That did not scare him. The work — four to six hours a day in the fields. He paused on that and pondered. His few days in Kentucky showed him that Florida did not have all the heat in the United States. Somehow or other, Gethsemani seemed hotter than Jacksonville. Could he stand that work in the fields under that hot sun? But then he thought of his brother, Jesse, and the long days he used to spend in the San Antonio orange groves. This would not be any worse; probably not nearly as bad. He could take it, he thought.

"The silence is unbroken," the letter said, "but the Superiors may be spoken to when necessary." The last half of that sentence rather than the first gave the boy real pause. How was he to speak in a language he did not know? He wondered why his father had not mentioned the fact that the monks were all foreigners. He finally consoled himself with the truth that he could at least learn the sign language the Master had told him about, and maybe in time he could pick up enough French to make himself understood.

The next paragraph called for long reflection.

"The food is poor and simply prepared. No meat, fish, butter, or eggs are ever given in the Community, but sometimes to the sick in the Infirmary. Vegetables, milk diet, preparations of flour and maize are all you will find in our Refectory. In summer there are two repasts; in winter, but one, and that at half-past two; while in Lent it is at quarter-past four. . . ."

His sister, Katherine, would become positively ill just thinking of that regimen for the boy she was always urging to eat regularly and well. Fred smiled now as he thought of how she used to scold him whenever he would hurry off with Frank Carroll or Will O'Neill. His smile grew broader as he thought what Will would say to a life in which you ate but one meal a day, and that at quarter past four in the afternoon after being up since two in the morning.

"For drink," the letter read, "is given cider or beer."

He had never tasted beer, and did not care for cider. Could he stand this life? he asked himself again. He shook his head in doubt until he recalled the thrill he had felt when he first read the final paragraph:

"Perhaps this setting forth of our mode of life may appear to you too rigorous. This is the idea that is formed in the minds of such as are not called. But should you say with St. Augustine: 'Why should I not do what such and such do?' and find yourself urged by the motion of the Spirit to undertake what is opposed to your nature, this inclination to penance will be a good sign, and with good will you ought to succeed here. This is all that is required for the admission of an applicant."

Father Faber's book was slapped against his knee as Frederic Dunne told himself he had all that was required; for he had a will. Had not his sister, Mary, often called him stubborn? And he still felt inclined to lead this "life of expiation," as the letter called it, despite the uneasiness caused by the thought of sleeping fully clothed in this August weather after six hours in the fields, seven or eight in the church, and only a meal or two.

In later life Frederic Dunne admitted that there may have been more of the motions of nature than of grace in this early determination of his to lead the life. "My father used to say that when a mule met me, the mule gave in. I was stubborn. But thank God I stayed."

He did stay. But on August the twelfth he saw something that made him think longer thoughts than any he had had in youth — and thoughts that could have ended his stay.

On the eleventh of the month Brother Alberic died. The very next day Freddie Dunne was in the cemetery attending his first Trappist funeral. He saw the body carried in on an open bier. He watched as it was lowered into the grave without so much as a board to support its limpness — just the lifeless body, clothed in the poor brown of the lay Brotherhood. He peered down curiously as the four who had acted as pallbearers began to shovel the clay upon the corpse. He noted that they let it fall as gently as possible and directed it first to the feet. Before they had reached the head, Fred noticed that the face had been covered with some sort of a cloth which had been tucked into the brown hood drawn over the Brother's head.

It was the first time Fred had seen a coffinless burial. It repelled him until suddenly he remembered that soldiers who had fallen on the field went into their graves in their uniforms — and only in their uniforms. He brightened. That very morning he had read the Prologue of St. Benedict's Rule and learned that the Patriarch of the monks of the West spoke only to those "who were ready to take up arms in order to fight under the Lord Christ, our true King." He watched the planting of the cross over the grave and knew he could consider the dead Brother as one who had fallen on the field of battle and gone into his grave as every such hero does — in his uniform and only in his uniform. A more spirited postulant went back to the church chanting the Penitential Psalms.

The following morning he was asking his Master what it was that the Abbot had said in the chapter room the night before. Dom Edward had spoken in French. All that young Frederic could catch was something about prayer. What he heard from the Master that morning made such an impression on him that he would repeat it a hundred times the next fifty years about men he, as Prior and Abbot, would bury. Abbot Chaix had said: "All Brother wants now is our prayers. He was seventy-three years of age when God took him — and had spent exactly half of his long life here at

Gethsemani. Of course we hope that he amassed untold merits during those thirty-six and a half years. But we know not the awful purity of God. So pray. If Brother could be sorry for anything now, it would not be for the hard life he led here, but only that it had not been harder. He regrets not a single cross he bore, but only that there weren't more and heavier ones. So let us all take courage from his example and accept our hard life with all its weighty crosses, not only willingly but lovingly. For we will all be one day where Brother is today."

That afternoon brought Frederic Dunne face to face with his first great temptation and crisis. It all began when the twenty-year-old American went out to the newly mounded grave and began to think. Strange as it may seem it was not of death, but of life, that he thought. He had been long enough at Gethsemani to know quite intimately just how Brother Alberic had spent the last thirty-six and a half years of his life. To a boy of twenty such a stretch appeared as an eon, and Freddie Dunne fell into what is perhaps the most common temptation a contemplative faces. He thought long on what looked like a life of utter emptiness and a human existence that was completely sterile. For thirty-six and a half years, summer after summer, Brother Alberic had gone out to hoe a field of corn or mound a few rows of potatoes. In the winter of those many years he had been out to the woods sawing down and chopping up trees. As the young postulant looked down on the heaped-up clay he asked what Brother had to show for those decades on decades of life. At seventy-three he had died with hands that were hard, but with hands that, to young Dunne, looked frighteningly empty.

Frederic Dunne was an American. He had all the American's passion for results and innate drive to accomplish something tangible. As a child he had seen a town grow under the hands of his elders. He had watched his brother Jesse turn a wilderness into an orange grove. As he grew he noticed that the efforts of the pioneers always brought palpable effects. When old enough to work he had taken hammer, saw, and plane, and learned the secret of making every movement count. Formlessness would take definite shape under the cut of the saw and the blow of the hammer. When day was done he had something to show for his labors. The same was true of his years with his father at Jacksonville. Trays of type lay before him — mere letters of the alphabet. But after selecting this one and that and putting them into his stick; after setting them all up and locking them into their form; after running them through the press, he had a book that might move the world. He had results that were visible and latent with unlimited possibilities. The devil knew all this better than did young Dunne. It is no wonder then, that he had the postulant looking down on the grave and asking himself if he had been grossly misled.

A subtler element came into the matter when he suddenly realized that he all but adored his father and now suspected that his filial devotion was at the base of his great delusion. In Captain Hugh Dunne Fred had seen what he considered manhood at its best. Bravery devoid of foolhardy boldness had been shown in the war. Real energy, enterprise, and efficiency had been displayed at home and at work. By sitting in on many of his business conferences the son had come to look upon his father not only as exceptionally prudent but as extremely wise. Hence, when the Captain had spoken so enthusiastically of the Trappists after his first contact with them, the boy had immediately conceived a lofty admiration for these strange men who had so moved his father. That was the beginning of his toying with the thought of becoming a monk. He now concluded that adolescent hero worship had led him to a place where a coffinless burial climaxes a life of emptiness.

He recalled now that his father had concluded one of his talks about the monks with the words: "They are men, those Trappists. With them I hope to make my final encampment before meeting my Commander in Chief — who is God." Maybe that was the day he, Frederic, had really decided to come to Kentucky. Maybe that was the day his admiration for his father had led him into making a great mistake. He frowned heavily, turned from the grave, and sought out his Father Master. . . .

A little over an hour later Fred Dunne came out of the Master's room. The frown was gone. There was starlight in his eyes. And in his heart he had a text he would use almost daily for the next half-hundred years: "If with this life only in view, we have had hope in Christ, we are of all men the most to be pitied" (1 Cor. 15:19).

In that hour he heard a history that never finds its way into ordinary history books. He heard ideals which modern man dismisses with a shrug of the shoulders and the smearing catch phrase: "Angelism"; but which medieval man not only conceived as worthy of their manhood, but by actual manly striving had realized at Citeaux, Clairvaux, and La Trappe — and which some of the more modern men had actualized at La Val Sainte, Melleray, and Gethsemani.

Father Henry told the anxious postulant how in the fifth century St. Benedict of Nursia had dreamed an impossible dream of how men, while still on earth, could do what the Blessed did in heaven — live in the presence of God, continually loving and adoring Him; then went ahead and made his impossible dream come true by founding the cenobitic form of life.

Freddie Dunne listened to the story of SS. Robert, Alberic, and Stephen and learned how in the early Middle Ages some very real Crusaders never went to the crusades, and how some truly chivalrous knights wielded only the sword of the spirit. The cloister began to assume a different atmosphere and the life within it appear in a far different light from the one in which he had seen it while standing at the new grave.

All that he had half glimpsed while sitting on the wharf at Tampa, looking out over a bay streaked here and there with phosphorescent beauty; all that he had half grasped while ambling alone in the woods at San Antonio; all that he had but dimly discerned while kneeling at the back of the church in Jacksonville, now became clear. That day he saw something he was not to lose sight of the rest of his long life, and something he endeavored to bas-relief for everyone with whom he had contact. It was that the Trappist life is a life of vibrant, vigorous, virile faith, or it is utter folly; that men in the cloister need faith and fortitude and very little else. But he never failed to add that of these they need a superabundance. They have to believe with all their heart.

Freddie Dunne was keen and imaginative. So as Father Henry talked, Freddie saw De Rancé, one of the most brilliant men of that dazzling age of Louis Quatorze outdazzle all his contemporaries by a renunciation that would be sheer madness had we not the Gospel story of Christ and the Rich Young Man. He saw this favorite of the King and darling of the King's all-powerful Prime Minister, the great Cardinal Richelieu, not only resuscitate the monastery at La Trappe, but revive the monasticism of early Citeaux — and all "that God might in all things be glorified."

It was extreme. It was revolutionary. But that day Frederic Dunne learned just how revolutionary was Christ and how extreme, Christianity.

He saw Dom Augustine Delestrange, at the dawn of the French Revolution, take a handful of monks and go to Switzerland "that God might be glorified." He saw that tiny handful grow into a veritable colony as men and women thronged to the Holy Valley that they might make reparation to the God who had made them free, equal, and His children; make reparation for the outrages committed across the border in the name of liberty, equality, and fraternity.

Freddie Dunne saw that the Trappist life was only for those who love God and their fellow man with a love that makes them completely forget themselves. Nothing else will explain La Val

Sainte or that monastic odyssey made when men, women, and children went from Switzerland to Germany; from Germany to Poland; from Poland to Russia — and all the way back again "that God might be glorified" in those days when Paris knew martyrs and Napoleon was striving to make himself lord of the world.

It would be years before young Dunne really mastered the history of his monastic ancestors. It would be only after a faithful application of those principles Mrs. Morse had taught him about the right way to read that he would be able to tell how, when, where, and why certain Benedictines became Cistercians; then centuries later how certain Cistercians became Trappists; and finally how these Trappists, after splitting into various observances, were reunited under Leo XIII to become again what His Holiness called "the true Cistercians," and hence, the Benedictines of Benedictines. But right now he saw that his sires were men of faith and fortitude; men of unselfish loves and lives. They all died as Brother Alberic had just died: empty-handed as far as human eye could see, but full-souled under the gaze of Omniscience, if Christ's words be the words of God.

By the feast of the Assumption Fred's will was set, and from that day until the day he died it never wavered. He asked only for faith and fortitude that he might live to God in Christ Jesus with no hope of reward in this life save that of an approving conscience.

It would be years before he was wise enough in the ways of God to see that He who is a Consuming Fire had placed a spark in his heart these first few days and so exceptionally graced him that this spark grew and grew until it burst into the flame which men would later speak of as "Dom Frederic's surpassing love for God and all that God had made," and of his devotion to the Cistercian Strict Observance that was a veritable passion. But one day he did see it. From that day on he advised all postulants and novices to "make an unconditional surrender to God and forget self entirely." He would unhesitatingly promise sure and steady progress in sanctity "if you will abandon yourself utterly to the good God." But in 1894 all he knew was that he was determined to give the life a man's trial "that God might be glorified."

On August 21 he was clothed in the Cistercian habit and began his canonical novitiate.

CHAPTER SEVEN

Greater Love Than This...

THE most common reaction to the description of what Freddie Dunne did on August 21 is the exclamation: "Didn't he have courage!" But that exclamation is meaningless unless it is used with a keen appreciation of the root meaning of words. It took *heart* to do what he did. Love is the only explanation of his deed that day and of his entire consequent life. A Trappist monk is a lover, a passionate lover, or his life is an endless lie.

For a young American, just attaining his majority, who owned property in Florida and had a trade with a most promising future, to give it all up and join a small community of rather aged monks who had come from a foreign land and spoke a foreign language, takes more than courage in the ordinary sense of that word. To stay on willingly after learning that this tiny community lived a life that was anything but American: observing a black fast for more than half the year, serving only cider or beer with the one daily meal, working their farm in utter silence and striving to give antistrophe to the ceaseless strophe of heaven's choirs, demands more than the ordinary American man has.

Frederic Dunne stayed and became "Frater Mary Frederic." What is the explanation? I said "love" up above and even intimated that it had to be a passionate love. But complete as that may be, it still needs explanation.

The keenly analyzing Cardinal Newman made the observation in his old age that much of our activities in early life, which we deemed due to grace, were really motions of nature. It is a very wise observation and it fitted in perfectly with his theory that the soul grows old just as the body; a theory he used in spiritual direction for himself as well as for others. He used to tell old men and aging women that they were not to be cast down when they felt less fervent than they had felt ten years earlier; and found spiritual acts which they did with ease in youth, now quite difficult. His explanation was that the soul was now left with no natural impulses, affections, or imaginations to rouse it; that it was cold, torpid, dejected, and knew real lassitude. Thus it comes to a true realization of its own nothingness, not because it has less grace than formerly, but because it now has nothing but grace to aid it.

It is a fascinating theory and undoubtedly holds much truth. We so easily deceive ourselves and take a natural impulse to be a divine inspiration; so often are subtly seeking self when we think we are being courageously self-sacrificing. The energetic man will call his innate energy zeal; the apathetic and languid will dare to term their natural laziness religious decorum and self-control. Newman tells truth when he says there is much of nature in what we deem to be grace; but what he failed to tell was the truth that the God of Grace is also the God of Nature — and that "grace builds on nature." Hence no one in his sixties is to regret what he did before he was forty, thinking it a case of having given the horse its head while deeming himself the expert driver. Our God-given temperaments are ours to use for a God-given purpose. We would never have the flaming St. Paul had there not been a fiery Saul; nor a rocklike Peter had there never been a stubborn fisherman named Simon.

But the point here is that what Newman found in his old age, would be reversed in the case of Frederic Arthur Dunne. Had he in his old age, analyzed, as did the saintly Cardinal, he would have discovered that much of what he took to be nature in his youth was really grace.

He wrote the bundle of letters he handed to Katherine and which he thought would be his last to the family. He purchased the ticket and rode to Louisville. He battled himself, the world, and the devil that first long afternoon and night. And finally he chose to remain even after learning just how un-American was this Trappist way of life. But the truer truth is that God not only graced him, He gifted him exceptionally that August of 1894.

The young aspirant did not know it then. Nor even in later life was he ever given to minute theological analysis of the action of God within his soul. But with an uncanny intuition — a legacy perhaps from his Alsatian mother — he divined that something more than his own will was in the action. So he went ahead with confidence.

I have said that Frederic Dunne was gifted that August of 1894. I have chosen that word deliberately, for already it has been said that he was graced. Now although every grace from God is a gift and every gift from God is a grace, in everyday life and in technical theology there is a vital and even vigorous difference between the two. And perhaps nowhere is that difference seen with greater clarity than in a Trappist novitiate.

Of course there is no such thing as physical consciousness of grace as there is of bodily health. "Man knoweth not whether he be worthy of love or hatred" (Eccles. 9:1). But there is altogether too great an unconsciousness of our baptismal endowment and confirmational grant; too great an unawareness of our spiritual assets and divine resources. Perhaps Frederic Dunne can alert us.

For Christians, every truth should be incarnated. For American Catholics, who are so much more at home with the quantitative than the qualitative, who are impressed by concretions and not by abstractions, this wrapping truth in flesh and blood is a neces-

Pontificating, 1947

In New York, June, 1948,
Negotiating for the fourth Foundation

Dom Frederic as Burnt Out Incense

Archbishop John A. Floersh with censor
This simple black box serves as bier for all Gethsemani monks

Procession to the grave
Abbot General Sortais at left in cope — Abbot Fox at right front of bier

sity. So instead of telling how every child or adult who is baptized receives from a lavish God not only grace but four cardinal virtues, three theological virtues, and seven gifts of the Holy Ghost; instead of insisting that these seven gifts hold a pivotal position in our supernatural organism, since they support the cardinal virtues and, as St. Gregory the Great teaches, even perfect the theological virtues; instead of showing that these seven gifts actually constitute seven steps to spiritual perfection; I will have you look not only at palpable facts but at palpitating persons.

There were four novices in the tiny room over which Father Henry presided the day Freddie Dunne crossed the wooden cloister to become an accepted postulant. None of them lies under an iron cross in Gethsemani's cemetery today. Why? — Why does Frederic Dunne?

It cannot be a matter of what some call "good will"; for I have yet to see a single postulant come to the Trappist novitiate without having the very best will in the world. Not all have the best understanding of themselves or of the life they have come to live, of course; so not all actually have a vocation. But granting that some have no vocation whatsoever; and even admitting that some have what is termed a "temporary vocation"; we are still faced with a mystery — and I use that word deliberately. Why do not all who have a real vocation persevere? To clarify the issue we can limit ourselves to those who actually stay, and ask the question: why is it that some actually glow with what is called fervor, radiate what can only be termed true holiness, as did Frederic Dunne while others just as earnest, just as anxious to serve God and grow in the likeness of Christ, seem ordinary?

The answer, I think, lies in the one word "gifts." But that solution only creates a greater problem; for it presents a far deeper mystery: that of the providence of God, His distribution of grace, and the selection of certain souls for special favors by Him who according to St. Peter and St. Paul is not "a respector of persons."

Father Henry watched his young American and his four older Germans and saw God the Holy Ghost at work. Naturally speaking, the four foreigners should have felt more at home than the newest arrival. They were older men, two of them were priests, and they were in a community made up mostly of their fellow countrymen. French was almost as much their native tongue as was German, and the asceticism of the monastic regime was in no sense alien to them. Yet, as the Master watched, he had to think of Teresa of Ávila and her description of the different kinds of prayer and the human activity characterizing each. He saw one of his men laboring with all the effort required to lift bucket after bucket of water by hand from a deep well to water a garden of no mean size. He saw another going through the same exercises but with perceptibly more ease. This man was like one who had a windlass to get his water from that well. Still another was taking the novitiate training with all the facile grace of a man who has diverted a stream into his garden and allows the irrigation ditches to do the work for him. But the young American, with all his native energy and enterprise, because of the enthusiastic manner he threw himself into the entire program, reminded the wise old Master of the one Teresa describes as letting God with His rain do the watering of the garden.

Had Father Henry been pushed for an explanation of the manifest differences, since, in the beginning, each appeared as avid for high sanctity and as generous in his efforts to conquer self and put on Christ, he would have had to borrow from Teresa and say that those who labor as strenuously as those lifting water from the well by hand are those who work with only ordinary sanctifying and actual grace. Those with the windlass have exceptional actual graces and a greater abundance given them with which to work, and they co-operate generously. The man who knows the effortlessness of owning irrigation ditches is the one who uses the infused virtues, both moral and theological, with greater consciousness, constancy, and effect. Actually they have and use more faith, more hope, and know more charity; they display greater prudence, fortitude, justice, and temperance. But there is yet a fourth class, and to this Frederic Dunne belonged. These are the ones to whom the supernatural life seems natural, who perform acts of virtue seemingly without effort, who have an instinct for things divine and a veritable intuition which enables them to see God in everything. It was of such and for such Francis Thompson sang in his *Kingdom of God:*

> O world invisible, we view thee.
> O world intangible, we touch thee.
> O world unknowable, we know thee,
> Inapprehensible, we clutch thee.

These are the ones in whom the gifts of the Holy Ghost are not only active, but dominantly so. For them the spiritual life is comparatively easy; for, to a great extent, God takes over.

Not all recognize this fact. But Frederic Dunne, perhaps by that same intuition I spoke of above, perhaps as the result of a little reflection on his own experience, came to know this truth, and as abbot would often use the example so frequently given by spiritual writers. He would liken those who work with ordinary grace to a child toddling after its mother, walking and often stumbling on his own wearying feet. "But there are others," he would say, "who are like the child the mother picks up and carries in her arms. We can be like that if we will but abandon ourselves entirely into the hands of God." I doubt if he knew it, but actually he was talking of the Gifts of the Holy Ghost.

Father Henry, however, was a deeper and more technical theologian. He knew what was going on. He saw the results of the gift of fear in this young American who was evidently fearless. In 1894 there was far less preoccupation with fear than there is today, so it may be necessary to state that the fear which was at work in the soul of Frederic Dunne had nothing cringing, cowering, or cowardly about it. Father Henry saw the exact opposite to these characteristics in his newest novice who took the silence, the coarse meals, the hard bed and short sleep, the wearying farm work, and the tedious house cleaning with an enthusiasm and joy that brought smiles to the bearded face and a sincere "Thank Thee, O God the Holy Ghost!" from his heart. The Novice Master saw fearlessness being bred in the soul of the young American, a fearlessness that had the boy curbing his nature with a relentless hand.

Those who knew the austerity of Frederic Dunne's life as Abbot will understand its source when they learn that the gift of fear, which is the beginning of wisdom, leads to the practice of great austerities for the purpose of rooting out completely what seems ineradicable — our selfishness and tendency to evil. It also spurs one on to the same austerities for the opposite purpose: that of avoiding the very semblance and shadow of what might be offensive to God, our Father.

The learned Dominican theologian, Father Arintero, has summed it up well when he says that under the influence of this gift the soul "seeks with great fervor to be crucified and transfixed with the nails of holy fear, that it may never be a victim of the Divine wrath." But that is not quite exact if we are to take it as a pen picture of Frederic Dunne. In the light of his last conversation with me, and of what I have learned of his early life, it is evident that he did make the cry of the Psalmist his own cry: "Pierce through my flesh with fear; for I am afraid of thy judgments" (Ps. 118:120). But Father Henry saw what Gregory the Great depicts as the proper action of this gift. He saw that the compunction of fear really leads to the compunction of love. So he rejoiced to find his newest novice growing in reverence and esteem for God, our Father, to whom we owe everything; for he knew that such fear would beget the virtue which is the foundation and the

crown of the Cistercian life — true humility. He even said what
the great Pope said before him: "The way to Perfection is from
fear to hope to love."

It is worth noting here that this kind of fear is not cast out by
love. The opposite happens. This holy fear is increased and perfected by charity. For the more a man is sanctified, and the more
a saint is deified, the more he understands God's great aversion to
sin. And because God is viewed as Father, fear of the one thing
that will offend that Father grows. Hence, ultimately and basically,
love is the substance of this, as it is of all the other gifts. That is
why Father Henry rejoiced and allowed the young American to
have his head, as it were, those early months.

That Dom Frederic never lost this gift can be attested by all
who listened to him morning after morning as abbot. His invariable
cry was: "Oh! Let us get rid of self. Let us be ruthless with
ourselves and root out every last vestige of pride!" The Book of
Proverbs tells that this gift "hates arrogance and pride," and
holds in detestation all deceit. More than that it gives an insight
into ourselves which makes imperative the practice of all Christian
virtues; for it sets us burning with the desire to rid ourselves of
whatever can separate us from God, and yearn to purify ourselves so entirely that we can attain union with Him who is all-
pure, all-holy, all-just.

The gifts make the spiritual life easy; but they do not enable
us to live it without effort. Frederic Dunne suffered those first
few months. It is inevitable; for entering a Trappist novitiate is
very like undergoing a surgical operation in which cords are cut —
and some of these are veritable umbilical cords! For many things
that actually furnished us with intellectual, emotional, and social
life are taken from us with all the finality of a real surgical
severance. Heartstrings that were entwined are ruthlessly and
radically separated. Family, friends, business and business associ-
ates, hobbies, interests, recreations, books, games, distractions are

all left behind, and the lone individual is found alone with his God — his Novice Master — and fellow novices.

The asceticism of the Trappist regime is sound and deep. It effects a complete detachment. But so is the psychology of the Trappist regime deep and sound. It presents the candidate a positive goal; it sets his mind and heart on attachment to God and the things of God, and thus keeps him forward looking; his face ever toward the sun. It has often reminded me of the experiment in physics used to demonstrate displacement. A solid is introduced into a liquid — and the liquid goes out. Trappist novice masters place the solid, substantial, eternal Christ into the aspirant's heart, and away go the weak, watery infatuations with things of time. But perhaps the cleverest bit of human psychology is displayed in the manner in which they keep the newcomer busy. He is so occupied, he has not time to think how radical has been his transformation from the life of a layman into that of a monk.

In 1894 Frederic Dunne was no more conscious of his great gift of fear of the Lord than he had been at the time of his Baptism. But he was very conscious of his pride, impatience, and a very real covetousness. He became a glutton for time.

He had to learn the French language. He had to master the Trappist sign language. He had to acquire some knowledge of the Latin tongue. He had to master the intricacies of the Breviary. And he would not have been the son of Captain Hugh Dunne if he did not want to make himself letter perfect in the thousand and one prescriptions of the Trappist *Usages*, prescriptions that govern everything from the proper way to address an abbot to the way you hold your hands while walking and your head while greeting a confrere. Time was at a premium — and time flew.

Just before his golden jubilee Dom Frederic made the statement that he had never spent one day of routine in the Trappist monastery. It is a startling statement when we remember that the monk's day knows next to no variation from one end of the year to the other save that of the seasons and the liturgical cycle. It is always: up for Office, out to work, in for the one meal, a few moments of reading, off to the Office again. Yet his statement is true and can be repeated by every monk who learned, as Freddie Dunne learned in his very novitiate, to throw himself heart and soul into every duty of the day; to live an intense intellectual life as he chants the Psalms or assists at Calvary's sacrifice; to see the symbolized in the symbol and have heart beating with the Sacred Heart from the *Fiat* of Mary Immaculate to the final *Fiat* of Gethsemani's grotto; then to go on living with the glorified Christ through the Resurrection, Ascension, and sending of His Paraclete. The life of a Trappist choir monk is one continual confrontation with the God-Man. He is their contemplation just as He was and is the one Contemplative. That is why there is and can be no boredom in a life that looks like killing monotony and death-dealing routine. There is and can be no boredom; for their life is not something but Someone — and God never bores.

Frater Frederic never had need to command "night to be sudden" or "dawn to be soon." His day was crowded and his night was short. That is why the weeks blurred into months and the months merged into seasons with an almost shocking swiftness. Most likely it was back here in his novitiate days that he coined the phrase we so often heard him use as his life neared its end: "There is so much to do, and so little time in which to do it."

It was spring in 1895 almost before Frater Frederic realized that winter had come. But as that spring flowered into summer, one who had witnessed his physical weaning arrived to see how his spiritual weaning was progressing. Captain Hugh Dunne had a motive even more personal than his son in coming to Gethsemani that summer. He was out to make his last encampment — and he would make it with God. When Frederic saw a printing press and bookbinding tools arrive within a few days of his father, he saw that Captain Hugh had come to stay and would not allow himself to be a burden on the monastery. The novice smiled to himself as he recognized the source of his own independence.

"How is the boy doing?" was Captain Hugh's first question to the Abbot — even in the presence of his son.

The Abbot smiled. "Well," he said slyly, "he has not been here a full year as yet, but he is running the monastery already."

The novice colored and caught his lower lip between his teeth — a gesture he would use all his life when aroused or embarrrassed. He wondered if the Abbot was referring to his pride. He hoped he had not been assertive. He knew he had frequently wanted to tell the Master how to do certain things about the farm and out in the woods; but he thought he had always refrained.

Dom Edward noted the reaction and decided to tease. "Yes, Mr. Dunne," he repeated, "not here a year, yet regulating everything in the community from morning till night."

Frederic blushed more deeply and frowned, but then as his father turned a look on him that was a combination of surprise, disappointment, concern, and condemnation, the boy burst into a merry chuckle.

"Oh, I see what you mean, Reverend Father. He's right, Dad. I do regulate everything and everyone in his monastery. I get them up, send them to church, call them in from the fields, line them up for dinner, and even put them to bed. I'm bell ringer."

"Quite a man, aren't you?" cut in the Captain. "But what kind of a monk are you?'"

"Shh!" cautioned the novice. "Public confessions ceased long ago."

"But not the Chapter of Faults," put in Dom Edward and his following laugh set his squat body shaking.

Again the novice colored and caught his lower lip between his teeth. When his father's eyes spoke his question, Fred told how in late October of 1894 he thought the world had practically come to an end and his monastic career was ruined beyond all repairing. For after accusing himself publicly in the Chapter of Faults of having made some unnecessary signs at work, he had been told to "take his dinner on the floor." This meant that he had to take a very low, backless stool, set it in the center of the refectory, seat himself on it, and try to eat his main meal of a watery soup and a bowl of unseasoned turnips in the gaze of all.

"Talk about being embarrassed, Dad. I thought I was disgraced forever by such a penance."

"Well, weren't you?"

"Only until the next day. For then the Prior had to do the very same thing."

"Had he been making unnecessary signs, too?"

"I don't know. But I concluded that if he was good enough to be prior, yet have such a penance assigned him, my plight could not be as hopeless as it first appeared."

"He'll do . . . I think," said the Abbot as he led Captain Hugh toward his room and sent the novice back across the cloister.

The truth is that Dom Edward was more than pleased with his first American novice: he was quite proud of him. In early February he had asked him to look after the sacristy. Before Easter he had learned that the energetic novice not only took care of the vestments for the eight priests, but the linens for the eight altars; washed the cruets; swept and dusted the entire church, sanctuary, transepts, and nave; made the altar breads; and bottled all the wine. When he found the youngster looking for more work, he had made him bell ringer; which meant not only regulating the duties of the community, but winding and setting all the clocks in the abbey.

How the boy found time to learn French is only an added proof of what an educator Mrs. Morse must have been.

From the very beginning Father Henry had insisted on what he called "an intense interior life." Frater Frederic did not fully understand all the aging monk meant by the phrase, but he did grasp the fact that attention to God dwelling in the soul was of paramount importance, and that a pure intention, by which everything from going to bed to kneeling for prayer was directed solely to the honor and glory of God, was absolutely essential. The advice was sound and sage. It laid a bedrock foundation for life as a cloistered contemplative.

The other great lesson of his early monastic life was devotion to Divine Providence.

"God's holy will be done!" touched off with an Irish brogue, had fallen on his ears since infancy. But the devotion he nourished in his novitiate, and which grew with him all the years of his long monastic life, was something far deeper and much broader than mere resignation under affliction; much more than the acceptance of the disagreeable with a more or less agreeable *"Fiat"*; it was something more virile and vital and truly virtuous than the supernaturalizing of a natural disappointment by "offering it up." Frederic Dunne's belief in Divine Providence in the last years of his life had in it all the baffling and even bewildering abandonment of the mystics who see God's hand in everything from an overcast sky to an upheaval in nature that brings us close to cosmic chaos. Were you to ask this man how he felt, his answer, even on the sickest day of his existence, would be: "Just fine! For I am just as God would have me — and that is better than fine." — And he was sincere about it!

It was a good thing that Father Henry insisted on such homely truths and had him cultivate such bare, bedrock virtues; for he had hardly celebrated the first anniversary of his arrival in Gethsemani when things began to transpire which disheartened monks of much maturer growth and many more years of monastic grounding.

The story has been told adequately enough elsewhere. Here we need but the salient details.

When Father Eutropius arrived at Gethsemani on December 21, 1848, he had forty-two men under him — and very little money.

When he decided to build the Protoabbey of the New World he launched a drive for funds through the lips of a certain Father Dominic, who enthusiastically promised that the monks "would build schools, and see that the children of the neighborhood were well educated." That promise practically wrote the history of Gethsemani for the next fifty years — and brought the monastery as near to ruin as it is possible to come and yet survive.

Dom Benedict Berger, Gethsemani's second abbot, rightly considered the community bound by the promise. He built a boys' school on the crest of what is called "St. Joseph's Hill," and after many experiments and heartbreaking endeavors, finally founded a school for girls a mile to the north of the abbey on a hillock called "Mt. Olivet."

In that sentence I have told the story of ten years of crushing disappointments and spirit-killing sterility despite exhausting efforts. But the schools were built, and the promise was kept. But then, just as what looked like a harvest was ripening, a storm broke which not only swept away the girls' school and the Sisterhood Dom Benedict had founded, but placed an interdict on the monastery and a stigma on the monks.

That tragedy was enacted just before Frederic Dunne was born. Its effects, however, continued to be felt in their fullness until just a few years before his entrance into the monastery. But now the trouble emanated from the boys' school, and was to sweep away not the abbey, but the Abbot.

Dom Edward's first big administrative act had been to get the state of Kentucky to elevate the tiny boarding school for boys to the dignity of a college and charter it with the right to confer degrees. His next move was to enlarge the buildings and lay out a real campus; and when students came not only from all parts of Kentucky, but even from other states, he thought he could give his full attention to forming a lay faculty.

This was one of the wisest projects of his short abbacy; for

cloistered contemplatives of the Cistercians of the Strict Observance can never be what they are vowed to be so long as they
have to conduct colleges. The teachers and prefects become hy-
phenates; they cannot be real monks.

Dom Edward thought Heaven had answered his prayers and
solved all his difficulties in the person of a man who called himself Darnley Beaufort and posed as an English nobleman whose
life had been blighted by the death of his only son in early childhood, and who now had but one ambition: to devote his life to
the education of poor boys. Dom Edward hired him. After a semester at the Mt. Olivet Convent, which had been converted into a
school for poor boys, during which he transformed the place,
Beaufort was appointed principal of Gethsemani College on St.
Joseph's Hill. That was the beginning of the end for Dom Edward
Chaix-Bourbon as Abbot of Gethsemani.

Early in August of 1895 Dom Edward set out for France and
the General Chapter of the Cistercians of the Strict Observance.
His ship had not cleared New York harbor before a warrant was
out for the arrest of Darnley Beaufort and a scandal was brewing
for the Kentucky Abbey.

Father Benedict Dupont, the seventy-four-year-old Prior, acted
promptly. He discharged Beaufort and let the public know that
the bogus nobleman had been stripped of all authority to transact
any business for the college or the abbey. Prompt as the action was,
it came too late. It was found that the books of the college would
not balance and several items had been charged to the monastery
which would bewilder any monk. Beaufort, who was now revealed
as a rogue with exceptional wit, was soon behind bars.

The older monks blamed the entire affair on Dom Edward. Those
who taught and prefected at the school had not only warned him
against the man, they had begged him for over a year to get rid
of him. They now decided to face the Abbot with some harsh
facts the moment he returned from France.

Dom Edward arrived on October 21.

The following morning young Frederic Dunne heard something which he told me completely bewildered him. He claimed he had known nothing of what had gone on up at the college or within the cloister. If that statement is true, it means either that young Frederic Dunne so minded his own business that he made it all-absorbing, or the seniors in the community were expert in concealing what was causing real friction between the Abbot and his Council.

On this morning of the twenty-second, Dom Edward made the astounding announcement that he had been requested to resign for the good of the community. He then confessed he was as yet undecided what to do about the request, but would appreciate the honest opinion of everyone in the house — novices and oblates as well as professed.

The next day Dom Edward Chaix-Bourbon boarded a train that was to take him away from Gethsemani forever, and Gethsemani, already stigmatized in the eyes of America because of Darnley Beaufort, would be seen by European eyes as having deeper and more unsightly stains because of the pressure brought to bear on the man who had been elected third abbot in 1890.

The Abbot departed in 1895 just as Frederic Dunne completed the year of novitiate required by Canon Law and was beginning the year imposed by Cistercian Constitutions.

Looking back from the vantage point of over fifty years, and knowing all that this man accomplished as prior and abbot in the face of what looked often like insurmountable difficulties, it is easy to discern God's purpose in all these untoward events and read the divine plan with much less difficulty than a blueprint. Steel is tempered by fire and water. Souls are made strong by temptation and trial. Frederic Dunne was being taught by God to live for God alone; to trust Him when trusting is the hardest thing of all; to go on bravely in blackness — even in blindness.

But it demanded the heroic exercise of the two virtues he prayed for most — faith and fortitude.

The Beaufort upheaval called for readjustments. Hence, before the year 1895 had died, Frederic Dunne found himself not only sacristan and bell ringer of the monastery, but secretary and bookkeeper of the college as well. The marvel is not how a young man with the little schooling Frederic Dunne had could discharge so many offices to the satisfaction of all, but how in a community of foreigners who spoke an alien tongue he acquired the sound spirituality he did and grasped so firmly those fundamental contemplative principles of union with God, denial of self, purity of intention, and the ready recognition of God's all-pervading providence.

Father Henry was a help — a great one. But he was now going blind — an infirmity which would not help him read the ever revealing countenances of his novices or aid him to detect a dangerous mood or catch a telltale movement.

The more one learns of the difficulties under which Frederic Dunne was initiated into the religious life, the more one is forced to conclude that God the Holy Ghost was lavish with His graces and gifts and the young novice was as generous in his co-operation as any of the monks of the Thebaid.

His constitutional year of novitiate passed ever more rapidly than had his canonical year. As the summer of 1896 waned he wondered when Father Benedict would admit him to profession. He was not only willing to pronounce his vows, he was somewhat impatient to do so; for already he had fashioned phrases he would tell his own subjects years hence. "We can give nothing to God but what we take from ourselves; so let us give Him all."

Frater Frederic was anxious to give his all; but Father Benedict was not nearly so anxious to receive it — even in the name of the Lord. His hesitancy had a twofold source; Gethsemani had been repudiated by her Father Immediate when he learned how Dom

Edward had been forced to resign, and as yet the General Chapter had made no official appointment of a *locum tenens*. The Prior was uneasy about his own status. But another and more serious reason for the hesitancy was the novice himself. Frater Frederic had lost weight, looked emaciated, and while he never complained about it, the infirmarian knew he had continual stomach trouble. The aging Prior wondered if the young American had the physical health required for the austere Trappist life — and he was not the only one in the community who entertained this doubt.

August passed. Frederic secretly hoped to pronounce his vows on September 8 — our Lady's birthday. But September and even October passed. The feast of All Saints had loomed as a possible date for his dedication, but Father Benedict maintained his disturbing silence. The novice grew concerned, but quickly turned and entrusted the matter to our Mother.

One day in November his father obtained permission to talk with him and asked him point-blank what was wrong. The only answer he received was a warm chuckle and the words: "Not a thing, Dad. God has His own time. Trust Him."

But the query sent the young man to his Master. Father Henry's eyes, fully blinded now by his cataracts, seemed to brim with tears as he said: "Frater, you are entitled to know that the Chapter is deliberating your case. Some are in favor of sending you home because of your ill-health. But I tell them you have no home. I point to your father and urge them to take a chance on you."

The novice was stunned. The blind priest sensed it. "Let us tug at our Mother's skirt like little children," he said. "She'll get us the vote."

And she did. On Thanksgiving Day Frederic Dunne was told to prepare to take his vows on December 8.

It was only several weeks after he had promised God to live poor, pure, obedient, and always striving for perfection in this Gethsemani community that he wrote to his sister, Fannie, who was now Sister Mary Carolina of the Sisters of the Holy Names.

Fannie had made her profession in August. The brother and sister had hoped to vow to God together. When Fannie sent word that she was to be professed on the fifth, Fred resigned himself to not sharing the actual day with his favorite sister, but still hoped that he might at least share the month. In his letter, congratulating her on her profession and first mission — which was to Key West, Florida — he told her so.

Then followed the months of suspense. When the good news was given him he was so hurried by preparation for retreat that he entrusted the joy of informing Fannie to his father. At Christmas he learned that she was still in ignorance of the fact. He sat down and wrote her the entire story. About the matter of his health he told her: "Ask God to give me health enough to be ordained. After that, He can do as He likes. . . ."

What happened after Sister Mary Carolina read that letter has been told by nuns, relatives, and by mere acquaintances in various tones of voice and with very different facial expressions. Some become dramatic and grow sentimentally pious. Others grow cold, hard, and even disdainful. But, as in the case of his mother's "vision" on her deathbed, Frederic Dunne would only state the actual facts and never draw a conclusion.

He told me that his favorite Sister had been sent to Florida because the cold of Canada had taken much out of her during postulancy and novitiate, and it was hoped that her native air would restore her to health, and that it was during the Christmas vacation of 1896 she received his letter. His gray-blue eyes would take on a faraway look as he would quietly add: "One of her companions told me that Fannie offered her life to God that I might be able to go on with my studies and be ordained. That was on December 27 or 28. On December 30 she was dead." — And that was all he would say.

But before me is a reprint from the Key West daily paper for

January 2, 1897. After a long paragraph detailing Fannie's birth, education, vocation, profession, and mission, it states:

Tuesday morning last, while on her way to the Post Office, she was taken with a fit of coughing and a smothering sensation. Her companions immediately took a carriage and brought her home. It was easily seen that the poor Sister was seriously ill. Doctor Sweeting was summoned, and for some time both he and the Sisters entertained the hope of saving the victim from death's cold grasp. The disease from which Sister suffered was pronounced to be congestion of the lungs together with failure of the heart. Towards midnight Sister's breathing grew more laborious and it was evident that the end was not far off. . . . Her last audible words were: "Let me go; I want to hear the singing of the Angels." A few minutes after midnight the Reverend Father D. Bottolaccio administered to the dying Sister the rites of the Church. . . .

You can interpret those facts as you will. As for me, all I can say is: "Greater love than this no man — or woman — hath!"

CHAPTER EIGHT

He Finds God

THE new year of 1897 had opened with sorrow for the young choir monk called Frater Frederic. He knew nothing as yet about Fannie's offer of her life for him and his ordination; all he knew was that his favorite sister was dead. Now granting that all Catholics know that death is the gateway to real life, and that religious will insist that every death is a resurrection, nevertheless it remains true that each death marks a final earthly separation — which leaves an aching void in human hearts.

But painful as such natural sorrows are, they cannot be compared to the anguish which sorrows that are spiritual or supernatural bring to the soul; and Frederic Dunne was to know many such sorrows this first year of profession. It is true that the taking of his vows lifted his spirits high, but there were other things happening in the monastery which drew those spirits down. Yet distance from the events allows us to see them in proper perspective and find them to be important parts of God's planning.

Morning after morning in his Chapter talks Abbot Dunne would cry: "Oh, see God in everything! Do not look at the mere men He uses as instruments. When you use a telephone how much attention do you pay to the receiver? None. For it is not the receiver through which the message comes that counts, but the message that comes through the receiver. Better still it is the person who sends the message. Be just as wise in spiritual matters; superiors are only God's transmitters. Don't look at them. See in them and hear in them only God." Little did we, who heard that cry, know when, where, and under what circumstances he had learned this lesson which is of such paramount importance for all who would be religious in fact and not merely in name.

With the same unceasing insistence the Abbot would teach us that we were to disregard our natural likes and dislikes utterly. Those who were well read in asceticism may have suspected that this was a gleaning from John of the Cross. But Frederic Dunne learned that lesson long before he even knew a John of the Cross had existed, let alone that he was a saint and a mystic who had written much about natural likes and dislikes.

Piecing together the facts he himself told me and the other facts I find in the monastery archives, the complete picture is seen; and it is found to be a picture of the hand of God.

Young Frederic Dunne had a natural liking for Father Henry — everybody loved the old man; but the young novice had just as natural a dislike for Father Gregory — a monk as rigid as the Code of the Medes and as cold as an Alpine peak. Just when Frater Frederic needed the sympathetic guidance of Father Henry the latter was removed from office because of his blindness and Father Gregory named as his successor.

Frederic Dunne had a warm affection for the saintly, jovial, ever placid Dom Edward Chaix. He was in no way attracted to the fiery little Frenchman, Father Benedict Dupont. But before the end of Frederic's novitiate Dom Edward's forced resignation was accepted, and he had to make his vows into the hands of Father Benedict Dupont.

Feeling the deficiencies of his schooling, the young professed yearned to devote all the time possible to the study of Latin, French, and philosophy. Yet he was kept on as sacristan, an appointment which ate into many of his study periods, and was further burdened with the office of secretary and bookkeeper for the college. The few short intervals of the day, which are free time for the ordinary monk, were denied him.

From the first he felt a powerful attraction to solitude and silence as aids to the love of his life: contact with God in prayer. Yet, shortly after profession, he found himself daily on the noisy campus of the college.

And so one might go on, but the obvious needs not to be belabored. Every natural like was denied Frederic Dunne; every natural tendency thwarted. And all in the name of God — under obedience. The young man *had* to become a perfect monk or else go mad. He had to look and look until he saw God in everything and everyone or else be seeing folly and frustration everywhere.

A review of his last few months as novice and his first few years as professed will reveal what veritable crises God had him face. In August of 1896 the Beaufort scandal broke and ran noisily through September. In October the Abbot was forced to resign. In November Frederic Dunne was told that his future as a monk was very questionable on account of his poor health. In December, six days after his vows, Father Gabriel died. Rumor had it that this was a manifestation of God's displeasure over the ousting of the Abbot. That rumor had just been set in real circulation when Brother Peter was taken by death. Two deaths in three days looked like confirmation of the claim. Three weeks later the first fatal accident in Gethsemani's history occurred when Brother Dominic Antoine was caught in the machinery at the mill and mangled to death. Less than three months later Frater Robert, the last of the pioneers among the choir monks, passed away. Four deaths in less than four months were both depressing and thought-provoking.

Then something worse than death began to affect the community and have an impact on the young professed. As a boy Frederic Dunne had read how even animals abandon sinking ships. He could not help recalling that fact now as he saw some of the older monks seek and obtain permission to leave Gethsemani and either enter another order or go to some other house of the Cistercian Order. Brother Lazarus went to the Carthusians. Father John Baptist sought peace in a Canadian Trappist monastery.

The young monk was too charitable to call such departures defections or desertions, but that they were depletions of the size of Gethsemani's community could not be blinked or bypassed.

He told me how one day in Lent he went out to the cemetery and stopped at Brother Dominic's grave — one of the newest. Soon, he said, he was standing at Brother Alexander's grave — the first in the new burying ground. These two, Alexander and Dominic, were brothers who with a third of the family, named Ignatius, came down from Canada in 1859 to become monks. In 1866 Alexander died and had the honor of being the first to be placed behind the newly consecrated church of the abbey. In 1869, after ten years of Trappist life, Ignatius obtained a dispensation from his monastic vows and went back to secular life. Brother Dominic, the youngest of the three, had just been killed — but the thought struck Frederic that he had died a monk and been buried as a monk, and would one day rise to stand in the ranks of the monks. Far better the fate of Dominic, he concluded, than that of Ignatius. And like another Job he swore: "Though He slay me, I will trust Him still. I'll die a monk of Gethsemani."

Like the person in the *Hound of Heaven,* Frederic Dunne might have looked up and asked: "Ah, Designer Infinite, must Thou char the wood e'er Thou canst limn with it?" The young monk was feeling the fire. But, if we are to judge from his entire later life, it would seem that he said something more like what Gertrud von le Fort sings in her *Hymns to the Church:* "I will go into deepest sorrow that I may find my God." Frederic Dunne found Him.

He had been told that the first duty of a novice is to seek God. In suffering and sorrow he learned that the first and last joy of a monk is to find Him.

Horticulturists tell us that roses which look so lovely in sunlight need darkness and the dew. I say: So does faith. Things were dark at Gethsemani this year of 1897. In June word came that Dom Edward's resignation had been accepted; but no word came appointing a successor. The older monks knew what such a silence meant. Dom Eugene Vachette, Abbot of Melleray and Father Immediate of Melleray's American daughter house, Gethsemani, had repudiated his offspring. The Abbot General in Rome was also silent. When no word came from the General Chapter most of the old monks felt that they not only saw the handwriting on the wall, but that they could read and understand it. Father Benedict was very uneasy about his anomalous position — and rightly so. He was prior without portfolio. Others thought the community was in the same condition. In such darkness, young Frederic Dunne looked to the stars. He had been told to seek God. He would look for Him where he was sure to find Him. He went where a light burned like a star before the Blessed Sacrament.

Unquestionably the appointment of Frederic Dunne as sacristan had been made by a man who was short of men. Dom Edward knew that no novice should hold so responsible a position. But in a monastery as large as Gethsemani with a community as small as forty-six, many irregularities had to be accepted as regular. Unquestionably, I say, it was the appointment of a man. But now, after listening to the Abbot Frederic Dunne speak on the Blessed Sacrament, we know that it was God who made the arrangement back in those "nineties," which were anything but "gay" for Gethsemani. In almost hourly contact with the altar, the novice had become more and more conscious of the Presence which never obtrudes Itself, yet is never completely obscure.

This steadied him when his whole world rocked.

That God writes straight with crooked lines is universally admitted, but that He makes assets out of liabilities is learned only when you study the life of a saint or a saintly man, and trace the growth in godliness. When Frederic Dunne came to Gethsemani he was handicapped, naturally speaking, by his lack of acquaintance with the French tongue. That natural liability became a supernatural asset; for he was forced to read Father Faber's works in his very first year of novitiate if he was to make any spiritual reading at all. After *Creator and Creature* he read his work on the *Blessed Sacrament*. Faber gave him more than the theology of the Eucharist. He actually gave him some Franciscan spirituality when, like another Bonaventure, he portrayed nature permeated with grace and had the young monk seeing God in everything from a particle of dust dancing in a sunbeam or a flake of snow falling from the skies, to that silent march of the stars.

Faber can make one marvel and cry with David: *"Quam admirabile est nomen tuum in universa terra."* But his purpose in this book was only to build to his climax which is the wonder of all wonders: God disguised in wheat and wine. Frederic Dunne came to see more in the dark church at Gethsemani than he had ever seen under Florida's sun or under the stars as he sat by the sea.

The next step was not too hard nor too high. If God could conceal Himself under a wafer of wheat, surely He could be in men who held office. From that moment on, Frederic Dunne went up to the college to keep books, not because he had been sent there by Father Benedict, but by God. The young monk would take time he ardently longed to devote to study and give it to the making of altar breads, not because Dom Edward had once made him sacristan, but because he knew God had given him this assignment.

Thus did his faith grow in what was real darkness — and peace came as gentle as any dew.

His father met him one day to indulge in the rare privilege of a few moments of conversation. Somewhat anxiously Captain Hugh asked his boy if he knew what was going on in the monastery.

Frederic smiled and with one of those understatements of which he was so fond said: "I have a hazy notion."

"Well, does it upset you?"

Blue-gray eyes twinkled behind steel-rimmed glasses as the head went down and the one word "Tremendously" came forth.

The father grew more anxious. He assured his son that the situation would soon improve. He begged him not to do anything extreme.

Again the head was lowered as the eyes behind those steel rims twinkled. "I'm going to quit," muttered Fred doggedly.

"Oh no!" exclaimed the Captain.

"Oh yes," retorted the son. "I'm going to quit worrying and quit being so poor a monk."

The relieved Captain clapped his son on the shoulder. "You'll never change," he said. "You'll be a tease to the day you die. But tell me honestly, doesn't this stir get you down?"

"Not at all, father," came the quick and earnest reply. "At first I was a bit bewildered. But now I just believe."

"Believe? Believe in what?"

"In God — who is our Father."

And Captain Hugh found himself looking into gray-blue eyes that held depths he had never seen there before. He did not know that in those dark months his son had grown from spiritual infancy to a real and a rare maturity. Nor did the son realize all the grace and gifts God had given him to bring about that growth.

But this unawareness is not surprising even in one as conscious of God as was this young religious. Most of us live for years and years utterly unaware of the workings of the divine life within us. Father Arintero, the celebrated Dominican theologian, has well said that "ordinarily the soul does not perceive the action of the Holy Ghost within it until it is far advanced on the path of virtue and so united to the Divine Will that it neither softens nor stifles the voice of God."

After fifty years of Trappist living, Frederic Dunne was so fearful of any shadow of pride or semblance of self-complacency, that he would not dare analyze his spiritual experiences to see if he could discover the workings of God the Holy Ghost. But he would often speak in such a way, and give such spiritual direction to individuals, that it was most evident to the alert that he was keenly aware of God's indwelling and knew that the Divinity was not silent nor sleeping in his soul.

Were one to scrutinize Frederic's life and actions in order to be able to give the technical term to his dominant trait, I believe most would be led to the conviction that the one word which alone will fit the facts is the word "piety" — that wondrous gift of the Holy Ghost which enables us to treat God with the filial and child-like affection, the confidence and simplicity a loving child displays toward its loving father. Or, if you have any antipathy toward childlikeness, then say it is the gift that allows us to look upon and love God the way a bride loves her beloved. Blessed as most of us have been with this gift from childhood, we have never realized the tremendousness of the endowment. Paganism and philosophy honor God as Creator, Judge, and Provider; Christianity alone cheers His Heart by loving Him as a Father. The thinker will appreciate St. Leo's remark that "the right to call God 'Father' is the greatest of all gifts!" Dom Frederic realized that; and I believe the realization was generated these dark years and grew in splendor until it was the light of his life.

The way the grown man would insist that we ever bear in mind that we were the "sons of God" and the tender way he spoke of Him who is Majesty and Power being "our Father" told the trained theologian that the Holy Ghost, by His gifts, had brought the man to the age of spiritual discretion and enabled him to feel, "taste, and see how sweet is the Lord."

That, of course, is all but inevitable if one will give himself to the Trappist life with the headlong generosity which character-

ized Frederic Dunne. For in the solitude and silence of the secluded
monastery and in the uninterrupted round of prayer, study, self-
examination, and the contemplation of Christ, a mystical meta-
morphosis is effected; a transformation so prodigious that the soul
of the man who would become a real monk is entirely renewed
and penetrated to its very deepest depths. The man is conscious of
his own efforts and may be called upon to battle self with a fierce-
ness that may have him thinking he is about to lose his mind or his
very soul. Yet the major portion of the work is done by the Holy
Ghost; and the chief factor in the accomplishment is the gifts.
When man yields himself as did Frederic Dunne he will soon find
that his intellect is radiant with light; his memory ever occupied
with things divine; his will a burning brazier which keeps the
body agile and the whole man docile to the Spirit; even his
imagination will be filled with supernatural phantasms and his
appetites with the divine impulses which the Holy Ghost communicates. The Trappist life is one in which the Holy Ghost can
work with a rare freedom, and that is why the novice and the
young professed, even as Frederic Dunne, find their faith enlivened,
their hope heightened and greatly heartened, their charity wonder-
fully inflamed. Though they may never know it, God the Holy
Ghost so endows them that there remains little or nothing of
earth in them and they live a life of radiant happiness because
they have been granted the gift of gifts: that savor for God and
the things of God which makes saints.

Père Hugon has given us insight into the development of
Frederic Dunne when he tells how those who have in their veins
the blood of heroes rush to the performance of great deeds as if
by instinct, and then points out that the Gifts of the Holy Ghost
enable us to do the same and even much more. "They are in us,"
he says, "as a seed, of which the flower must be heroism." True
Dominican that he is, he then goes on to say that St. Thomas has
insisted that there belongs to every form a proportionate tendency.

Thus, from the indwelling of the Holy Ghost, there results in us those divine instincts or impulses which are called "gifts." These are a sort of superhuman heritage, a divine blood which courses through our veins and which, after the fashion of a noble hereditary form, impels us to noble and heroic action proper to a divine race. This is the mystical heritage of the children of God — and is capitalized when one is generous.

Frederic Dunne capitalized it; for he was generous.

Père Lallement, the spiritually wise and deeply penetrating Jesuit, just about sums up these early years of Frederic Dunne's life as a Trappist when he says: "We must be courageous and fearless in the service of God if we would advance in perfection and become capable of doing great things. Without the Gift of fortitude no notable progress can be made in the spiritual life. Mortification and prayer, which are its principal exercises, demand a generous determination to overcome all the difficulties to be encountered." The lone American amid a group of foreigners, some of whom were defaulting, no one of whom was not fearful, walked his way with a calm and a courage that tell of a generous and strong heart being helped by a strong and generous God.

The accomplishment is made clear by the words of Teresa of Ávila: "His Majesty desires and loves courageous souls if they have no confidence in themselves but ever walk in humility."

Now I am quite positive that Frederic Dunne never read that line from the great woman who had the heart, the mind, and the pen of a man, yet I am equally positive that no one could sit for a single week under Frederic Dunne without hearing at least seven times: "Oh, we must rid ourselves entirely of every last vestige of self-confidence, and place all our confidence in God. If God be with us, who can be against us? We can do all things in Him who strengthens us. Fathers and Brothers, we can have confidence, even great confidence. We must have it. But in God, not in ourselves."

That is why I have been so insistent on the work of the Holy
Ghost and especially of the workings of His gifts. And why not?
Here is Frederic Dunne in an atmosphere and amid happenings
little conducive to spiritual growth, yet we find him not only growing, but growing rapidly and well. The linguistic difficulty would
have been obstacle enough, but when we add all the others, the
scandal and its consequents, the taking from him of the two men
who could have helped him most — his Master of Novices and
his Abbot — the defections and the defaults of the older men
who grew fearful, the uneasiness of the Prior, the depression
that fell on the entire community, we have not only an
atmosphere that is unfavorable, but the very soil seems utterly
unsuited for anything like proper growth. Yet Frederic Dunne
arrived at full bloom. What other answer can be offered than that
given by the Masters who say that "in the beginning of the spiritual
life grace remains hidden, though operative; and we, it seems,
have to take the initiative. Grace here seems to adapt itself to our
'human mode' of acting in prayer and in all things else. We are
then very definitely in the ascetical life. But as the spiritual life
deepens and develops, the Gifts of the Holy Ghost take the ascendancy over the virtues — and life becomes far less complicated and
much easier. When the Gifts take that ascendancy, one is in
the mystical way; when the same Gifts dominate habitually and
in a manifest manner, one is in the mystical life; for that has been
well defined as 'a life under the habitual direction of the
Gifts of the Holy Ghost' in what St. Thomas calls their 'superhuman mode.'"

I stop there, for I can hear Dom Frederic "shushing" me as he
deprecatingly gestures and scoffs at the "fluoroscoping of a soul"
and tells me there is no such thing as a "thermometer for spiritual
temperature taking." But facts are stubborn. And the facts are
now before us. In extraordinarily unspiritual circumstances Frederic Dunne showed extraordinary spiritual development. The only

explanation to fit the facts is God and the Gifts of the Holy Ghost.

The young professed did not allow the technicalities which so harassed his Superior, Father Benedict, to bother him. That poor man might worry about his possession of authority, since he had received no other delegation than that of the custom of the Congregation. But Frater Frederic would see in him and hear from him — God.

Blessed though he was with this clarity of vision and purity of intention, he was as greatly relieved as all the rest when, in June of 1897, two abbots came to Gethsemani to make a special visitation of the troubled house.

Dom Carthage Delaney from Mount Melleray, Ireland, assisted Dom Eugene Vachette, the irate Lord from Melleray in France. Their first official act was to regularize Father Benedict's position by appointing him officially the superior *pro tempore.*

The visitors were intent upon a study of the affairs of the abbey, especially those concerning the school and the scandal connected with it; then a more intimate study of the men and the minds of the community and the reasons for Dom Edward's resignation. But they were not so intent as to have no interest in America's first recruit for the choir — the young Frater Frederic, so recently professed.

Dom Carthage granted him a private interview during which he asked the young monk what he found most difficult in the monastic life and received an answer that showed him he was dealing with an Irishman.

"The most difficult?" repeated Frederic thoughtfully; then smiled as he replied, "That which presents no difficulty."

"And what is that?" asked the Abbot.

"Seeking Him who can be found everywhere, yet is never sufficiently discovered."

"Where do you look for Him?"

"Well, Reverend Father," replied the young monk honestly,

"when I want to be absolutely sure of finding Him, I go to the church. In the Eucharist — the Mass and the Blessed Sacrament — I know I have Him. But I can also find Him in my superiors, in my Rule, in the order of the day, in my brethren, my occupations — everywhere." Then after a slight pause he added, "But nowhere more surely than in suffering."

"Do you suffer?"

"My stomach gives me some trouble." Then came that characteristic quick chuckle, "But my temper gives me more."

"Oh, you have a temper?"

"My father is Irish. My mother was French. How could I be without one?"

The Irish Abbot sat back, stroked his flowing beard, then quietly said, "Frater Frederic, I had a very interesting conversation with one of your American industrialists — that's what he called himself — on the way down from New York. We were riding through Pennsylvania, I think it was. I saw some mighty stacks and asked what they were. This man told me they were chimneys for what he claimed will yet revolutionize the world — steel. He told me many wonderful things about this metal. But do you know the most impressive thing he said?"

"What?"

"He said steel is useless unless it has a good temper. I think men are just like steel. Thank God if He has given you a good one. But try to remember that just like steel, you'll be useless when you do lose it." Then as he blessed the young monk, he added, "Use that temper rightly and I promise you you'll find God."

CHAPTER NINE

New Century—New Appointments

TO ANYONE interested in the Trappists, Gethsemani, or Frederic Mary Dunne, 1898 is an unforgettable year; for it was a year seeded with events that would bring a rare harvest to each of the above named.

In the Old World it marked the eighth centenary of the founding of Citeaux; and the Trappists, newly united into an Order by the amalgamation of the separate Observances, made it more memorable by purchasing the ancient site (which the French Government had confiscated during the Revolution), refounding the monastery, and making it again the mother house of all true Cistercians.

In the New World this year marked the golden jubilee of the arrival of forty-three Frenchmen at Gethsemani, determined to create on this continent a Citadel of Silence, that America might have one spot where men could listen to the beat of their hearts, hear the stirrings of their souls, and catch the quiet voice of God as it speaks to them in the depths of their being.

But for Frederic Dunne it was made most memorable by the arrival of a man who was to influence his entire future life, and the departure from this life of the one who up to now had dominated his entire existence.

On March 25, 1898, the man who was to inject a new spirit and create a new era for Gethsemani arrived at the Kentucky monastery. He had been appointed *Administrator ad tempus* by the General of the Order, on the recommendation of the two abbots who had made that special visitation in 1897.

It was on the feast of the Annunciation, the forty-fourth anniversary of the laying of the cornerstone of Gethsemani's abbatial church, that the dark-haired, dark-eyed, burly Alsatian, Father Edmond M. Obrecht, walked into the life of Frederic M. Dunne. Little did the young monk know all that this man would mean in the shaping of his soul and his search for God. But already he had learned what someone has called the "A B C's" of all religious living — but which is often forgotten by too many both within and without the religious life — the thrilling and comforting truth that every single happening in our individual day is the hand of God upon us. It would be years before this sublime simplification of life would have so penetrated to the marrow of his being that without ever tiring he would be teaching incessantly that every detail of our lives is a loving means arranged by a provident Father to lead us to Himself, and that each event of our earthly existences can be rightly viewed as a "coming of Christ." But even at this early date he could look at Edmond Obrecht and see God behind him; listen to heavily accented English and recognize the voice of Christ; for this man came vested with legitimate authority — and that comes only from above.

With the rest of the community he thought there was relevance in the fact that the new Superior arrived on a feast of our Lady and the anniversary of the laying of the church's cornerstone. But while he shared with others the joy in this gift from God, he was alone a week later in the grief caused by some divine thievery. On April 1, his father, Captain Hugh Dunne, died.

Whenever he spoke to me of this event his eyes held lights far different from those I would see whenever he would tell of his mother's demise, and his voice held stronger tone. Admiration for human bravery and gratitude for divine bounty tell briefly and best the source of those lights and the cause of that tone.

Edmond Obrecht had not been in the house a week when he deemed it wise to tell the aged and ailing family brother that it was high time for him to put his earthly affairs in their final form. The look he received was anything but what he could have expected. It was not disdainful exactly, but it certainly was cool. The eyes of the prostrate man were clear and luminous with understanding and the words that came from his lips showed the new Superior he was dealing with a man who was fully conscious and utterly unafraid.

"Time?" said the Captain. "I've got much less time than you think. My soul is right. Get a notary and I'll make everything else right."

Edmond Obrecht liked such terseness. He was terse himself. But young Frederic thought he should apologize or explain his father's directness. So as they left the room to summon the notary, he began, "My father was a soldier . . ."

"No need to tell me," broke in the Superior. "I saw it in his eyes. I heard it in his speech. His requests are commands. I'd like to see him die a soldier of Christ."

"What do you mean?"

"In the habit."

"Oh!" exclaimed Frederic as he stopped at the head of the stairs, "speak to him about it. I'm sure . . ."

The Administrator wheeled about, walked back to the Captain's side, and began to outline the advantages of dying in religious garb. Again he got more than he could have expected when the old soldier interrupted his outline with "I came to live *among* the monks. Get me a habit and I'll gladly die *as* one."

After telling that much of the story Dom Frederic's eyes would glisten, his whole countenance light up, and with a shake of his head he would say: "A soldier to the end. Not foolhardy. Not really fearless, I secretly believe. But calm and coolly brave. It's wonderful to see a man go to meet His God with such perfect command of self. But, Father, it was more wonderful for me to see him lowered into the grave clad in the simple brown of our humble lay Brotherhood. That, to me, was God's stamp of supreme approval on his entire life."

But Frederic Dunne, like Augustine for his sainted mother, Monica, never offered a Mass without making memento of the soldier-monk who was his father. And I always found it touching to watch the aging but ever energetic Abbot stop before the simple iron cross with the legend: "Brother Hugh — Obiit 1 April, 1898," bow his head in prayer, then bless the grave as he departed. It told that the heart of the boy still beat in the breast of the man. It also told me that life for those who love grows ever more lonely.

With the final note of that ever plaintive *"Domine, miserere super peccatore,"* which ends every Trappist burial, life and living took on a new aspect for young Frederic Dunne. His father, mother, and favorite sister were now dead. The living members of the family, Katherine, Mary, and Jesse, had married; and each was engrossed in that all-absorbing task of raising a family. Frederic felt that life would now become exactly what he had envisioned it the day he left Jacksonville — an existence for and with God alone.

Two months after the funeral, Frater Frederic felt really alone as he stared at an empty ceiling from a bed in a lonely room at SS. Mary and Elizabeth Hospital, Louisville. The new Administrator had inquired into his chronic stomach trouble and wished it traced to its source.

For the first time in four years Frederic Dunne was in contact with what religious call "the world." He felt strange riding in on the train, but not nearly so strange as when, after arriving at the hospital, he had been led from one white-capped nun to another, then from one corridor to another, until finally he arrived on "Sister Camillus' Floor."

That first night was filled with meditation. The young monk stared at the bare ceiling and tried to puzzle out why it was that all day he had felt so empty. Why did he feel so strange, lost, and alone in this tiny world of a hospital which literally teemed with activity? He had had hardly a moment to himself since arrival: nuns, doctors, nurses, attendants — someone was always in his room asking him something. Then why had he felt so alone?

It was late when he finally saw that Gethsemani is truly "out of this world"; that it is a world within itself where one lives a life more different from the ordinary man than is the life of seraph or angel from that of the ordinary monk. The same sun shines on the two worlds; the same winds and rains buffet them; the same physical phenomena of life and death are seen in the birth of buds, the blooming of flowers, the maturing of fruits, and the falling of leaves; but the thoughts, ideals, aims, aspirations, interests that move the men of the two worlds make them as different as high noon and deepest night. Truly, Frederic Dunne had been "out of this world" for all of four years. No wonder he had felt so strange!

He smiled at that empty ceiling as he suddenly realized that attention had been focused all day on something he had given slight consideration for all of the four years — his body. That smile widened as he recalled all the kindnesses of the nurses and their genuine solicitude for his comfort — something he had given no thought since 1894.

At this point in his analysis there came a gentle tap on his door followed by the quiet entrance of the floor supervisor.

"Sister Camillus," exclaimed Frederic, "not food again!"

"Just a cup of cocoa to help put you to sleep."

"But, Sister, that will make about the fifth time I have eaten today! If I didn't have stomach trouble when I came in, you'll give it to me. You'll kill me with your kindness."

"That's why we're here, Frater. We either kill or cure."

"You'll destroy my Trappist vocation."

Sister Camillus had set the steaming cup on the bedside table and was bending over the tiny cabinet along side when Frederic made his charge. She straightened now, smiled, and asked: "What in the world ever brought you to the Trappists?"

Frederic had liked this nun the moment he met her. She was capable, affable, and yet could keep one at a proper distance even while being most sociable. He envied her the ability to unbend and yet maintain her religious dignity. For all her lightheartedness he suspected there were rare depths to her soul. He decided to probe a bit.

"The same thing that made you leave home," he answered.

Sister bent over again and got her utensils, then as she rubbed her patient's back she said: "I wonder if it was. I could say I did not like men, but I did like nursing. You couldn't say that."

"No. And I notice you don't say it either."

"But why a Trappist? That's so strange a life."

"Any stranger than yours?"

"Oh, Frater! Perpetual silence. Perpetual penance. Almost perpetual fasts. Work . . ."

"What time did you get up this morning, Sister?"

"Long after you."

"How long? . . . What time exactly?"

"Four fifty, if you want to know."

"It's now after nine thirty, and you've been on the go every minute of the day. I wonder if you don't work harder than the Trappists."

Thus it began the first night — banter that was serious soul-searching; wit and merriment that had depth and substance. It continued throughout the days; each searching for the source of what they recognized in one another as a radiant spiritual personality.

One morning, as she was leaving the room, Sister Camillus said, "You're not so bright as I thought. The answer to all your questioning about my vocation and my life lies in my name. I am a Sister of Charity."

When she came with his dinner tray, Frederic accused her of having told him nothing by telling him her name. Sister set the tray down and while arranging the dishes gave explanation that provoked laugh after laugh but ended with a remark steeped in seriousness. She told how stupid humans had clouded over and not only obscured but completely confused the real meaning of the word "charity." They take it to connote mere human kindness, a boy-scout act each day or a dime for a cup of coffee to a beggar or a panhandler. She went on with examples, giving Frederic plenty to think about as she ended with "Charity means love. We Sisters of Charity are Sisters of Love."

Frederic kept Sister that night until she was late for bed, but her arguments showed him not only that she knew what she was about, but that he would be living a tragic delusion if his religious life was anything but a life of love. From then on their conversation was really a comparing of notes; a comparison that showed we all believe the grass to be greener in our neighbor's yard. For when Sister envied the Trappists their "leisure to love," Frederic countered with the statement that "Love serves — and is best shown in deeds, not words." There the argument, if it can be called such, stood. Each was smiling. Neither was yielding an inch.

By such teasing of Sister Camillus, Frederic Dunne came to see that it is God who fills the horizon for every true religious, and that implicit in every Rule is what St. Benedict has made so explicit in his; namely, that "nothing whatsoever is to be preferred to the love of Christ." More than once Frederic Dunne said to me: "Sickness can be a blessing, Father. I know my stomach trouble opened my eyes." It had opened them to a total dedication of self to God as seen in the life of a Nazareth nun.

A friendship was formed on that floor of SS. Mary and Elizabeth Hospital that was to end — at least in its earthly phase — only with the death of Sister Camillus a half century later. On that occasion Abbot Dunne wrote:

February 28, 1948.

My dear Sister Superior and Community:

I was deeply grieved to learn of the death of our dear Sister Mary Camillus. . . .

In the first place I wish to offer you all my sincerest sympathy. I know that she was not in condition of late years to be of any material help, but I am sure that her exemplary life, her prayers and the suffering she endured in her illness were of more value to you in bringing God's blessing upon your work than much physical labor and ingenuity.

You know how closely she was united to me ever since my operation nearly fifty years ago; and our relations have not lost anything in the passing of the years and the decades.

I have recommended Sister to the prayers of the Community repeatedly, and especially in her last sickness. This morning my Holy Mass was a tribute of affection and gratitude, and offered for the repose of her precious soul.

Begging God to bless you and your great work, and to let you feel something of the intercession in heaven of good Sister Camillus, I am

Very sincerely yours in Corde Jesu

That was not the first nor the final Mass Frederic Dunne offered for Sister Camillus; for on the first of March for almost fifty years a letter would arrive at Gethsemani containing an offering and the brief but thought-provoking message: "Mass in thanksgiving for your priesthood. And don't forget our bargain!" It was always signed "Sister Mary Camillus, S.C.N."

The story behind that addendum is that Dr. Ouchterlony diagnosed Frederic's trouble as a duodenal ulcer and spoke of surgery. When Sister told the young monk and asked him how he felt about the prospect, he smiled and said: "I have no will but the will of God, Sister. Yet, if I am allowed a wish, I'd like to live long enough to say one Mass."

"Let's strike a bargain," was Sister's reply. "If you'll remember me in every Mass you'll say, I'll pray that you say many."

"Done!" cried the young monk with enthusiasm.

But I feel sure that Frederic Dunne was reminded of more than his bargain by those letters. I believe the mere sight of Sister Camillus' handwriting served to remind him of the lesson he had learned at SS. Mary and Elizabeth's Hospital: *Devotion to duty to the utter disregard of self is the safest, surest, shortest way to sanctity.* I even suspect that his own devotion to duty, which often mounted to the heroic, was patterned on what he had seen of Nazareth nuns in that Louisville hospital.

Actually, Frederic was not operated on that summer; but neither was he cured. He would be back to SS. Mary and Elizabeth's. But it would be only after having attained the desire of his heart and discharging some of his debt to Sister Camillus.

On July 15, 1898, Frederic was allowed to return to Gethsemani, but with orders to maintain a strict diet. The first week in August, however, he received something which had much greater therapeutic value than any diet; for that week he knelt at the feet of Thomas Sebastian Byrnes, Bishop of Nashville, Tennessee, and received minor orders. On receiving the news Sister Camillus wrote: "It won't be long now before you begin paying me what you owe."

Sister was right, but Frederic Dunne would have to pay much more than the good nun ever demanded. For in October of that year, Edmond Obrecht was elected fourth abbot of Gethsemani. For six months as administrator he had been studying the community, and what he had found in Frederic Dunne so pleased him that he decided to hasten his ordination as much as the canons would allow. Immediately after his election he asked the young monk how long he had been studying theology.

"Just started, Reverend Father. But, really, I haven't rightly finished philosophy."

"Trappists aren't scholars," came the somewhat gruff reply. "De Rancé was right about studies for monks. The less they have of them, the better monks they are. Go on with your theology."

That would have been burden enough, but Dom Edmond added

to it by relieving him of the sacristan's charge only to make him vice-president of the college — before he was twenty-five.

Had Frederic Dunne not labored to acquire true and deep humility from the very first, the appointments given him in these early years could easily have ruined his entire monastic career. Had he not been so mentally pliable, the accumulated duties could have broken him. He did admit in later life that studying theology in the dormitory during the time of the midday siesta, contributed in no slight degree to the nervousness so noticeable in his advancing years.

Father Leonard took him through the course of theology as well as he could in the time allotted and as the circumstances allowed. After each semester he reported to the Abbot. Every time he claimed that his charge was doing exceptionally well, but that there were genuine grounds for lament in the limitation of time.

The Abbot's reply was ever the same: "Trappists are not supposed to be great theologians."

On February 2, 1900, Dom Obrecht allowed the young vice-president of the college to pronounce his solemn vows as a monk. Frederic rejoiced that it was another great feast of our Lady that was to be the day of his dedication, and he begged the Immaculate Mother to present him in the Temple of Inaccessible Light just as she had presented Jesus in the Temple at Jerusalem — as a victim for sin and sinners.

He chuckled merrily as he told me: "I was relieved that day; for at simple profession I took the Order, but at solemn profession I felt that the Order had taken me. I felt secure at last. But that happiness of February was forerunner to a greater happiness in April. Then the Lord really took me." He was referring to the seventeenth and eighteenth of that month, when Bishop Byrnes conferred on him the Sacred Orders of subdeacon and deacon, bringing him within one step of the priesthood.

Week after week he now donned vestments and assisted the celebrant at the conventual Mass. The dream of his youth and the desire of his lifetime seemed at his fingers' tips. But still he was burdened with offices that took him from his books. In December of 1900 Dom Obrecht named the young Deacon secretary of the abbey and guestmaster of the house.

"Hope you'll be responsible for my theological ignorance," said the new Secretary shortly after his appointment.

"You be a Trappist," came the sharp retort. "Let Jesuits and Dominicans be theologians."

But before the month was out the Abbot himself grew a bit concerned; for when he asked the Bishop of Louisville to ordain the young Deacon to the priesthood he received the hearty response: "Most willingly, provided he passes the required examinations, which will be held in the Cathedral rectory before the end of January. We will expect the young man to defend all dogma and be ready to answer any question in moral theology."

Dom Obrecht studied that signature "William George McCloskey" for some time before saying aloud: "He's within his rights. The Canons allow it. But it is stiff."

On January 10 Frederic journeyed to Louisville. He did not enjoy the journey; for what awaited him at its end was really an ordeal. His time for preparation had been short; the matter for examination was wide — as wide as God. But he went and faced the vicar-general of the diocese and its two leading theologians.

They did not spare the monk. They were under orders to examine. Frederic told me they really probed. But would that Mrs. Morse could see what lies before me this moment. It is the testimony drawn up by those examiners. It reads in part:

This is to certify that we, the undersigned, a Commission appointed by the Rt. Rev. Wm. Geo. McCloskey, Bishop of Louisville, for this purpose, did examine Frater Frederic M. Dunne, O.C.S.O., of Gethsemani. . . .

We hereby certify that the said Frater stood the test of the examination *Magna Cum Laude*. . . .

What a vindication of Edward Chaix-Bourbon's words: "Intelligence is better than education." What a proof of Frederic Dunne's powers of application!

On March 1 he again went to Louisville. But the Cathedral and not its rectory was his goal. Therein the Bishop performed that silent wonder of the laying on of hands which brings God the Holy Ghost down from heaven and imprints on the soul of the candidate that Christ-Character, which will last so long as God is God. Frederic Dunne was made a priest forever — a priest according to the order of Melchisedech.

His mother was not there. His father could not be present. His favorite sister did not attend. But there was a Nazareth nun at the ceremony; and after it, received a blessing from the newly ordained whom she reminded of the bargain they had struck not quite three years earlier. It was a very happy monk who laughed at Sister Camillus and whispered: "Shylock!"

To his dying day Frederic Dunne claimed there never had been, and there never was again, a spring like that of 1901. No almanac will bear him out. Kentucky had as variable weather that year as any other year — and that is most varied. Chilling rains, late frosts, sudden bursts of heat came. Gradually the world grew green; the orchard became a toss of white blossoms which hummed with bees; flowers burst their buds to make field and roadside gay with color. But when Frederic Dunne spoke of this as the "most wonderful of springs" he was not referring to nature's recurrent miracle; he simply meant that this spring the miracle or miracles was wrought in him and by him: he had become Christ, could renew Calvary daily, hold in his hands a consecrated Host, and all but feel the beat of the Sacred Heart. His devotion to the Blessed Sacrament deepened into a longing to adore unceasingly the God who is disguised as wheat and wine. This longing became a physical ache. But the ache was not to be eased nor the desire satisfied. His duties took him from what he considered man's only duty. . . .

When Frederic Dunne became a cloistered contemplative, a monk in the most penitential Order in the Church, he had chosen "the road less traveled by." And now within the cloister and within that Order, he would have to walk along a path that is but lightly worn; for few are the feet that tread it. St. Bernard has said that in every monastery there are a few Marthas who must be "busy about many things," there are many Marys who can sit at the feet of the Master and contemplate His loveliness, and there are Lazaruses who live — and spend their resurrected lives in penance. Thanks to the whisperings and the gifts of God the Holy Ghost, Frederic Dunne walked the much less trodden road as he became all three in the unity of his personality. Office after office was given him, each of which kept him from the Focus of his heart and the Polar Star of his life — the Christ in the Eucharist. But by cultivating an extraordinary awareness of the omnipresence of God, he became a contemplative in the best sense of the word; for he could find God in everything and everyone.

In the early 1900's Gethsemani did not have the number of guests she has in the 1950's, but the Guestmaster had more than enough to do taking care of the priests, both secular and religious, who boarded at the monastery for anywhere from a week to years. Perhaps it was while ministering to these that he first conceived his tender, affectionate interest in these "shepherds in the mists." In every letter he wrote to Dom Edmond while the latter traveled the world, these boarders received special mention. And when he himself became abbot, there was nothing he would not do for a priest. Germanic though he was in his insistence on punctuality and attendance at choir, he had one exception — priests. If they came and asked for a confessor, they always got one, no matter what the hour of the day or the night. The one assigned to that office for the year might be out at manual labor, he might be in choir, he might even be in bed taking his few hours of needed rest . . . it made no difference; Dom Frederic would have him summoned. A priest was calling — no one greater on earth could call!

But even in those days — as in our own — there were always a few very curious visitors. One such was cured by Frederic's most frequent prescription — his sense of humor.

"I hear you monks dig your own graves," said this one. "Is that a fact?"

"Absolutely," replied Frederic.

"Is it true you dig a part of every day?"

"Every day." Frederic's eyes were sparkling now. He knew what he had on hand.

"Well, how much do you dig?"

Frederic edged closer to the stranger and said in a lower tone "I'm going to tell you something I would not tell everyone. You look like a very intelligent man. We take off one thirtieth of an inch every day."

"One-thirtieth of an inch!" gasped the visitor. "That certainly isn't much."

"It makes a full inch every month except February."

"But what's that?"

"A foot a year."

"Of course, but what's that for a grave?"

"Think man! We buried a priest yesterday who had been here for fifty-four years. How deep was his grave?"

The stranger stared at the young monk a moment, began to answer then caught the twinkle in the blue-gray eyes. Clapping his hands in real appreciation he laughed aloud and said: "How stupid of me. What a report to circulate."

That story does not register on paper. It needs the jumping eyes, the expressive hands, the ever changing facial lights and shadows, and the clever shift of key in the Frederic Dunne voice. He was a perfect raconteur.

If the newly ordained priest secretly lamented the many assignments which burdened him and took him from the silence and solitude he loved, he had reason in early May of 1901 to exclaim: "A monk never knows when he's well off!" For on the twelfth of that month Dom Obrecht recast his panel of officers and named as Prior of Gethsemani — Frederic Dunne.

At that moment Frederic was but twenty-seven years of age; had been a monk only seven years, and a full-fledged member of the Gethsemani community, made so by solemn profession, only one year. He was a priest of but two months' standing. Yet he had to assume the rank of prior over men like Father Benedict, who was nearing eighty, had been at Gethsemani for forty years and more, and had been an ordained priest before ever coming to the Kentucky monastery. He had to command his former Master of Novices — Father Henry — who was now sixty-five years old. He had to assume full responsibility for the entire abbey whenever Dom Obrecht was away or incapacitated, and at the same time had full run of the college on the hill. Yet he was only twenty-seven years of age.

It is easy to see why he *had* to find God; why he *had* to become a perfect monk.

CHAPTER TEN

Like an Oak

BEFORE me are more than two thousand letters written by Frederic Dunne while prior of Gethsemani. Practically all of them are addressed to Rt. Rev. Edmond Obrecht. They are the daily report Frederic would make to the traveling Abbot about his community back in Kentucky. I have read most of these letters three or four times and have caught myself exclaiming again and again: "How the boy grew!"

Just recently I found myself changing that exclamation into a question. I had now become curious about the how rather than the growth. It has not been an easy question to answer; for I was not asking about the means only but also about the manner. The means are quite obvious: generous human co-operation with divine grace and gifts. But as to the manner . . . I was defeated until out of the past there came to me an echo. I heard the voice of the great Lacordaire as he said: "Monks, like oaks, are eternal."

That figure pays fitting tribute to a very powerful fact; for what St. Benedict of Nursia began at the time of the fall of Rome seems destined to stand until the fall of the world. Of course, like all comparisons, it limps. Neither oaks nor monks are eternal. Yet, as I looked for something to which I might liken this growth of Frederic Dunne, I saw that, in all nature, I could find nothing better than the sturdy, strong, solid-hearted oak. For that, I know, sinks roots deep into the ground, spreads strong arms wide in sunshine and in rain, yearns ever upward to the sky and the stars — and it is durable. Frederic Dunne, I also know, became deep, strong, heaven-bent — and he was durable.

My obvious difficulty may puzzle you, and my solution may not seem to solve. But here is the situation: I knew only the matured man and the mellowed monk. For thirteen years I lived in intimate contact with him as abbot. In that time I saw him in almost every circumstance possible to a Trappist. And I saw his actions and reactions. I knew *Abbot* Dunne. But these thousand letters, running from 1902 and 1903 to 1933, show *Prior* Frederic. And the difference between the first letters written by the boy-prior and the last composed by the matured monk is astonishing.

In these early years his all-out devotion to duty is as evident as it was in his last years as abbot, but his judgment of men and events, his attitude toward the weak and complaining, his indignation over the commission of faults mark him out a nervous youth whose towering ideals and utter inexperience have him unmindful of the fact that monks, after all, are only men, and that wherever there are a lot of humans, there is always a lot of human nature.

At the dawn of the century his judgments were severe, his penances harsh, his tolerance almost nil. Here is a letter from the boy-Prior to his Abbot. Humility and obedience are in evidence; but the kindness and understanding, the tolerance and patience that mark the matured . . . are not.

Aug. 30, 1902.

My dearest Reverend Father:

I was glad to see that your boat reached port on Wednesday morning. That certainly means a very good trip across. I suspect it was the speediest voyage you have ever made over the Atlantic.

Yesterday we gathered our grapes. There are enough to make about 75 gals. of pure wine, but as the quality is not good, Bro. Albert will doctor it so as to have table wine for feast days. It will be all right for that purpose, though not good enough for Mass.

The other farm work goes pretty well. Bro. Conrad bought

20 head of sheep this week, and is now trying to sell 2 old mules — which will be a good thing. He also says you told him to drain some more fields. But you told me expressly, in your last instructions, that there would be none of this work done in your absence. So nothing will be done, at least until we hear from you, so as to be sure what you wish.

I regret very much to have to say that Fr. S—— became very angry yesterday morning, and manifested much temper again at the afternoon work. So this morning at Chapter I presumed your will in the matter and forbade him to say Mass until the Feast of the Nativity of Our Lady and said he was to wear the Oblate Habit until we had heard from you. This Father does not seem to realize he is a priest and a religious.

Fr. A—— is giving trouble again in Choir. Yesterday he took one of the large Choir Books to Chapter and began to study the Monitum. So I fear he is planning more trouble. I am trying to have peace, but if he commences to give scandal, I shall certainly forbid him to say Holy Mass and take the holy Habit off him. It would be a blessing from God if this man were out of the house.

All the sick, or rather the infirm, are the same or better. Even Fr. N—— says he will soon be able to follow the Community Exercises. At the visit of the infirm this morning Frs. Mary, Patrick, Sebastian, Bernard, Nivard, Gregory, Francis, and Anselm, as well as Bros. Gregory, Joseph, Jerome, Pius, Mary, Edmund, and Philip came to speak of their ailments — real or imaginary. Not one was of any importance.

There have been no changes in the Hotel since I last mentioned the "boarder-priests." They seem to be behaving well enough.

The weather is extremely warm. I do not think I have ever perspired so freely as at Conventual Mass today. The underclothing, habit and scapular were wringing wet; even the shoulders and sleeves of the cowl were more than moist. I hope Our dear Lord will remember it and forget our sins.

I hope your own good health, as mentioned in your last letter, continues.

Your loving child in the Sacred Heart,

fr. Frederic.

The close of that letter, wherein he speaks of God forgetting and remembering, is about the only passage in which I can recognize the Frederic Dunne I knew. But he was not yet thirty years of age when he wrote it.

Now let us look at one he wrote twelve years later and note the advance of the boy into a man, a monk, and a better superior.

June 27, 1914.

My dearest Rev. Fr.:

I thank you very much for your letter of the 24th which reached me this morning. The letter to Mr. Flattery has been attended to; the Masses have been entered, etc., etc.

The threshing doubtless will be completed some time this afternoon, and as they had 897 bu. of wheat by noon, we will get our hoped for 1000 bushels or very near it. It is perhaps the most difficult time we have ever had on account of the great heat. All who have been working there are just about exhausted; two of the seculars had to quit yesterday; but our monks have held on. . . .

Mr. Hettler, cousin to Bros. Wendelin, Dominic and Joseph, has been here for a few days, but left this morning. He proved himself a very nice, quiet old gentleman.

Last night the young Italian from Orange, N. J. reached the monastery, and this morning Frank Spaich (I'm not sure of the spelling) came from Louisiana. It is hard to say at the moment how they are disposed, but I am in hopes that both are well-intentioned. They seem to be men of *Faith* — and that is most important.

Mr. Herrmann was unable to give us any information concerning the disease on the grapes, but advised continuing the Bordeaux mixture. This we are doing. I sent a sample of the infected grapes and vines also to the Secretary of Agriculture at Frankfort, so as to have their opinion. Father George is much discouraged; but should not be. There is no call for that: *"Deus dedit. . . ."*

We kept the Feast of John the Baptist, singing the Office as on Sunday. This gave the Brothers a little more free time. I was glad to make it a bit easier for them, for the threshing the last few days has been very hard on them, not only because of the work itself being harder and longer than usual, but because of the heat.

Fr. Heibel in the Hotel had two fainting spells this morning. Just what the trouble is we do not know, so I have summoned the Doctor, who is with him now. In the Community there is little change. Dear old Fr. William sometimes gives quite a bit of trouble to those who attend him; but, poor man, it is not his fault, for he is seldom fully right in his mind. Fr. Mary says he is unwell (though he does not look it!) Still, in this kind of weather, scarcely anyone is really well.

I sincerely hope it is not as warm there as it is here. Not only is it warmer than usual, but a hot, dry wind is blowing, which makes it worse than usual; but — the Good Lord will care for us!

Well, I must try to make a little visit to the Blessed Sacrament, so with the prayer that everything continues to go well with you, I am

Your loving child in the Sacred Heart,

fr. Frederic.

How much more like the man I knew are those judgments on men who are at fault and those who complain they are ill. How much more God-conscious and prayerful the monk has become. How much kinder the superior.

But to see the matured man of God, we go to letters dated twelve and even thirteen years later; for supernature, like nature, does nothing with a rush. The climb up the mountain is not made by leaps and bounds, but one slow step after another slow step; for often we are climbing up the sheer face of a cliff! Look at this for an opening to a letter dated August 26, 1928, the feast of the Most Pure Heart of Mary. . . .

My dearest Reverend Father:

The grace of another sweet feast is granted us today in order to strengthen and console us in our exile; reminding us of what awaits us after we shall have been admitted to our true home. What a joy it will be to see our Mother!

The soul of the monk had deepened. And his heart has been attuned both to human beating and to the throb of the One whose feast he was celebrating. Recall now his remarks on Chapter and the sick when he was a boy. Compare them with these observations of the man, given in the same letter:

> At Chapter this morning Brothers Thomas, Peter, Albert, Labre, Joseph, John and Nivard were the only ones proclaimed, and none for anything serious. At the visit of the infirm Frater Denis came up to say he was well enough to attend Community Exercises, but the good young man suffers so much from his asthma we are keeping him in the infirmary for a while longer. Brothers Ambrose, Jerome, Stephen and Mark were up for the visit, but their complaints were not serious, just ordinary ailments to which we poor mortals are prone. I gave them what aid I could.
>
> As for myself I have a boil in my right ear, making it uncomfortable to sleep on that side; and the rheumatism in my left shoulder makes it just as uncomfortable to rest on that side. But neither of these things will kill me, will they? And the loss of sleep will have been a memory — I hope one in God's unfailing memory! — by the time this reaches you.

That is more like the Frederic Dunne I knew; the man whose mere presence created an atmosphere, and one that puzzled people who did not know the effect of a radiant spiritual personality. But he had not grown so spiritual as to forget the materialities. Here is a letter of just a few months later:

> . . . The wine harvest gave us 458 gallons — nine barrels and an 8-gal. jug. That leaves us with a stock of well over 900 gals. in the Winery. — A small patch of potatoes has been dug, yielding about 50 bushels; but the larger part of the crop, in another field, remains to be dug. — We have 37 barrels of cider in the cellar, besides a good quantity of apples stored away for the winter, plus about 50 gals. of jelly. So if everything else was short, we would still have plenty to be thankful for in our apple crop.

Walker Bowling succeeded in bringing over a fine bull calf at the end of September. This will replace our big bull next year. Like his predecessor, he is a registered animal of our own breed — 'short horn.'

The weather is very peculiar. Seldom have we been so long without rain. Most of the springs have ceased to flow, and the place is parched. What little wheat has germinated is in danger of burning up in this drought. While I am writing this the thermometer in your room registers 88 . . . and this is the middle of October. If you were home you would have to change your shirt many times a day.

But the good God has an infinitely wise plan and a real good in view whilst permitting this; and we lovingly submit to His ever-adorable Will.

No, indeed, he was not "out of this world" entirely as he grew and grew in ever greater awareness of the all-pervasive presence of Him who is the Son of the other world. And I find a typically Frederic Dunne touch in the final paragraph of a letter of the following week, dated October 16, 1928. "Speaking of politics," it runs, "and that is the topic of the day, I am compelled to withdraw all my objections to your friend, Al Smith. Of course I have long esteemed him as a splendid man (although running in very bad company!) but just today I learned that the maiden name of his better-half was Catherine DUNNE — and, of course, anyone with a better-half from that stock must be above and beyond all objections."

On Armistice Day, a year later, Frederic wrote a letter which reveals the kindness of Christ coming out of the man and the consciousness of Christ dominating the thinking of the monk.

My dearest Rev. Fr.:

We can only try to keep united with you in prayer, and this we do every day; so I trust that our dearest Lord will protect and preserve you, and not be unmindful of us at home — that we may always do His holy Will. We are always anxious for

word from you, but when it does not come we know that you
should not tire yourself in an absence that should be as much
of a rest as possible.

There is no change at home. After the rain of yesterday we
had a very heavy fog this morning; hence, everything is wet.
But this afternoon all are digging potatoes: the religious in the
garden and the novices in St. Joseph's field. We have very seldom
been so late with this kind of work, but as the heavy frosts
were late in coming, there appeared to be no danger; now
however, we must work fast, for there is peril to the crop. The
sky is still covered with clouds, and it is liable to resume
raining at any minute.

Now, my dearest Reverend Father, do not worry about the
Community. I suppose we are making the usual mistakes, but
I do not think there is much bad will in anyone; or at least, if
any exists, it is in the very few. We are but poor human creatures, very frail ones at that, but the predominant thought is to
do the Holy Will of God always. If only we could realize this
better, how much more perfect we would be!

The book in the refectory is very good: a fine commentary
on the Rule of St. Benedict, a little elevated in style at times,
but it ought to do us much good, since it tries to impress on us
the great thought of our Legislator: to seek God alone and in
all things. I think that all are as much pleased with it as I am,
judging from those who have spoken to me of it.

About myself: I believe the "old boy" must think I am going
to die soon, and he wants to get in his work; for it is a long
time since I have been so much tempted to impatience: impatience against almost everything and everyone — even myself.
I suppose, though, if I had the proper spirit of Faith, I would
regard this is a good sign, an indication that our dear Lord has
not altogether given up my poor soul, and that the devil,
knowing this, is trying to snatch it away from Him. I have some
other temptations, too; but they are mostly to unnecessary or
rash judgments of others. So please pray for me that I may win,
or rather, that our dearest Lord may win in this conflict.

I know that you may find things less odious up there than
you anticipated. Still, you know, that if you do the work of

God He will be satisfied, even if men are less pleased. I shall constantly pray that you will succeed in doing His Will in whatever comes before you.

Begging your paternal blessing, I am, in the Sacred Hearts of Jesus and Mary,

Your loving child . . .

What has happened to the boy who formed such harsh judgments about minor human failings and passed out such severe penances to his fellow priests? What has happened to the Superior who once wished certain men out of the monastery, and had such little patience with those who complained of being ill? — There is only one answer: He has been washed in the light of God, showered on by Him who once fell as flame, sunk his roots into a soil into which three generations of Trappists have verily tilled the spirit of holiness. Frederic Dunne has grown like an oak. He has become discreet.

Discretion should be as native to Benedictine superiors as wetness to water or energy to the sun; for St. Benedict put it in his Rule in large capitals, then underscored it. But that was all St. Benedict could do. It takes the Holy Ghost to complete the work; for Discretion is not only the fruit of the infused virtue of Prudence, it is also a function of that precious gift of Knowledge. Thanks to this great gift one is able to do the right thing, at the right time, and in the right way. But if ever we are to see how natural the supernatural is, this is the time; for God the Holy Ghost used the Rule of St. Benedict as channel for His gift, and as casting for the molding of the man into a real monk and something of a mystic. Here are my reasons and my reasoning. . . .

To those of us who have grown gray in religion, and spent most of our years in the Cistercian life, Frederic Dunne presented a puzzling problem. We saw the man as regular as the Book of Regulations. If his stall was ever empty during an hour of the Office, we could be reasonably sure that if circumstances allowed it, he was chanting that hour with us — just as the Regulations suggested. But to be as regular as that in his attendance in choir he had to spend between seven and eight hours of his working day in the church. The rest of the time he was at the beck and call of everyone in the community, from the Brothers in charge of the boilers and the carpenter shop, to the professor of theology and the prior of the house. Moreover, no extern ever transacted an iota of business with anyone in the monastery save Abbot Dunne. Add to this the fact that his telephone was seldom silent and would be carrying anything from the voice of a mother in the neighborhood asking prayers for her sick child, to the wire from some executive in Washington, Chicago, New York, or even San Francisco, asking final word on some contract with the abbey. And on top of all this we saw him incessantly slitting mail which might hold anything from an ad for a Wiltex Roman collar to a communication from the Sacred Congregation of Religious or the Holy Father himself.

We knew that just as surely as "faith comes from hearing," knowledge of the spiritual life comes from study. We wondered when Frederic Dunne studied. That he had a truly intimate knowledge of the spiritual life, an unshakable grasp on all its principles — and an insight that ordinarily comes only from wide reading and long study — was evident to all who heard him converse and most manifest to us who sat under him as he lectured morning after morning in the Chapter Room.

In 1941 it was natural for some of us to conclude that he must have acquired his knowledge in his early years as a monk. But when we learned that this sort of thing, this total immersion in work, had been going on since 1901; that for forty years he had been living his days in this same merciless manner; that he had been prior, guestmaster, postmaster, and Abbot Obrecht's plenipotentiary since his ordination to the priesthood, our problem became much more puzzling.

Those who analyzed his teachings soon saw that his was not

only the identical spirit, but the identical doctrine of St. Bernard of Clairvaux. The masterly rhetoric of the "Mellifluous Doctor," of course, was not there; but the substance of what Bernard put so artistically was given in Gethsemani's Chapter Room morning after morning by a man we knew had no time to study St. Bernard.

He did not make use of all of St. Bernard's premises perhaps, but the great medieval Master's conclusions were hammered home day in and day out. Before me is a set of notes taken down while Frederic Dunne talked. It covers a month of his daily instructions. Studying it I find a scheme every bit as scientific and exact as anyone ever drew up after a scrutiny of the sermons that transformed the Valley of Wormwood in that nursery of sainthood called Clairvaux.

With the surety of a master surgeon cutting to the very focus of infection, Dom Frederic would place his finger on the root of all religious imperfection as he would cry: "Oh! if we could only get rid of *self-will!*"

So insistent was he on this point that some of us grew restive and even remonstrated with him. I well remember the day I told him I had a suspicion that he must be descended from Calvinistic stock, or else had consorted long with Manichaeans in his youth. For a split second there was an interrogation in those ever lively gray-blue eyes. Then came the characteristic lift of the head, the flashing smile which so transformed that entire countenance, and then the very humble and spiritually sound reply: "I lived with myself all my youth, Father. I've lived with myself almost three quarters of a century now. I've come to know a little about myself. I know both Manes and Calvin were wrong. We are not a mass of corruption. But I also know Francis de Sales was right when he said self-will and self-love will die just a quarter of an hour after we do."

It is only too true that Dom Frederic omitted that basic and utterly essential Bernardine teaching about the dignity of man.

Never did we hear him speak formally as did the Abbot of Clairvaux on the *nobilis creatura* which is man, or that *dignitas* which, in a sense, is the alpha and omega of St. Bernard's doctrine. Yet it was implicit in all Dom Frederic's exhortations. If he insisted on the *curva,* as St. Bernard calls it — that almost ineradicable tendency in human nature to seek its own way, its own will, its own honor, glory, and love — it was ultimately for the same purpose Bernard had in mind when he spoke to his community on the very Canticle of Canticles. Dom Frederic was a pragmatic American, and knew that if we were ever to know God with that knowledge which not only sanctifies but actually beatifies, we must first know ourselves — and very especially be cognizant of our lower selves, which spiritual writers have termed self-love and self-will.

Those who know the Bernardine system will recognize it in the doctrine of Abbot Dunne. His first step was the acquisition of knowledge of self so as to know what we were, what we are, and what we are to become. If St. Bernard would pause here to insist that we are *noble creatures,* since we were made to the very image and likeness of God, Dom Frederic would hurry on to stress the truth that we are *defaced* images. But in doing this the American Abbot had simply placed heavier stress on St. Bernard's second fundamental point, he had not departed one iota from the Abbot of Clairvaux's doctrine.

Dom Frederic taught, as did St. Bernard, that our misery lay in the fact that we, by self-will, had covered over the very likeness of God, and that, consequently, our first great task as Cistercians was to clear away the ugly defacement wrought by selfish sin. "Know thyself!" he would cry — and might even quote it in Greek. But it was not to focus our gaze on our greatness as images of God that he would thus cry; but to set us staring at the defilement of the likeness of God we had made by self-will. Thus he grounded us, as Bernard would ground all at Clairvaux — in humility.

Step by step we can trace Dom Frederic's path from knowledge of self and its consequent humility, up through fear of God and detestation of self-love, to love of God and fear only of self-will. Finally this love of God would grow to be so all-absorbing that we become utterly unmindful of self-will and self-love as we became ever mindful of God and His creation.

Of course Dom Frederic never used the technical terms Bernard employed, and he would shy from all talk of mysticism and ecstasy as he would shy from a snake; yet his goal was nothing short of the one set for all at Clairvaux by the Mellifluous Doctor. To hear this American Abbot exclaim: "Oh! if we could only love God as He deserves to be loved! If we could only love Him with every fiber of our being! More today than yesterday, but not as much as tomorrow! Oh, if we only knew who God is!" was to understand that, without ever using the phrase, Dom Frederic aimed at, and would have all of us aiming at, that love of God which so transforms the mind, heart, and whole being, that it is called "transforming union" and "mystical marriage" by the initiate.

Now there precisely is the problem. How did this American, who for forty years was typically American inasmuch as he was ever active, acquire such a knowledge of the ascetical and mystical life and arrive at such a perfect system? It was Bernardine — and therefore, strictly Cistercian; but it was acquired by one who had no time to study Bernard or learn from books the system of Citeaux.

While Dom Frederic lived I never solved that problem, though I probed it often, and probed as far as I could. More than once I asked him what he read and when he read, and more than once I received as answer a twinkling smile and a silent gesture. Hands would go out to the litter on his ever littered desk, as if to say: "What time have I for reading?" My practical conclusion in those days was that he paid very close attention to the books read in the refectory during meals and absorbed all that was read in Chapter before Compline. All during his abbacy those books were truly select. Further, he never allowed a year to pass without having something from Bernard or something about Bernard read. So my conclusion was most practical; but it could hardly have been more wrong.

Dom Frederic's grasp in 1941 and 1942 of Bernardine ascesis was acquired by Prior Frederic back in 1901 and 1902. Here is how it happened. . . .

In May of 1901 Dom Obrecht named the young American as prior of Gethsemani. In July of that year the Abbot packed for his annual journey to Citeaux and the General Chapter of the Order, leaving the young man of twenty-seven to govern the monastery and conduct the college on the hill. That meant that one of his duties was to give a talk to the assembled choir monks every morning immediately after the chanting of Prime. Those talks had to center around and be based on St. Benedict's Rule.

That is how he came to a knowledge of the fundamental Bernardine principles without any formal study of St. Bernard himself; for it was in explaining this same Rule that the Abbot at Clairvaux had arrived at his own clear understanding of the basic principles of the Cistercian life. The central idea running through the Rule is that anyone who comes to serve God under it, must as a first and indispensable duty renounce his own will. This he can do most effectually by living under constant and complete obedience to an abbot.

Both Bernard and Frederic found this truth in the very Prologue to the Rule. Then in chapter after chapter, the third, fourth, fifth, and on to the seventh, St. Benedict rings the changes on the one same theme. "To you, therefore, do I address myself," he says in the Prologue, "to you who renouncing your own will, take up the strong and shining armor of obedience." That is the melody which will be heard again and again as he goes on. In his first chapter he names the kind of monks his men are to be: "Cenobites — men who live in a monastery and fight under a Rule and obedience to an abbot." In the third it is "let no one in the monastery follow his own will." In the fourth he gives his Instruments of Good Works, number ten of which is "To deny ourselves," and the fifty-ninth "to hate self-will." On and on he goes until he reaches his famous seventh chapter with its Twelve Degrees of Humility — steps that will lead to a perfect love of God; but steps that will never be climbed until first we have walked all over our self-will and self-love. Four times in the first degree are we told we must give up our own will; four times again in the second; in the third and fourth it is of obedience that the Saint speaks. So the lesson cannot be missed. No one who so much as reads the Rule from that Prologue which is addressed to "those who will renounce their own will," down to Chapter 72 where all are urged to "vie with one another in the practice of obedience and never to do what is profitable to self but rather what will profit another"; no one, I say, can miss what Frederic Dunne learned; namely, that two loves dominate our lives — and that it is only by denying our love of self that we can show our love for God and come, through Christ Jesus, to an all-absorbing love for the Father who made us.

In 1941 and 1942 we were listening to the matured man, the monk who had mastered his doctrine. But in 1901 and 1902 that monk, practically an untried tyro, had to take the text and think it through. It was that thinking through that made the man the monk he was, and ultimately transformed the monk into something of a mystic.

More than once I have called Frederic Dunne a pragmatic American. That adjective tells why what should have been a dismal failure turned out a phenomenal success.

The community this mere boy had to address was made up almost of the same people who six years earlier had forced a fairly aged abbot to resign. Why was it that they listened so docilely to one whom most of them could have rightfully called a boy? It was not that Frederic Dunne was something of a born diplomat and blessed with truly charming ways. Diplomacy played small part in the process and charm meant next to nothing. It was not that they could take advantage of his youth and inexperience; for he proved himself a stickler for the Rule and placed everything on a supernatural plane by making it all a matter of obedience. Yet, these men not only listened to his chapter talks, they followed his advice! Why?

The answer lies in the one word *sincerity*. Men of any age and men of all nationalities will ever pay tribute to one who is sincere. In a Trappist monastery this is doubly true. For here character rates higher than intelligence, creative ability, or personal charm. And if the old men could see anything in the earnest young Prior, who they knew was really only just learning the Rule he was trying to explain, it was character.

Frederic Dunne was not an intellectual genius, nor a physical giant. His receding chin may have led some to believe that he lacked virility. But to see him live every hour of the day the principles he had proposed that morning as deriving from the Rule; to see him give without counting the cost; to watch him obey the injunctions of an absent abbot, and be as tenderly considerate of others as a mother while utterly relentless toward self; to find him the first to take the menial and repulsive tasks while assigning others to what was more agreeable; to listen to him asking advice from seniors and making polite requests when he could have issued orders, was to watch a young monk grow like an oak, and see a theory reduced to everyday practice. Humility ceased to be the name of a virtue for Frederic Dunne as it became the very blood of his veins. But not without cost. Just as we can fancy it costs the oak . . .

To push roots deep into the ground the oak must patiently worm its way around stubborn rocks, pierce hard clay, sometimes travel through a bed of dry gravel to get down to moisture. To throw those sheltering arms for a wide shade and lift its head to the skies, the oak must bear with bleak winters and scorching summers. To stand stately requires patience, fortitude, and faith.

❖   ❖   ❖   ❖

Father Frederic was happy to see Dom Obrecht return that November. Being prior for an absent abbot can cause tension, and it was only after Dom Edmond had resumed the chapter talks that young Frederic saw how taut he had been since late summer.

But that first year, with its three full months of responsibility, was only brief apprenticeship for something not even Dom Obrecht could have envisioned. In 1902 Gethsemani's Abbot was commissioned by the General Chapter to make the regular visitation of the Trappist community in Bosnia. That meant a slight prolongation of his usual three months' absence from the Kentucky monastery. In 1903 he was asked to do the same for the Canadian houses. But in 1904 the General Chapter made him Visitor Extraordinary to the monks of Marianhill in South Africa, and Rome added dignity to the assignment by appointing Dom Edmond Apostolic Administrator of the distant mission field. It was a burden for the Abbot, but a very light one compared to what it entailed for the young Prior back at Gethsemani. The work consumed the best part of four full years, which meant that Frederic Dunne, before he was thirty, was ruling a Trappist monastery and running an American college.

It affected Frederic; but not as most humans would expect it to. His eyes were affected, not his ego. The more the Abbot exalted him, the more humble he became. The more numerous the material enterprises he had to oversee, the sharper became his spiritual sight. He became expert at piercing disguises and finding beneath each creature, the Creator; and in every human, the divine. Wine and Wheat, once consecrated, had never deceived him. Neither now would flesh and blood. Every command from Dom Obrecht was a commission from God. Every member of the community was a member of Christ. Every guest to the monastery would be received as St. Benedict wanted them received — as Jesus.

God often works by opposites. He blinded Saul that Paul might see. He burdened Frederic Dunne with more activities than the busiest business executive just that He might lighten the weight of life's inherent weariness. He cluttered and complicated his cloistered existence just to simplify his contemplative life. Frederic Dunne *had* to find God in everything from stone and cement to singing the Conventual High Mass — or foolishly fritter away a God-given existence.

The years most marked by Dom Obrecht's long absences were exceptionally busy years at Gethsemani. In 1901 the cow barn had burned down. But livestock cannot be left unhoused. So work was begun immediately on what was to be a much larger building. Dom Obrecht commanded that it be 180 feet long and 40 feet wide, with walls of stone 2 feet thick. The loft was to be high enough to hold a two years' supply of fodder for 100 head of cattle. Father Frederic had to see that that command was carried out to the letter. He had to become superintendent of construction along wih his other offices. As soon as that barn was roofed excavations began for a building of identical dimensions but a far different purpose. This was to hold the monastery's shops, laundry, and dairy. Before this was finished the enterprising young American Prior was sinking a huge cistern at the top of a high western hill. This was not filled when he was experimenting with cement stucco in an effort to make the American monastery look more monastic and much less American.

In late 1907, when Dom Obrecht returned from his long stay in South Africa, he found a far different looking abbey standing on the very spot he had last seen a rather unsightly red-brick building. It looked much like the abbeys of the Old World with their hard faces of home-quarried and often crudely cut stone.

The change was due to the daring and enterprise of the young American Prior.

As the burly, black-headed Alsatian Abbot looked at his Prior he was struck by the fact that everything about Frederic Dunne would prove deceptive to a stranger. He was thin, but he also looked slight of build. There was no great spread to his shoulders, and his arms looked weak and small. But Dom Obrecht had seen this seemingly slight man dig and wheel dirt with an energy that looked tireless; had watched him quarry stone and roll boulders out of the way with a strength that was surprising; while the way Frederic wielded an ax in the woods and a hoe on the farm caused a laughing Abbot to christen him "his American dynamo." But the deceptiveness did not stop there. To catch Frederic in a moment of pensiveness was to look on features one would class as belonging to an earnest but not overbright student; for weak eyes behind thick-lensed, steel-rimmed glasses topped a very weak-looking chin. Actually there seemed something extremely delicate and even womanish about this slight-appearing monk.

But if his physical strength caused surprise, his unyielding moral stamina evoked real wonder.

The older monks of the community knew the principles of the spiritual life and the depths of the Trappist spirit. Day after day they saw this young American put those principles into uncompromising practice and send that spirit radiating out from his person in everything he did from the singing of the Divine Office to the distribution of work. It was soon seen that Frederic Dunne was not only fearless in his application of principle, but utterly unbiased in his adjudication of facts. He would not trifle with the ideal upheld by so many generations of Trappists. That is why the community saw him in the absence of the Abbot not only welcome aspirants and give the habit to postulants, but dismiss those who would not be generous with God or true to the Trappist standards. They found their young Prior somewhat inflexible when a principle was at stake, and they marveled that one who could be so considerate of the feelings of others and even tender in his dealings with the weak, could prove so adamantine when convinced that God's glory or the good of the community was at stake.

In a letter dated August 29, 1904, I find an example of what set these older men marveling:

> . . . Word was sent me that Brother B—— was seen down by the railroad talking to some people early this morning. I gave orders that he be brought to the Gate House immediately. When he arrived he found his clothes, money, and possessions awaiting him. These he took, and left without being allowed to speak with anyone save the gate keeper. I feel sorry for the poor man, but the Rule must be kept! . . .

Perhaps any other abbot would have grown concerned to learn that the community he had left in 1901 numbering eighty had dwindled to seventy before the South African administratorship had been concluded. But Dom Obrecht had seen oaks grow. He knew the soundness of their hearts. He had watched this seemingly weak monk grow very like an oak. He would trust his judgment to be sound.

What especially gratified, even as it mystified, the returned Abbot was the way Frederic Dunne had simplified life for himself despite the mounting complications of his monastic existence. While in South Africa Obrecht had told himself that Frederic had reduced all life and living to the catechism's answers to the first few questions. God made man to know Him, love Him, and serve Him. Frederic had reduced that trinity to unity by making his arduous service a service of ardent love for the One who had made him out of love.

As the daily letter arrived in South Africa telling the Abbot about everything that transpired in Gethsemani — even to the sudden changes of Kentucky weather — Dom Edmond read between the lines and saw how his Prior was supernaturalizing the natural and thus sanctifying himself. He rejoiced that his protégé was growing in more than administrative experience.

This letter of August 20, 1912, is as good an example as any to show how he kept his Abbot informed on everything that took place in the monastery — although almost any one of the more than two thousand that I have would serve to illustrate the same.

My dearest Reverend Father:

We have just finished the Night Office, which went on pretty well, though perhaps a little slow, as it was practically 4:30 when we were through.

I was very glad to receive word from you yesterday, especially to learn that you are so much better. I hope that in your entire trip you will be as well or better. I expect that you are spending today at Our Lady of the Valley. That will at least make one part of the work over.

Father Robert's good friend, Father McCluskey, reached the Abbey last night, and Abbot Athanasius will come this morning; both intend leaving this evening. Father Courier comes this evening, but I do not know how long his stay will be. Doubtless it will be short.

Mr. Wilson sent us a copy of the new Insurance law, which was passed on the 4th of last March. This leaves the regulation of the rates in the hands of a Committee of State officials. If this is proven to be constitutional it will take much power out of the hands of the Companies. So soon as the case is settled he will give us the advantage of any reduction that may be made possible, but his superiors will not allow him to act until then.

We are having a very warm spell just now. Fr. McCluskey says that more than a thousand men had to drop out of the parade in Louisville on Sunday, some received bad cases of sunstroke. I am broken out with the heat rash from my shoulders to my knees. This is the first time I have ever had this, or at least the first time I have ever had it so bad. But I believe they say it is a sign of good health, so I need not complain.

Fr. Benedict is making his first week as Hebdomadary, and is doing very well, only he is inclined to give his voice higher than the Choir can follow. He will overcome this with more practice.

Fr. Patrick's brother is still here, and will remain until his week is out. Brother Leo's brother was also here to see him, as he had some business in Louisville. He came Tuesday and left Wednesday.

Otherwise there is little change amongst the sick or the other members of the Community. The work is still at the weeds principally, but soon we ought to have another cutting of hay. Then there may have to be some extra work.

Praying our good Lord and His Blessed Mother to guide and guard you, I am

Your affectionate child in SS Corde Jesu.

But I select this one of July 3, 1914, to show how easy it was for the absent Abbot to follow the spiritual growth of his son and see the one who was hardly more than a boy when he appointed him to the priorship, mature into a holy monk, a real man of God.

My dearest Reverend Father:

I am rather worried that we have not received word from you since your letter of the 27th ultimo; however I suppose that it was only occupations incident to the Visitation, and that you will be in Louisville tonight, and out home tomorrow, as indicated in your letter from Lonsdale. I hope especially that your health is not giving you any trouble, at least not more than the usual stomach trouble.

Our good Father William has passed into his Eternity. This morning they called me at 1:30, but by the time I reached him he was gone. However there was nothing that we could have done, that had not already been done — except to pray for the repose of his soul. I sang the Requiem after Prime, and we will have the burial after Vespers this afternoon. He died without a struggle, just burned out like an exhausted candle — as should we all! — God grant him speedy rest.

Our Italian postulant has left us definitely. He was only a few days in the Community when he found the life too hard, and the attractions of home too strong. I am glad to say, though, that the Bohemian is doing very well; takes hold of the life in earnest, and finds nothing too hard.

I am expecting every minute to receive a telegram from you, but I see now that it will not come before I have to finish this, so I will say "Au revoir."

Your loving child in the Sacred Heart

Anyone who has his life so integrated that he can conceive it as a candle burning before God, has certainly simplified life. And if he desires only to burn out like an exhausted candle, he has simplified and supernaturalized death. Abbot Obrecht reading such lines, and between them, must have rejoiced.

It was fortunate, however, for Frederic Dunne that he had so simplified and supernaturalized life, for Abbot Edmond kept complicating it. It was in these years that Gethsemani obtained the Batz Memorial Library. Father Frederic had to supervise the reception and shelving of over 10,000 volumes, then begin their indexing. It was in these years also that all precedent was shattered and the Governor of Kentucky was received within the cloister with a gubernatorial suite that was heavy with women. Father Frederic was not only the reception committee, he was the banquet and entertainment committee, and guide to all the guests. It was in these earliest years of his priorship, too, that the refugee monks of Fontgombault, fleeing the Masons of France, found asylum at Gethsemani. Prior Frederic had to arrange quarters for them by making a Trappist monastery out of what had been a girls' school and a Sisters' convent up on Mt. Olivet.

That meager summary of Frederic Dunne's activities during his early years as prior will give some vague idea of the puzzle presented to one who would account for his magnificent growth in genuine holiness. The human mind has only a "one-point consciousness." We can give full attention only to one thing at any one time. So one wonders how Frederic Dunne as prior of a large monastery, president pro tem of a thriving little college, super-intendent of construction of massive buildings and dangerous architectural ventures, receptionist for the State's leading man and leading ladies, responsible head for the religious observance by young and old in the community, manager of the widespread farm, etc., etc., could keep God ever before his eyes as a contemplative should.

The answer is not the one Dom Obrecht framed for himself while off in South Africa. Frederic had not simplified his life by adopting the dicta of the catechism. He had learned the secret of sanctity and genuine happiness while giving morning chapter talks on the Rule of St. Benedict. He was growing daily like an oak — and very specifically like the twelfth-century oak which dominated all other growths by growing in his retreat at Clairvaux in a love for God that would one day win for him the only title worth having and worth a lifetime of striving — that of saint. Like the Abbot of Clairvaux the American Prior learned life's greatest lesson, and life's only real object, in the five words St. Benedict has placed at the close of his Chapter 57. A chapter, strangely enough, which deals with commerce! Benedict says: *ut in omnibus glorificetur Deus* — "that in *all things* God may be glorified." So Frederic Dunne would be anything from a mixer of mortar and hod carrier to postmaster and college vice-president "that in all things God might be glorified."

Thus would he grow — not so much like a tree as like Him who died upon a tree. Thus did he grow in the likeness of Christ: by doing what he was told by men, but doing it only for the love of God.

CHAPTER ELEVEN

"If Any Man Will Be My Disciple..."

THE tragedy of our times is that we say Christian without ever saying Christ. It begins too often at Baptism and can carry on until death. If that "i" in Christian were long, we might have a greater realization not only of the transforming power in that gift of God called Baptism, but of the very power and person into whom it transforms us. That would change life for many; for it would give them possession of the truth which possessed Frederic Dunne. He not only heeded the command given by St. Leo the Great: "Christian, know thy dignity!" but accepted and fulfilled the obligation such a dignity imposes. *Noblesse oblige.* Being a Christian, he knew he had to be Christ. The Trappist way of life proved to be just what he needed to accomplish this end; for the first word as well as the last word the God-Man spoke is the first and last word any true Trappist can speak. It is the word of obedience.

Through the Psalmist God the Holy Ghost has God the Son saying to God the Father: "Behold, I come. In the head of the Book it is written of me that I should do thy will, O God" (Ps. 39:8–9). In the Gospels Christ Himself says: "My meat is to do the will of him who sent me" (Jn. 4:34). At the beginning of His Passion, as at its end, it was still the Father and the Father's will: "Fiat" in the Garden; "It is consummated" on the Hill.

Be it admitted that Frederic Dunne was not a scholar, and that time enough to become a real student was denied him. Nevertheless, with the intuition of genius and the instinct of a lover, when analyzing the character of Christ, he pierced to the center's central core. He did this also with the Rule of St. Benedict. And thrilled to find them both the same. He saw every virtue in its perfection in Christ Jesus; yet looking more deeply in this many-sided, all-beautiful character, he found that humility was the bone and the very marrow of the bone which made the Man-God what He was — and he found that humility expressed most perfectly in His obedience. Reading then the Rule of St. Benedict, which is addressed to "those who will take up the shining arms of obedience," he found that the palpitating heart of this Rule is humility; that the two words "humility" and "obedience" were so easily interchangeable throughout that he would not be wrong if he likened them to the systole and diastole of that heart. He rightly concluded that if he would be what he was called to be by Baptism, and what he had chosen to be by religious profession, he had only one thing to do. He saw that he would not only be like Christ, but actually, in the very real, but in what is called the mystical order, he would be Christ, if he obeyed.

In his thirteen years as Abbot, hardly a week, certainly not two weeks, passed without him reminding the community of this truth. When he learned it first, no one now can say. But that he lived it with a simplicity, a sincerity, a generosity that was nothing short of heroic from the moment he was appointed Prior until Dom Obrecht's death, no one who has seen the records can deny.

If one is seeking the secret of this young man's success as Prior with the ever demanding Abbot, Dom Obrecht, and with the community; if one is seeking deeper, and searching for the secret of his success with God, I believe he will have discovered both when he has looked at his ever prompt obedience. For God loves obedience. When His love had spilled over into what we call Creation, He set as law for that universe obedience to His will. And when He allowed His only-begotten Son to effect a re-Creation, it was by a fulfillment of the same law — obedience to His will. Hence He cannot but love and greatly bless any man who will be humble enough always to obey, and be obedient enough always to be humble. Frederic Dunne was exceptionally blessed during his thirty-two years as Prior under Dom Obrecht. Unquestionably his generosity, his sincerity, simplicity, and humility won gifts and graces from God; but nothing won more than his obedience.

One of the greatest puzzles of life and deepest mysteries of theology is the way God distributes His gifts and graces. It is a revealed truth that the "Spirit breatheth where He will"; yet when we study the life of a saint, or even of a saintly man, usually we can trace a pattern and learn the price Divinity demands for certain great endowments.

Frederic Dunne was Prior of Gethsemani from May 12, 1901, until July 16, 1933; then from November 1, 1934, until February 6, 1935 — a total of thirty-two years and five months. During that time his Abbot was absent from the monastery on an average of three and a half months every year; and some very long absences contribute to that average. The South African visitation absorbed the years from 1904 to 1907. In 1908 Dom Obrecht visited the Trappist monastery in Palestine. Naturally he made a pilgrimage to the Holy Land. So it was late in the spring of 1909 when he returned to Kentucky. In 1910 and 1911 he was sent to investigate the foundation made in Oregon by the exiles from Fontgombault. In 1912 and 1913 he traveled to the Far East as visitor to the Trappists and Trappistines in China and Japan — a work absorbing more than four full months. World War I prevented his annual trip to Europe for the General Chapter of the Order; but from 1914 to 1918 he was away from Gethsemani from three to six weeks every year as he made the visitation of his daughter house in Rhode Island and of the Canadian Trappist monasteries. In 1919 he was absent for four consecutive months; in 1921, for five and a half months; and in 1922, four months again.

Those details are necessary if we are to arrive at an approximate estimate of the price Divinity demanded for the gifts and graces He would give Frederic Dunne. Absentee landlordism ruined Ireland and deeply affected the entire Irish race. Absentee lord abbots did the same to monasteries and monasticism in the late Middle Ages and at the dawn of modern times. Now here was an abbot who was absent annually anywhere from six weeks to over six months, yet we find his abbey progressing all through his long reign.

The explanation of that marvel cannot lie in the men who made up the community; for the bulk of them had made up the community which had ousted an abbot who was seldom absent from his cloister. Nor can it lie in the personality of the reigning Abbot. The only answer seems to be: the American Prior who was God's grace to Gethsemani.

It may not be generally known that it is much more difficult to be prior in a Trappist abbey, than to be abbot, especially when the abbot of that monastery is a man of Dom Obrecht's stature and is summoned by higher authorities to works which demand frequent and long absences from the abbey. For then the poor prior has all the responsibility with next to none of the authority. He must carry all the burdens of the first superior without being able to command all the respect of the first superior, since he is still only a subordinate. It was none other than the Abbot General, Msgr. Marre, who sympathized with Father Frederic on his priorship by saying he well understood from long experience how it was that "whenever anything goes wrong in an abbey, everyone blames the poor prior." Laughingly he told Frederic that, because he was prior, he could expect to be "an anvil on which all would hammer."

If that comes as a shock let it only be recalled that "wherever there are a lot of humans, there is always a lot of human nature." And while human nature can be very lovable, it is also true that since Adam listened to Eve, it can also be very petty — and at times somewhat mean.

A prior in a Trappist abbey is placed between the abbot and the community; and while he almost always finds himself prized by both, there will be occasions when he will find himself pressed by both. And unless he is made of stern stuff he may very soon feel himself somewhat squeezed out.

How did Frederic Dunne maintain his position for over thirty years? How did he manage not only to placate, but even to please both the Abbot and the community for that length of time?

Some of the ancients in the community, who lived with Frederic twenty and even thirty of those years, speak of his innate tact, prudence, and even mention his patience. I have to smile at that last trait; for in the last year of his life on earth, Dom Frederic told me that his temper still bothered him and that his impatience was his greatest cross.

I recall vividly the day he had granted me permission to visit an old lay Brother, who had been confined to the infirmary for years and was now nearing his death. Brother Andrew had been on the stage most of his life, and had gone all the way from song and dance man in "honky-tonks" of small western towns to Broadway — and that includes years as clown in a circus! Even in his old age Brother Andy could still clown and entertain royally. But this particular day he was suffering and seemed quite low in spirits. Abbot Dunne was leaving as I arrived, and in his usual cheerful manner asked Brother if there was anything he could give him.

"You might give me a little patience," grunted Andy before spreading his mouth in a real circus-clown smile.

"Sorry, Brother," came the instantaneous reply from the Abbot, "but I need every ounce I have for myself."

But never would I have known he had a temper, far less that

he had trouble with it, had he not confessed it. In thirteen years of very intimate association with him I was privileged to see him in many trying situations, but never once did I note the semblance of a flash of temper, let alone a real outburst.

It was not until I had read about fifteen years of correspondence between himself and Abbot Obrecht, while the latter was traveling, that I got an inkling of the real secret of his success, and realized the meaning of the passage of Scripture which says: "The obedient man shall speak of victories."

Frederic Dunne was a young, exceptionally energetic, and quite enterprising American when Dom Obrecht was in South Africa, Palestine, China, and Japan. The urge, so characteristically American, to do things and to get things done, is evident in letter after letter of their almost daily correspondence. But what makes me marvel is the evidence before me that Frederic Dunne never did a single thing in all those years except in explicit obedience to his Abbot.

There is a splendid example of this in a letter containing a request which shows not only the obedient monk, but the American monk. It is dated August 29, 1924, and runs in part:

> Today the enclosed letter was received from a company of lawyers in Minneapolis re. St. Mary's Abbey, and in which they offer to represent the affairs of our Abbey. They have been answered to the effect that you are absent for the moment, but that on receipt of word from you, they will be notified of what is to be done. You will notice that their letter is not typewritten but printed, showing that they have written similarly to others. This may be a good idea, for the one Company representing so many creditors may have the greater power to enforce a just distribution of the assets. If you should wish them to be authorized immediately to represent the Abbey (since they say things are to be settled in thirty days), I would understand this from the one word "Authorized" sent by cable. But before anything will be done, inquiries will be made as to the standing of this firm of lawyers.

This rather modern way of expediting business by cable is found in another letter written during this same absence of the Abbot and the same month of August. It is dated the twenty-fifth and is one of the most crowded letters I have read. He covers everything from Chapters of Faults, visit of the sick, and the manual labor for each day to the retreat master for the Knights of Columbus and his own reactions to him as a preacher and to the effect he had on his hearers. But in the midst of all these comes the, to me, surprising way of doing business by Trappists. It reads:

> As you had only a minute to reply to the note that reached you on board the ship, you could not have read all of my note, so did not give all the directions I asked for. However, I understand your directions for further charity. If a cable arrives with the one word "Charity" it means that I am to send you ten drafts of the value of five hundred francs each; and none is to be sent if no wire arrives.

There was another bit of business, though, which shows Frederic Dunne's spirit of perfect obedience which was not transacted by cable. It had to do with water for Gethsemani — an ever pressing problem. At the time these letters were written summer droughts had just ruined two Gethsemani potato crops — and potatoes form the main vegetable on the Trappist menu the year around! In those days when an individual wished to wash up after work he had to go to the single tap, draw his water in a basin, and walk with it to the lavatory. Despite the lesson taught by the destruction of the cow barn by fire in 1901, there was still no fire protection around the monastery. Frederic Dunne had noted all this and now humbly begged permission to sink some artesian wells. Dom Obrecht granted this request readily enough. But when all efforts to sink a shaft proved fruitless, Father Frederic proposed the building of a large cistern on the highest hill to the west, which he would fill by piping the many springs on the property to one point and then pumping the water to the hill. Dom Obrecht was not enthusiastic. But after a series of letters containing intricate explanations of the project, the Abbot finally blurted: "Go ahead with your cistern if you promise to sit on it all winter to keep it from freezing."

It was a strange permission; but it was permission. Father Frederic went ahead, and for all the years of his long priorship Gethsemani profited greatly from his wise foresight — while never once did he have to sit on the hill to keep the water from freezing.

That kind of thing, that continual respect for authority, and that patient waiting for abbatial authorization, wins what never can be commanded — admiration and loyalty from men, and graces and gifts from God.

Still it can be said that Frederic Dunne who always obeyed his Abbot never once obeyed Edmond Obrecht. In more than thirty-two years no one saw a sign of servile subservience or obsequiousness in the submission tendered by Prior Frederic. It was always that sublime virtue of religious obedience, that act of faith which sees flesh and blood, knows it is looking at a human, as fallible if not more fallible than himself, yet cries in his inmost being as cried the doubting Thomas after he had put fingers into the place of the nails and hand into His side. It is absolutely true that Frederic Dunne never once obeyed Edmond Obrecht, for he was ever obeying the voice of God made articulate by the black-haired Alsatian who had been elected to rule America's protoabbey.

Faith, of course, is a gift from God. But man must work with it! In a way it can be said that obedience like Frederic Dunne's is also a gift from God since it depends so entirely on that faith. But again, man must work to acquire it. The beauty of it all is that these two things compliment one another, so that the greater a man's faith the more ready and unquestioning his obedience; and the more ready and unquestioning his obedience, the greater will be his faith. That is a circle about which there is no viciousness. And skilled spiritual directors will tell you that in proportion as a soul draws nearer to God the power of faith increases in that soul, until what is actually blind obedience is very near faith's crown of vision. The man not only hears God in his superior, he all but sees Him face to face!

But note the price Divinity places on such gifts. . . .

Still very much alive among Trappists is a practice as old as monasticism, but which most moderns have allowed to die — the Chapter of Faults. This is a practice in which you are not only allowed to accuse yourself publicly before the community of your external violations of Rule, but in which others are allowed to accuse ("proclaim" is the technical term) you of such violations. You can imagine how humiliating it is to accuse yourself; but to have others accuse you — !

Well do I remember dear old Father Augustine, who was a Protonotary Apostolic and rector of a major seminary in Canada before becoming a Trappist at Gethsemani, telling me in his seventy-fourth year, that proclamations still pricked him.

At La Trappe De Rancé had added a refinement that will be appreciated by few. He used to proclaim for faults that had not been committed, then further humiliate the monk by a tongue-lashing for the uncommitted fault that would wound the well-nigh invulnerable. In the Reformed Cistercians this refinement has been done away with; but the spirit that brought it into being and the end aimed at by De Rancé still flourishes. Humility comes through humiliations; and humility is the goal of the Chapter of Faults every bit as much as regular observance and external discipline.

During Dom Obrecht's absences, Frederic Dunne would conduct these Chapters — and after each proclamation issue what he deemed a fitting penance to the one proclaimed. But on Dom Obrecht's return, Frederic Dunne was just another monk — albeit the first monk, or prior — and hence liable as everyone else for proclamations. Being human, he made slight slips during the Abbot's absence. Being among other humans he was proclaimed for them on the Abbot's return. But the stinging part of the process for sensitive human nature lies in the castigation given for an inadvertence, and being held guilty for something that was obviously involuntary. Now God alone knows what motivated Dom Obrecht, but the external fact, known to all present, is that on every such occasion, as public reward for the yeoman service Frederic Dunne had rendered him and the community during his absence, the Abbot gave full vent to his irony, which was strong, and to his sarcasm, which could be truly keen.

Recently I had occasion to consult one of the oldest members of the community about Mass at the high altar of our basilica. This, in our day, is reserved exclusively for Conventual Masses. In a letter from Father Frederic to Dom Edmond I find him asking his Abbot if he might not assign two priests to offer their Masses there each morning to obviate the necessity of appointing some priests to the altars in what was called the "secular church" — a portion in the rear of the basilica, originally used as a parish church, but for all of this century reserved for private Masses by the monks, at which their relatives could assist. It was a request that shows the Prior's anxiety to keep the community together. I am told that it was granted. But on the Abbot's return the Prior was proclaimed "for introducing innovations by using the High Altar for private Masses." When I asked if the proclamation was accepted, this old monk chuckled and replied: "Not only accepted but used as peg to hang much more on." Then he gave me the gist of what Dom Edmond had to say, and I was back in La Trappe in the days of De Rancé, even as my heart ached for Dom Frederic Mary Dunne. "Yes," Dom Obrecht had said, "that is the usual thing, I understand. I hear that my back is not turned when everything here is overturned. Before I reach Louisville, so I hear, you have changed everything." Then he would go on to quote that section of the Rule which speaks of certain priors who thought themselves "second Abbots" — and end by reminding Frederic that St. Benedict made a very strong recommendation on how to treat such men.

When abbot, Frederic Dunne himself told me laughingly of another such occurrence. Dom Obrecht had sent orders to reprint the names on each cross in the cemetery. Only the other day I came across the letter in which Dom Frederic, then Prior Frederic, had replied by saying that the work had been started immediately; that he himself had gone to the printery and shown the monks there how to set up the type, adding that he had stayed there so long that he could now write only a short letter. He had added the line that it would be as easy to print the same name one thousand times as print it once, since each name had to be hand set. He had closed by saying "It will take time, but we have made a good start."

Dom Frederic was showing me how God purifies a soul this particular day, so he went on to tell me how he himself had gone to the printery day after day to help the workers there. They had finished all but three names when Dom Obrecht arrived home. At the first Chapter of Faults after his arrival the Prior was proclaimed for "not carrying out Reverend Father's orders" — a very vague proclamation, and one that ordinarily would not be accepted without further clarification and specification. But Dom Obrecht seized it this day to tell the entire community about the printing job he had ordered done and which had not been done. "That's the way it goes," he said, "you start nothing until you hear I am back in Louisville already. Let things go to the last minute. That's how my orders are carried out."

Now understand the background or you will misunderstand the deed entirely. Seen in any other light than that of La Trappe, colored by De Rancé's own concept of what human nature needs in order to be divinized, and you will see it awry. It will not only lack perspective; it will be completely out of focus. Let it be added here that De Rancé had justification for his action in a line of St. Benedict's Rule which urges all his followers to read the Fathers of the Desert in order to learn from them how to live. It was far from unusual for those old hermits to mete out to aspirants humiliations which now shock us and seem impossible to justify in the light of truth and charity. But the facts are there — immutably.

Edmond Obrecht had made his novitiate at La Trappe. The odor of De Rancé will never completely leave those hallowed halls. It would seem to be inevitable then, that when Edmond Obrecht became abbot he should employ some of the methods that made his original monastery famous.

Thus, in the light of what we know of monasticism, St. Benedict's Rule, the spirit of La Trappe, and Edmond Obrecht's early training, we can account for the happenings. But in the light of what you know of human nature, you can easily surmise what such treatment does to any sensitive human heart. Naturally speaking, that heart would be broken. But, in a prefix, you have the whole story. Trappists do not live naturally; their lives are lived on the *super*natural level. That is why Frederic Dunne's heart did not break. But let no one imagine for an instant that it did not ache. And again the same prefix tells you the entire story. The supernatural is exactly what it is named — a life built on the natural. St. Thomas' axiom about "grace supposing nature" and even "perfecting it" is sound. The wondrous human nature that a generous God gave us is the foundation, the substratum, and, in a certain sense, the very substance of what we call supernatural. Grace builds on nature. Scratch a monk and you'll find a man. Were that not so, you would never have a monk, who is, after all, nothing more than a man of God.

The humanity in religion is the source of most of the suffering in the religious life. It is also the foundation of all the sanctity found among religious. And the relation between suffering and sanctity is so close that while we may never call suffering the cause of sanctity, we can frequently name it more than a mere occasion; we can rightly say it is a *"condicio sine qua non."*

Our world is full of pain. The religious world is not free of it. Yet men go on speaking of the mystery of evil and the problem of suffering. The solution is obvious from a glance at the two Adams. There was sin; there had to be a Saviour. There was sin; there had to be suffering. Infinite satisfaction was demanded by Infinity for sin's infinite outrage. So there was a Christ of God who became the Jesus of men. There is sin today. There will be, there must be suffering today and tomorrow. But thanks to the doctrine of the Mystical Body of Christ, Christians no longer find evil a mystery or pain a problem. With St. Paul they cry: "I fill up in my flesh those things that are wanting to the Passion of Christ." And more than one stanch follower of Him who anguished in the first Gethsemani can say: "I fill up in my mind those things that are wanting to His Agony in the Garden." The mental sufferings of the Christ are shared by many a Christian — and not all of them are outside cloister walls. Thus do I see Frederic Dunne.

But the point I make here is that the divine Sculptor was at work on the delicate, thin-veined marble in the soul of Father Frederic. He saw it needed polishing were it to shine with all the brilliance of which it was capable. The abrasive was ready at hand in the monks who proclaimed and the Abbot who penanced. Frederic took it silently and with a brave smile; for his faith was such that he could pierce appearances and see in his brethren members of Christ and hear in the Abbot's voice the very accents of God.

In his *Apologia for Monasticism,* after insisting that no founder of a religious order or legislator for the religious life ever assigned

the cultivation of the soil, the copying of manuscripts, the progress
of arts and letters, as the special aim of his disciples, and asserting
that institutions simply human and powers purely temporal might
confer the same benefits on society, Montalembert points out that
religious orders and rules do what no human power can do:
they take the man of the world, even if he be wasted by sin,
and re-create him to virtue, disciplining not only the body, but
the very soul itself, transforming it by chastity, subduing it by
obedience, elevating it by sacrifice and humility and thus produce
prodigies of evangelical perfection.

Now in that passage whose every phrase glows with truth, the
one that brands itself into the attentive soul is that which says
humility and sacrifice elevate. Benedict knew this, that is why
he portrays humility as a ladder with twelve rungs. Frederic Dunne
accepted him wholly, then learned by experience how truthfully
his master had taught. Humility exalts. So if man would be high
in heaven he will go down low on earth. Frederic took God at
His word: "Learn of me for I am meek and humble of heart."
He accepted Christ's challenge: "If any man come after me, let
him deny himself, take up his cross daily, and follow. . . ."

Thanks to his painful experiences in Chapter Frederic Dunne
saw how foolish it would be for anyone wearing a religious garb
to work for the approbation of anyone less than God. He philoso-
phized. He analyzed. He meditated. He saw that ambition, which
is as natural to man as breathing, can have no place in the
religious life unless it be the sole ambition to grow in the likeness
of Christ. He saw that the cause of a thousand painful experiences
which often come as surprises, and which really form the tissue
of so many lives, lay in the failure to reduce everything to unity.

He had hardly arrived at this conclusion, and the Abbot had
not as yet reached France for the annual General Chapter, when
the Prior was handling a case which substantiated all that he had
argued to. The letters show how easy it was for Dom Edmond

to follow happenings step by step, even though he was thousands of leagues away. Thus on September 1, Father Frederic was writing: "Frater A—— has had another cranky spell, but I do not know what he wants. It appears to me that he wants to be put in the Infirmary, but there is absolutely no reason for it. He is in as good health as he ever was, but made up his mind that he would not eat. After being obliged under virtue of Obedience, he began last night at supper to eat as usual." On September 13 the Prior was writing: "Last Sunday Frater A——, who had been on special diet for a few weeks, came to say that he was all right and did not need the extra food. But yesterday he came to our room saying that he was all broken up, weak and failing in every way, asking to be put in the Infirmary, at least as far as the refectory part of it is concerned. I told him that he would see the doctor at his next visit; but he objected to this, as he feared the doctor would stop his studies. He certainly shall see our medical advisor at his next visit, and should it be suggested by him that studies be interrupted, [the doctor's] directions will be followed to the letter. Almost every day our good Frater has a new idea, but studies, studies and higher studies, are the obsession of his mind. They will cause him to lose that mind if he is not careful."

The Abbot may have smiled at this last, but the very next day he received a letter, one portion of which read: "Doctor Greenwell, just as I expected, said that Frater A——'s trouble comes from excessive application to study. I know that the boy spends nearly every moment of his time bent over a book, not taking enough time even for his devotions, never walking in the yard as the other students do. So, with his nervous disposition, his head is not able to bear the strain. This does not mean that he must discontinue his studies, but only that he must shorten his time at them, occupying himself with things that require less concentration. There is no question of more food, the doctor said; our ordinary diet, supplemented with milk is amply sufficient."

The Prior had diagnosed the case before the doctor had been called in on it. He saw ambition eating into the vitals of one whom God had not endowed with what was necessary to achieve that ambition. He warned the boy. But the next letter shows the patient not improving. "Frater A——," it runs, "is not quite satisfied with the directions given by the Doctor. He told me yesterday that he did not want to take milk, as it only makes blood; he did not want to take vegetables, as there was no nourishment in them; what he wants, he says, is plenty of meat and fish, for they are *brain food*. It seems to me that he is always thinking about himself, his health, his studies and the books he will write! I reason with him about his obligations as a religious, and for a while he appears to give a certain consent, but then relapses into the same old trouble. Such false ambitions for a young religious!"

The case ended on a happier note, for the Prior appended a few lines to a letter the young monk was sending to his mother, and those few lines suggested what the mother should say to the son in her reply. She followed the suggestions carefully, and three weeks later we find Father Frederic writing to Dom Obrecht: "Frater A—— is doing very much better. If he continues in his present dispositions there will be no complaint to be made against him. Of course the devil will attack him again, but the result will depend on his fidelity to grace and to his resolution to rid himself of false ambitions. If he would only get the ambition to be another Christ, what a subject he would have. But, as I say, just now he is giving very high satisfaction."

God directs souls even through the souls that are being directed; fashions older monks by the ones they are fashioning. It was through others as well as through trials within himself that Frederic learned the necessity to reduce everything to unity.

This presented a problem until he saw how easy it would be for all religious to know real heavenly peace and real harmony in themselves and with their God, if they would capture this unity by the practice of constant obedience. He saw how this one virtue would not only give unity, simplicity, harmony, and effect exalting humility in the soul, but bring a deathless peace even as it meted out death to the old man and brought about the resurrection of the new man "in Christ Jesus."

Trials opened Frederic Dunne's eyes as nothing else could. They showed him that if he gave one split second entirely to a man, it would be a waste of something of infinite worth; and this made him realize, with a blinding vividness, that there was no infinitesimal fraction of time that a religious could not devote entirely to the infinite God — by the practice of obedience.

In later life he would say: "We cannot be praying in the Church all the time. We cannot be doing physical or even spiritual penance all the time. But there is one thing that we can be doing every hour of the twenty-four and every second of each hour. We can always be obeying."

He had learned that salutary truth from sorrow.

CHAPTER TWELVE

The Silversmith at Work

MARCH 8, 1926, found the entire Gethsemani community lined up on the gravel walk which stretched from the main door of the monastery to the gatehouse. Father Frederic was in the tiny post office looking through its barred window every now and then to see if there was any activity on the road. He wanted to catch sight of the Abbot's car the moment it turned into the lane so that he could signal for a loud pealing of the bells and alert the waiting community for a warm reception. Dom Obrecht had been away from Gethsemani for almost seven months — and had given the community its greatest scare since his arrival in 1898. He had been to Europe and had there been seized by a severe cardiac crisis which caused word to be sent to America that the monks had looked on their Abbot alive for the last time.

That ominous report had reached Frederic in late August. Summer withered into fall and winter came on without another word from Europe. Even the heart-warming feasts of Christmas, Circumcision, Epiphany, and Holy Name failed to dispel the chill that had settled on the monastery as that silence deepened. It had been a trying time for the Prior. But it had ended gloriously.

He looked at his watch and glanced out that tiny window again. How often during the past twenty-five years he had stood in this same little room while the community waited in the yard beyond. He had been prior only a month when he first had to take this position so as to ascertain the moment Governor J. C. W. Beckham with his party would take that final turn and come down the lane for that visit when, for the first time, an American governor was given the privilege reserved for emperors and kings — that of bringing his suite, even though it contained many women, within a cloister for men. With a start Frederic suddenly remembered that that was exactly twenty-five years ago. How time had flown! . . . And what a strange life he had led! He had come expecting silence, solitude, seclusion, penance, and uninterrupted prayer. He had come to live with God alone as well as for God alone. Yet, for twenty-five years, what had he been and what had he done?

How well he remembered his sister Katherine writing in 1901: "You seem very young for so responsible a position as prior." Little did she know the responsibilities that would devolve on him because he was prior under a man like Edmond Obrecht. Because of the color in this man's character Frederic Dunne had stood in this tiny post office time and time again awaiting important visitors. Because of this man, Frederic had talked with the four Apostolic Delegates to the United States: Martinelli, Falconio, Bonzano, and Fumasoni-Biondi at Gethsemani. With this last he had struck up a real and a very warm friendship. Thanks to Dom Obrecht, Frederic had entertained almost every governor of Kentucky from Beckham to Fields within the cloister. Thanks to the same dynamism he had had personal contact with cardinals, archbishops, and bishops from both sides of the Atlantic; had chatted with numerous abbots of the Order and even with one abbot general; and had met many of the so-called great in the ecclesiastical, political, and financial world right here in this tiny post office. It had been a strange quarter of a century for a cloistered contemplative monk, replete as it was with surprising activities and utterly unexpected events. He chuckled to himself as he recalled that the man who had given off the happy phrases:

"O beata solitudo. O sola beatitudo" was a man who had had a very similar experience. Bernard of Clairvaux would have smiled, and sympathized with Frederic, as he stood now in the little room reminiscing but not really regretting anything. God had been in it all.

In 1944, at the time of his golden jubilee, Dom Frederic made the statement that he had never known a single day of dull routine while a Trappist. If he could say that without reservation in 1944, imagine what he could have said in 1926. Had Dom Obrecht never been sent to Africa or Asia, the things he accomplished in America were such as to keep his able lieutenant from ever knowing an hour of dull routine. Had he never used Frederic as errand boy, or allowed him out of the cloister to be his agent with bankers and brokers in Louisville, but kept him as superintendent of the work within the walls, the Prior could still claim he had never known routine; for in twenty-five years Edmond Obrecht had planned or approved plans for works that completely changed the monastery Frederic had entered in 1894.

I once heard Frederic say: "I thank God very especially for my last few years as a secular." The remark had not been addressed to me, but when the Abbot saw surprise in my eyes he explained that the experience he gained in those last few years had proved of inestimable worth to him as a monk. It was not until I had the obligation of studying his years as prior that I came to understand that remark fully. But when I found that the heavy construction work which began in earnest after the fire of 1901, never really ended in Dom Frederic's lifetime, I could see how his experience as a carpenter on St. Leo's Abbey near San Antonio, Florida, helped. When I learned that he had to transact most of the business of the monastery and heard a broker in Louisville say that in all his years of such transactions — and they really amounted to over forty — he had never seen Frederic Dunne make a single mistake, I could see how his time under his father at

Jacksonville, where he learned much of business methods and businessmen was of tremendous value. He had reason to thank God for those last years as a secular; they were prelude to his peculiar life as a monk.

Frederic had reason to ponder on the strangeness of his years as he stood awaiting Dom Obrecht's return. But as he stands there smiling to himself — and even a bit at himself — he presents us with a greater strangeness. We want to know how it was that this boy from Florida, who had literally been immersed in absorbing activities for over twenty-five years, had managed to grow into such a perfect Trappist monk. How had he managed to grow in soul when it seemed that all the faculties of that soul were entirely engaged in things so many spiritual writers claim will stunt?

Spiritual growth, like physical growth, is often, if not always, an unperceived process. Usually it is not until we have to lay aside clothes which once fitted us perfectly that we recognize the fact that there has been a physical change. So, too, with the soul: when a man awakes to the fact that he is more controlled, more tolerant, more kindly, more gentle, more ready to forgive instantaneously and forget entirely; when a man finds himself not only resigned to disappointment and reconciled to suffering, but even ready to accept them and be even somewhat joyous in bearing them; when he finds himself thinking of and turning to the Christ of Calvary when real humiliation comes his way; when he finds himself in actual pain and perhaps even physically ill when he hears of sin, then he can be sure his soul has outgrown its youthful garments, and, like Frederic Dunne, that he is maturing spiritually and mellowing into something of the likeness of Christ.

Then two truths will flame for him: first, that God is a Silversmith — just as Malachias has pictured Him — refining His silver, burning out whatever dross would mar the image of Christ in the human soul; second, that man must let God have His way, if man would grow to Godhood. How often Frederic Dunne stressed these truths! As he neared his golden jubilee he repeated them almost daily. But I suspect he learned them about the time of his silver jubilee as prior.

God would continue the process for another quarter of a century, but during that time Frederic Dunne would understand the purpose of it all and recognize in everything that burned his soul the hand of the perfect Refiner. Secretly he would rejoice to find himself still the object of so much heavenly concern. With rare wisdom, Frederic Dunne saw that the God of nature is the one true God who also rules the supernature. Hence, he rightly concluded that just as nature is never hurried, he is wrong who expects supernature to be so. A baby does not become a six-footer in six years; how can any man expect a monk to grow to the stature of the God-Man in a hurry? It takes years before principles, that were received almost instantaneously by the intellect, will really beat in the blood and become as much a part of the man as his breathing. Dom Frederic never minded the seeming endlessness of this process of spiritual development either in his own soul or the souls of others. For he realized that a life's work is done only in a life's time — and the reproduction of Christ is the life's work of every Christian, but very especially of the Christian monk.

Many marveled at the patience displayed by Frederic Dunne as abbot with men who did not seem to grow. They did not know that as prior he had a lesson every director of souls needs to learn faultlessly; namely, that before any human being can change his innate egocentricity into genuine Christocentricity, there must be a *metanoia* which is complete and absolute; and that is as much a work of God as was the raising of Lazarus from the dead or the changing of Cana's water into wine. We must wait on God.

But it was not from books that Frederic learned this truth; it was from himself. The Frederic Dunne who was loved by everyone who had any close contact with him; the man who charmed with his smile and fascinated by the naturalness of his genuine supernaturality; the one who radiated otherworldliness even as he manifested a keen aliveness to all that was transpiring in our passing world; the Abbot, whose mere presence made everyone God-conscious, was not the product of an abbatial blessing, or the by-product of discipline, diplomacy, and a dignity. It took God and himself fully fifty years, and required constant and close co-operation every moment of those fifty years, to make the man and the monk we knew. And what Frederic knew for years but what we are just now coming to realize was that the man and the monk who was now coming down the lane was the instrument God used most constantly in the perfecting of His first American Abbot.

The meeting between Abbot and Prior was enthusiastic on that March day in 1926; but it would be impossible to say which studied the other the more intently. Dom Obrecht was now in his seventy-sixth year. He had already given the community two scares as his aging heart flared up to remind them of his mortality and counsel him about his immortality. Father Frederic peered intently at the lined face and studied the sunken eyes. But what he found there surprised him. This latest brush with death seemed to have given new life to this threefold Jubilarian — Dom Edmond had just celebrated his silver jubilee as abbot, the golden jubilee of his entrance at La Trappe, and the diamond jubilee of his birth.

For a few moments Frederic was at a loss to explain the rejuvenation. It was true that his Abbot was always glad to get home and that the welcome extended both by the college boys and the community acted like a wine and exhilarated him. But this time there was no college band nor any college boys. In back of him rose a bleak hill with a bare statue on its summit. The College had gone up in flames in 1912 and Dom Edmond refused to rebuild, saying it took the monks away from their one work:

the direct adoration of God. It was not until Dom Edmond had said *sotto voce:* "Well, you were right about the little Carmelite; and I was all wrong," that Frederic was able to account for the young voice and the youthfully gleaming eyes which looked at him from out an aged face.

Frederic's head went back as he laughed his quick, infectious laugh and asked: "Do you forgive me now for having had *The Story of a Soul* read?"

"Not only forgive you, but I'm going to repeat the performance shortly."

Once again the Prior's head went back and that quick laugh of his set all the others smiling, even though they had not heard all that was said, nor did they know all that lay behind the remarks.

In late 1912 and early 1913, while Dom Obrecht was in China, Father Frederic had selected for table reading the autobiography of a young, then quite unknown, Carmelite who had called herself the "Little Flower." When the Abbot returned and heard of it, he gave Frederic what the latter termed "Hail Columbia." He could not understand why his Prior would hold up as model for men a little girl who had entered the convent when she was just fifteen, and who was dead before she had reached twenty-five. But now it was the Abbot who was afire over Soeur Thérèse. He had reason to be, as the Prior learned later. "She cured me," said the Abbot now with rare conviction. "It was a miracle."

Later he told how the Abbot of La Grande Trappe had obtained permission for Gethsemani's ailing head to enter the cloister of Lisieux. It was the last permission Pius XI, who had canonized Thérèse, granted before publishing a strict prohibition about visitors to the Carmel. Dom Edmond went to the infirmary where the Saint had died and came out cured. Now he was saying enthusiastically: "That little girl is a great saint."

But even as he was speaking the Abbot was noting the changes time had wrought in the appearance of one he had appointed prior when Frederic was little more than a boy. The hair was sparse now and no longer sandy; the thin goatee beard was as white as snow; there was a pronounced curvature of the shoulders which with the forward inclination of the head spoke of a calcification of the topmost vertebrae. Frederic looked distinguished as always, and even more delicate than before, yet the snap in his eyes, the flashing hands, the rapid speech told of the throbbing energies of youth in the man's soul despite the definitely aging body.

When they were alone after a truly heart-warming welcome, the Abbot claimed he was a new man.

"You look it, you sound it, you act it," was the Prior's quick comment.

"And you look like an old man to me. Was the strain as bad as all that?" asked the squinting Abbot.

"Not at all," laughed Frederic. "And as for getting old, I'll be fifty-two years *young* next month. And I'm growing younger every day."

The Abbot chuckled. But little did he realize the tremendous truth the Prior had told in his jest. He had been and still was growing younger spiritually even unknown to himself. It is something all but inevitable in the cloistered contemplative life. I would almost say in the consciously lived Christian life. For if Christ taught anything by His life and His death, He taught *piety* in its native force and meaning: loyalty, love, devotion, and devotedness to the Father. Once the Christian soul is possessed by this gift of the Holy Ghost, life becomes what God planned it to be from the beginning: a divine romance. Troubles, of course, will come; sorrow will be no great stranger; but the individual will accept both as part of the Father's all-wise and love-filled plan, confident that in them and through them will be fulfilled St. Paul's bold dictum: "To them that love God, all things work together unto good."

Frederic Dunne was anything but a demonstrative character

and so jealous was he of humility that he would never use the pronoun "I" if it could possibly be avoided. So it is only by pondering long on his actions that we can ever plumb the depths of his ever sensitive and steadily growing soul. I wonder if, from the books he chose for table reading, we cannot get insight into what was churning in those secret places where man is most himself and where he holds rendezvous with God.

To find this energetic American selecting the Little Flower's autobiography long years before Rome made one of its comparatively speedy moves canonizing the girl 28 years after her death; to learn that Gemma Galgani was another favorite of his at a time when Gemma was the favorite of few; to find Frederic interested in saintly children and fond of such simple souls as Bernadette Soubirous — and all this long before some of these causes were introduced — tells us of Frederic Dunne's intense hunger and thirst for God. It also tells us why he was so constantly repeating the text: "Unless you become as little children, you shall not enter the Kingdom of Heaven."

Actually these selections are indicative of the truth that Frederic Dunne was living the doctrine of spiritual childhood long before he had ever learned it from little Thérèse; that he had been practicing holy abandonment years before Lehodey had written his book; and that he had brought to perfection the Irish inheritance of trust in Divine Providence and devotion to God's will.

Less and less time for private study or leisurely reading was his with the advancing years, yet he always managed a short period daily with Thomas à Kempis and God the Holy Ghost. The *Imitation of Christ* and the *Bible* were the two wells whence he drew living water. And those two sources explain that happy combination found in him as abbot whereby he could satisfy and even inspire the more robust and virile characters who might have shied from what they would have wrongly considered saccharine sentimentality and even dubbed a trifle effeminate — the doctrine of Soeur Thérèse as presented by too many writers. For these the Abbot had his dynamic, driving, and even vehemently virile St. Paul — that fiery tentmaker who was all manly love and manly loyalty for the God-Man. For these he also had the ever uncompromising À Kempis who can be as demanding as John of the Cross and yet as convincing as the ever logical Aquinas.

As Frederic Dunne aged, a new timber crept into his voice and a deeper resonance sounded in his doctrine. And while he could still be as simple, as tender, as childlike as Thérèse, the steely strength of St. Paul was always accompanying it. Of course someone has lately described the Little Flower as a "core of iron wrapped in cotton," and I have already alluded to Frederic Dunne as a sword of steel sheathed in silk; but the combination of which I am now speaking seemed something a bit different. I can only view it as the Holy Ghost's way of preparing the Prior for his abbotship. He was shaping the soul, the mind and heart of Frederic Dunne so that many different hearts and minds might react to his.

It was fortunate that there was so much of Paul in the Prior these days; for the next decade of years would witness the final preparation of his soul for his greatest work under God. He needed all the love of the tentmaker from Tarsus to take it aright.

Dom Obrecht had not been home a fortnight when flu broke out in the community. In three days between fifty and sixty of the eighty-two monks were in bed. Ten days later, on March 22, there was a funeral. Father Malachy, the well-known guestmaster, had few attendants as he was lowered into the grave. Father Frederic read the prayers. There was only one choir religious to answer them. And a mere handful of novices chanted the plaintive *Domine, miserere super peccatore.* Four days later the same scene was enacted. By this time perhaps the sickest man in the house was Father Frederic, but he was determined to carry on in order to spare the lately returned Abbot. It was the Frederic Dunne

will in characteristic action: forcing the body which sheathed it
to forget its aches and pains as it obeyed.

If asked how he felt his usual "Just fine, thank you," would ring
out, followed by his explanation: "For I am exactly as the good
Lord wants me to be." Inwardly, however, he was telling his soul
something that was even more habitual than this outward cheer;
he was saying: *Cum Christo cruci affixus sum* — "With Christ I am
nailed to the cross."

By the end of the month the epidemic had passed. The two
deaths alluded to above were the only fatalities, but the sickness
had taken such toll of the strength of the monks that Dom
Obrecht would not allow the usual Holy Week services to be performed. This aftermath was much worse on Frederic than the
actual onslaught; for Holy Week had become to him what the
Liturgy ever meant it to be — the *Great* Week.

It was true that the Abbot had fought his way out of the severe
heart attacks of 1925 and 1926, but it is even more true that he
was not the same man after the fight. Hence more and more responsibility had to be shouldered by the Prior — his biggest responsibility, of course, being the Abbot himself.

There was no dissuading Dom Obrecht from the fatiguing journey to Citeaux and the annual General Chapter, but Frederic
could draw some consolation from the fact that now every trip to
Citeaux meant a trip to Lisieux, and the Little Flower was doing
other things to the heart of the aged Abbot besides returning it
to some semblance of normal functioning. After each immediate
contact with the living sisters of the little Saint, Dom Obrecht
showed himself more gentle, more kind, more mild, and much
more given to spiritual simplicity.

This greatly cheered Father Frederic who for years before her
canonization had been more than admirer of Thérèse Martin. But
she had to prove herself a real sister these years and send more
and more roses of patience along with his and her cherished

humility; for as the physical powers wane in a man who has ever been active, he can prove a problem.

In 1930 Dom Obrecht began his last great bit of construction — the enclosure wall. It was a tremendous undertaking for unskilled labor; for it was to be more than a mile long, seven feet high and eight inches thick, with pilasters two feet square and eight feet high every fifty feet. The Abbot managed to get out to the scene of operations almost daily — even if he had to be wheeled there; but the real responsibility for the work fell on the Prior.

Not only the work on the wall, but much of the other work, even the spiritual work of forming the young and maintaining the fervor of the old, became the responsibility of the Prior; for Edmond Obrecht was aging fast physically even though his mind and spirit stayed young. The body was tired after its more than eighty years of generous service.

Diabetes and the awful heart condition were not enough, it would seem, to slow the octogenarian, so God allowed him to feature in an automobile crash. It happened in the late winter of 1933. For a time there was talk of amputating the Abbot's gangrenous leg. But the Little Flower intervened and, something that Doctor Greenwell would not call a miracle, but which he did pronounce as something beyond scientific expectation or explanation, took place. There was no surgery, but Dom Edmond Obrecht showed the effects of his shake-up. For months Father Frederic had to function as head of the house.

He had been prior for thirty-two years now, so he knew the ins and outs of the office, and showed his knowledge quite expertly. But the ins and outs of the human mind are known only to God, so the community was treated to one of those manifestations of the human in us, which, to those who really believe what they profess they believe and actually live the *Credo* that falls from their lips, is always recognized as a movement of Divinity. On July 16, 1933, Father Frederic was removed from the office he had held since May 12, 1901. No explanation was given. The sudden removal could hardly be construed as a commendation!

It was God's final refinement before assigning Frederic Dunne to the great task of his life — the full Americanization of the New World's first La Trappe.

CHAPTER THIRTEEN

First American Abbot

FREDERIC DUNNE was beginning his fortieth year as a monk when Dom Obrecht removed him from the office of prior and appointed him confessor of the novices. Since the novices were not numerous, for the first time since he was ordained priest Frederic Dunne tasted that which is the essence of the monastic life and the quintessence of the Trappist existence — leisure to love God. Now he could awake at two in the morning and tell God that the day could be and would be spent not only for Him alone, but with Him all alone. He could retire at seven in the evening, pitying Father Robert who had succeeded him, but grateful that he, Father Frederic, had been allowed the seventeen-hour day with God alone — and not with the hundred and one things of God that a prior must care for and think about in an ordinary Trappist day.

He confessed to feeling lost for a few days. But when he found he could spend the intervals — those periods of from twenty minutes to three quarters of an hour which come between certain exercises — in the church, talking with Christ in the Blessed Sacrament, he found himself. This was a pleasure and a privilege he had not had since 1901. He reveled in the opportunity.

It was stocktaking time for Father Frederic. He was now in his sixtieth year of life, and while he said he awoke every morning feeling like a boy of twenty-five, he knew life's hourglass could not hold as many grains in the upper half as had already dropped to the lower. He took a very clear-eyed and steady look at life itself, at his own life and then at the life called Trappistic, and saw that the explanation of all three was love. Youth was before him in the novices who knelt at his feet. Middle age was about him in the mature monks who went about their work with a calm that spoke of surety. These men had confidence, not only in themselves but in their mode of existence. There was about them the untroubled air of masters. Old age was before him in the Abbot. And in the full compass, Frederic saw love. For if that was not the explanation of what these men, the young, the middle aged, and the old, were doing, their life was a lie — and he felt that Gethsemani held no prevaricators. It was the home of the sincere.

The first few weeks of this, to him, novel mode of existence, saw him gathering books he had long since promised himself he would read. But that promise went unfulfilled; for his old favorites: Faber, À Kempis, and the Bible, proved more than sufficient. And now, more than ever before, when he had to shape souls on the pattern given us on the Mount, when he had to form other Christs, he found St. Paul his main attraction.

St. Benedict had made his Rule strictly Christocentric, and while tradition has consecrated the phrase *"Ut in omnibus glorificetur Deus,"* as the Benedictine motto and the epitome of his Rule, one would be as justified in taking "Let nothing be preferred to the love of Christ." That is why Father Frederic found the Epistles of St. Paul a commentary on the Rule, and the Rule an exegesis of the Epistles. More and more his own soul was taking the cruciform shape; for Paul's burning eloquence, his contagious, flaming love for the Christ of Calvary, was enabling Frederic Dunne to crystallize his entire existence in the phrase: *Cum Christo cruci affixus sum* — "With Christ I am nailed to the cross."

Looking back now, the development seems not only normal, but inevitable. He had entered Gethsemani when the Trappists were still separated into the four Observances; and he had found his way into a house that belonged to the Observance which was the strictest. Further, the protoabbey of the New World had been founded and formed by men of exceptional austerity. Dom Eutropius, Dom Benedict, and Dom Edmond Obrecht were abbots of the Rancéan school — and the spirit of the abbot is the spirit of the house. Finally, we must take into account the personal character of the man himself: being generous and energetic by nature, and extremely sensitive of soul, the all-out love of Jesus Christ, shown by its climax on Calvary, fired Frederic Dunne to an all-out love in return. That is the explanation of Frederic Dunne. Those who considered him a penitent were using as substantive what can be used rightly only as adjective; Frederic Dunne was incarnate penitential *love*.

In the foregoing you have insight into the apostolic and catholic heart of the man and the monk. There was little in his own life that he had to expiate; for his pioneering days down in Florida had been days filled with simplicity, and his years as monk had been lived with utter sincerity. But he had come to know the Heart of God, and that knowledge set his own heart beating in sympathy for the One who had taken the sins of the world on His sinless Self. Frederic Dunne would emulate Him. Being in love with Christ, he was in love with everyone for whom Christ had lived and died. Hence, though he kept his body within Gethsemani's cloister, his heart went out to every soul in the world.

These few months out of office were really the divine Silversmith's moments of cooling the refined metal and allowing it to harden into its final mold. Frederic himself characterized these months as the happiest period of his life. In 1944 he told me that this period was very like the time in retreat before his solemn profession in 1901 when he felt a nearness to God which had him exclaiming as Peter once exclaimed on Thabor: "Lord, it is good for us to be here!" He claimed he hated to see that retreat come to a close. "And that," he added, "is exactly how I felt the year that I was nothing but confessor to the novices and some sort of a figurehead on the financial committee. It was heavenly."

But this bit of heaven ended on All Saints Day, 1934. Frederic Dunne had been out of office just a bit over fifteen months when Dom Obrecht entered the Chapter Room for what was to be his last public appearance. And his last public act was a recasting of his panel of officers at the head of which he renamed Frederic Mary Dunne as prior.

Twelve days later the reappointed Prior was bending over the man he had served for thirty-three years, administering to him the last rites of the Church. Six weeks later the two were even closer together as the old Abbot gasped his last few breaths and fell back into the arms of Frederic Dunne. It was January 4, 1935.

As the Prior looked down on the marble features of the man who as monk had traveled around the world; chatted intimately with four different popes and received special commissions, privileges, and blessings from them; was close friend to cardinals, archbishops, bishops, and countless abbots; had exchanged pleasantries with the president of the United States, many governors, and princes from foreign lands; who was regarded by his Order as administrator extraordinary and savior of the Protoabbey of the New World — as he looked down on the dead Abbot he suddenly realized that all this meant nothing if Edmond Obrecht had not referred it all to God through Christ Jesus.

When Cardinal Dougherty addressed the community the night before the burial, and reminded them of all the power, prestige, honor, and fame that had been won for the abbey by this ever colorful character who had been their Abbot, Frederic Dunne was saying to himself something similar to what the wisest of men, Solomon, had said of similar things in his old age: "Vanity of vanities — all is vanity" — save to love God and work for Him in Christ Jesus.

As he stood beside Bishop Floersch and saw the mitered corpse lowered into the damp clay, Frederic Dunne, the American Trappist, was cognizant of the fact that can be frightening in a world such as ours. He was telling himself with Léon Bloy that there is only one genuine happiness for any human being — and that is to be a saint.

He had admired Dom Obrecht in life, and had profited greatly from his wisdom and wide experience. But it was in death that the aged Abbot was teaching Frederic the greatest lesson of their long and intimate association. He was telling him what both the little and the great Thérèse teach: that motive, and motive alone, really matters; that the smallest things can be made great if done with great love. Frederic Dunne came back from the funeral with the Trappist ideal shining before him with a clarity it was never to lose so long as he lived. He saw that sanctity is its goal, and that is to be achieved by a simplicity which is motivated by an all-absorbing love.

On February 6, 1935, the members of Gethsemani's Chapter assembled for the solemn duty of electing a successor to the man who had saved the monastery from spiritual and also from material ruin. Many in Europe pitied them, and considered them faced with an impossible task; for the masterful Obrecht had made his name and that of America's protoabbey synonymous for the past thirty-five years. While those across the water conceded that the monastery would stand, they considered it a foregone conclusion that it would never be the same without that ever colorful head who had so dominated it for decades. But the voters in the American abbey manifested no hesitancy, nor did they reveal any trepidation as they approached the chalicelike receptacle to cast their ballots. The long process, which is identical with that for the election of a pope, was cut as short as possible by the electors when, on the very first ballot, they chose as Gethsemani's fifth Abbot the first American to persevere as a choir monk — Frederic Mary Dunne.

When the President approached and asked him if he would accept the office, Father Frederic lowered his head and in a voice that was hardly audible answered: "As the will of God, I accept it; but only because it is the will of God."

Not many in that Chapter Room, and most certainly not the President of the election, realized that with those words Gethsemani began a new life — and had been assigned by God a new role. All unknown to them, a leadership was being thrust upon this abbey, which would have repercussions the world over; and the man at the head of it would be responsible for that influence. God had shaped His instrument. The time was at hand. And without knowing how finely shaped he was, Frederic Dunne yielded himself to God with the same finality that is found in that magic word *"Fiat."*

With regret, I note that most of Dom Frederic's diaries were destroyed, but by one of those providential acts which we dull humans so often call accidents, the one for 1935 fell into the hands of a collector of mementos. He tore the page bearing the title *"February 6 — Wednesday"* out and threw the book away. Last week he presented that page to me. I transcribe it verbatim. It can speak for itself and tell the story of the heart of the man God was now going to use for a gigantic task. It reads:

> The Election for a new Abbot took place today. Rev. F. R. Cotton acting as Notary, with Revs. J. H. Willett and D. J. Driscoll as witnesses. Prime — 5:15 — Conventual Mass, sung by Dom Corentine, at 7. Entered Chapter at 8:15. At 12 noon Fr. Frederic was declared elected. May God have mercy on and help me. Mary, I put my trust in thee.

And what was God's first act of mercy and demonstration of help? — An epidemic of influenza three times as violent as the one Dom Obrecht had brought home from Europe in 1926 — and five times as fatal. The Abbot-elect had not time to make an entry on the reverse side of the page quoted above when Death walked among the men who would now call him "Reverend Father." On February 15 Father Columban died. His body had not been washed when Brother Placid breathed his last. Two days later, Father Anselm, the oldest priest in the community, died. He was being buried on the eighteenth when Brother Michael died. Four deaths in less than four days would shock the most hardened. But since most were so sick that they were indifferent, the full burden of the blow fell on the shoulders of the newly elected Abbot.

He felt his position keenly; for until his election had been confirmed by Rome, he was without full jurisdiction, and could not function as father to his sons. Father Robert, whom he had appointed as prior, did the anointing; while Dom Corentine, the Father Immediate who had come to preside at the election, presided at all the funerals. Yet these were Frederic's own men! The one thing he could do, he did: he was in the infirmary constantly. He might be without canonical jurisdiction; but he was not without his fatherly heart.

It was just after Brother Michael's death on the eighteenth that word came from Rome, confirming the election and empowering Dom Corentine, Abbot of Melleray and Fr. Immediate of Gethsemani, to go ahead with the installation. The French Abbot waited not an hour. He knew dying men wanted to address their old prior as "Reverend Father," and that Father Frederic wanted the official title of Dom Frederic so that he might minister to his men.

On the very day of the installation Dom Frederic used that power: he anointed Father Anthony. A little over twenty-four hours later he crossed the limp hands of this good Father in their final fold. It was the fifth death in six days. And still Death was not satisfied. On the twenty-second it took Brother Nivard and, on the twenty-fifth, Brother Matthias.

Seven burials in a single fortnight was God's ceremony of initiation for Dom Frederic Mary Dunne.

In early March, Dom Corentine felt he could leave his daughter house, for the fury of the onslaught had spent itself and medical authorities announced that the epidemic was not only under control, but being driven out. When he cautioned Dom Frederic to spare himself as well as his men, he received a characteristic reply.

"I'll always try to spare my men, Reverend Father, but as for myself I'll ever strive to be the servant of these servants of God."

"That sounds as if you want to be pope."

"That only sounds as if I want to keep my Rule, which tells the abbot that he should ever strive to give others a lift rather than show them that he is lord."

"Where does the Rule say that?"

"In Chapter 64 'De Ordinando Abbate.' I've been meditating that chapter ever since February 6. I love the strong admonition of St. Benedict: 'sciatque sibi oportere prodesse magis quam praeesse' (let him know that it behooves him to serve his brethren rather than lord it over them). He then repeated the last four words: 'Prodesse magis quam praeesse' — that is my motto from now on. I think I shall put it in my coat of arms."

That coat of arms was not seen until May 1; for Dom Frederic postponed his abbatial blessing until the community had fully recuperated after its severe experience of February and early March. But the Abbot did not wait until May to show that he intended to minister rather than master.

He had rearranged the panel of officers, but while he named a prior and subprior, he appointed no cellarer or procurator. He would keep those offices for himself; for those were real burdens and entailed endless distractions. The government named no new postmaster for Gethsemani's tiny post office, so the name of Frederic Dunne went on every voucher. There was a guestmaster, but as soon as he had received the guests he led them to the Abbot's office, where they were made welcome and warmly entertained. The Prior soon found that he was president of the work — and little more. And the novices quickly found out that they had a master in the Abbot as well as in their own Master of Novices.

For more than ten years Frederic Dunne had chuckled as he heard friends tell how they had come to the old Abbot and asked for a few minutes with the Prior only to hear: "I'm Abbot here. I'll do all the business." And whenever they would call on the phone and ask for Father Frederic, a loud voice would reply: "The phone is in the Abbot's office not the Prior's. What do you want?" If they made bold enough to say: "Father Frederic," the old Abbot would cry: "I asked *what*, not *who*," and then hang up. But now Dom Frederic was able to see and talk to these men. He did both. But it was only to spare all the other monks the distraction. Every telephone call came in to him. Every single business transaction was negotiated by him. He became factotum of Gethsemani when he became abbot; for he would live his motto and spare his monks; he would be their minister more than their master. *Prodesse magis quam praeesse* was woven into his life and shone forth in his deeds much more brilliantly than it had been worked into his abbatial coat of arms.

Only seventy monks saw him mitered on the first day of May; and two of these had died before the year was out. But with the sixty-eight left from Dom Obrecht's reign he began something that is still causing wonder not only in America but everywhere it is known about. I do not refer to the physical fact of mere numbers — though that is amazing; for that sixty-eight of 1935 had risen to eighty-two in 1936, then to one hundred and twenty-six before World War II had begun, and, before that war ended, stood at one hundred and forty-five. Twenty of these he sent to Georgia to make the first foundation in America from what was now really an all-American house. But still the marvel continued. In 1947 there were one hundred and seventy-two at Gethsemani and about forty at the Georgia foundation. In July of that year thirty-six left Kentucky to settle in the mountains of Utah. But every emptying of Gethsemani brought about a greater filling. Fifteen years after Dom Frederic had received his blessing and begun to rule sixty-eight monks, Gethsemani had made four foundations with a total enrollment of just under two hundred monks, while she herself was figuratively bursting at the seams as she housed two hundred and sixty-six men who aspire, as Dom Frederic aspired, to live for and with God alone.

As amazing as this physical growth is, the thing to which I referred above is something deeper, more substantial and much more amazing still. And it began that May 1 when Frederic Dunne was blessed as fifth Abbot of America's protoabbey. It was and is the fulfilling of an ideal.

When, where, or how the ideal was generated I know not; for I found it full-blown when I first met Dom Frederic Dunne. That was one year after his blessing. By that time he was openly preaching that he wanted Gethsemani known in the Order as the most regular house of the Order. He wanted his American abbey to be an oasis both for God and man. He wanted it to be a garden spot where God would be loved with a total love by generous, virile hearts; a spot where He could live among men who lived only for Him. As for men, he wanted Gethsemani to be an oasis of prayer and penance in a world that has been turned into a dry-as-dust desert because of its headlong plunge after pleasure both sinless and sinful, and made extra dry by its total lack of penitence. That was his ideal.

Being an American, the Abbot would make it real. He would be practical. He would actualize all his desires by making Gethsemani God's seeding ground for sanctity. In St. Benedict's Rule along with the Constitutions and *Usages* of the Cistercians of the Strict Observance he had his plow, harrow, fertilizer, and cultivator. To him these were not lifeless lines of print; they were the pulsing will of God — of the ever living God. And he knew if he could get his men to see eye to eye with him, if he could fire them to the blaze of his own faith and fortitude, Citeaux would have an American abbey that would be what the first founders of the Order — SS. Robert, Alberic, and Stephen — desired: a solitude where men could hold rendezvous with God, a City of Silence wherein the Divinity could be heard speaking. And the Strict Observance would have a house which was living up to its title.

As he began his task he carried about with him much of the aura which had clung to the men who had once written *Collis Armatus* on their escutcheon. He was brave. He was determined. And true leader that he was, he would never ask his disciples to do anything he himself had not done. In fact he always outdid the men under him.

Being a twentieth-century American, he lost no time in putting his plans into execution. He asked the community to take the Book of Regulations and see if they could not observe it literally, doing away with every semblance of mitigation which had crept in during the years. It was a bold request. But when he told them the purpose behind it, he had won his cause. He said that he felt they owed God this; and he felt sure that if they paid Him this debt, He would repay them by prospering their monastery.

It could have been diplomacy. It could have been his innate delicacy. But I like to think he took it to be part of the Rule and the Constitutions when he demanded nothing, but consulted the community before each big move and even took a vote on the matter. Thus the records show that many votes were taken the early days of Dom Frederic's abbacy. He said that deterioration could set in through two avenues: the refectory and the parlor.

This was not only an idea with him, it was a fixed idea. Perhaps that is why his earliest request was that the community vote on the question whether they would maintain the prescription of the *Usages* which stipulates that from September 14 until Lent the monks be granted a "frustulum" each morning after Chapter, or continue taking the "mixt" which Dom Obrecht had allowed.

With that charity which was in his bone and blood he cleared Dom Edmond's name by pointing out that the Rule expressly grants the abbot the competence to grant whatever indulgence he deems necessary. Then he added that the excessive heat of Kentucky during the long summer and the many heavy labors performed by the monks while building, certainly justified whatever indulgence Dom Obrecht granted. But now he asked if they could not sacrifice a little bit more for God. The answer came in a practically unanimous vote to take only the "frustulum" — a mere two ounces of bread with a cup of the usual beverage, in place of the "mixt" which allows six ounces of bread with an occasional dish of fruit or a serving of butter.

Not long after this, he pointed out that the Rule said the drink was to be "the common drink of the country." He admitted that, strictly speaking, America had no common drink such as France, Italy, and other European countries have. He even added that he knew the men who had come from across the sea would be making a real sacrifice to give up what they had had since childhood. Nevertheless he said that if any one drink was more common than any other it was coffee. Hence, he would take a vote on whether they should not make this sacrifice and adhere more closely to the Rule and Regulations. More than one American in the community may have wanted to tell the Abbot what he already knew, namely, that the barley brew which was then being served was not coffee. But he anticipated them by admitting that it was not exactly what passed as the more common drink in the country but insisted that it did look like it at times — and would always prove more nourishing. The vote again was practically unanimous.

Things were now moving. Soon it was noted that most of the special dishes, which had been served to individuals because of some chronic complaint, had disappeared. The men had caught the spirit of the Abbot and voluntarily offered to forego this indulgence and be satisfied with the common diet.

Once the refectory was in accord with the *Usages*, Dom Frederic turned to the parlor. Realizing that Trappists are allowed visits only from their immediate families — and that but once a year — realizing further that the visit had to be made in a small bare room in the low cement building called the Gate House; realizing finally that women could never so much as cross the garth which separates the monastery proper from this Gate House, one might well wonder what danger visits could cause to regularity. But Dom Obrecht had allowed his men to take a meal with their relatives at each visit. Dom Frederic proposed that this be allowed only on the day of solemn profession and the day of a newly ordained priest's first Mass. For the third time the vote was again practically unanimous. The community saw that this man wanted that simplicity, seclusion, and silence which are the very foundation stones of the Trappist observance and were now ready to follow him to the last detail.

This return to the literal observance began very quietly; for Dom Frederic was an enemy to all fuss and histrionics. By placing everything on the plane which was second nature to him — the supernatural — he forestalled all arguments and precluded all debate. With the two big dangers to regularity now barricaded, he turned to other matters.

For some years now, when the great feasts fell on a Saturday, it had been the practice to rise at 1 a.m. for the feast, but to grant some recompense for the lost sleep and the extra energy expended in singing the long offices, the community was allowed to sleep until 2 a.m. Sunday morning instead of rising at one thirty, as the *Usages* prescribe. It was a very slight indulgence, indeed. But Dom Frederic had eyes for the noun, not the adjective. He had no sympathy with any deviation from explicit rule or regulation. The community was up at one-thirty every Sunday morning. And when Holy Week came in 1936, the marvelous and moving liturgy of the last days was executed in its fullness, and, as far as human frailty would allow, without a flaw. When Easter dawned the community was tired, yet had never known such a thrill as was theirs this feast of the Resurrection. The price had been paid; blessings were being delivered.

The Abbot recognized this fact — and few in the community missed the connection between cause and effect. They were now anxious for whatever the Abbot suggested, and admitted that instead of innovating he was only renovating; for everything he had so far asked was there in the books: either that of the Rule or the Regulations. A more joyful spirit settled on all.

In the summer of his first year as abbot he had granted what some took to be an innovation and an indulgence when he threw open the door of the Batz Memorial Library to the professed choir religious every Sunday afternoon. But when he then inaugurated monthly conferences in Church History and Sacred Scripture, the men assigned to give these conferences saw that the Sunday afternoon "indulgence" was very nearly an incumbrance, since they were expected to consult numerous authors in that library before giving their public conference.

The reorganization of the seminary proper was done even more quietly. Father Augustine had been president of a major seminary in Canada for years before coming to Gethsemani, and had been a professor in that seminary even a greater number of years. So when Dom Frederic appointed him Prefect of Studies and urged him to make out a curriculum as strictly in accord with the Code of Canon Law as the Trappist regime would allow, an old hand was set to a familiar and greatly loved task.

Dom Frederic realized that the contemplative life is grounded on the intellectual, and that while it remained true that contemplation in its highest and purest form is a free gift of God bestowed on whom He wills, he, as abbot, had the obligation to see to it that a suitable receptacle for this great gift was as perfectly prepared as possible. To put it another way: Dom Frederic felt that his was the duty to prepare intellects properly so that God, if He so chose, could drop these seeds of contemplation in soil that was perfectly prepared. He might still agree with Dom Obrecht that the Jesuits and Dominicans are the theologians of the Church, but he would never agree with the wrong inference some shallow minds have drawn from that fact. Dom Frederic wanted every monk to know as much theology as he possibly could; for devotion not based on dogma is questionable devotion to say the least.

"Oh, if we only knew God!" was the Abbot's constant cry. And the story he repeated most frequently was that of the boy, Aquinas, running around the monastery at Monte Cassino, tugging at the sleeves of the monks and asking: *"Quis est Deus?"* — Who is God — or What is God like?

To any who asked why all this insistence on study — and there were a few who so questioned — Dom Frederic had but one reply: "If we are to love Him as we ought, we must first know Him."

Contemplation — close union with God — at least acquired contemplation, was the end Dom Frederic had in view in each of his moves.

The more reflective in the community soon awoke to a strange fact; Gethsemani had become more penitential than ever, yet her spirit was much more joyful, and her monks radiated a happiness and a peace which attracted rather than an austerity which might have repelled. It was a puzzle and a paradox: there was a marked increase of cheer in the community with each removal of something which had been granted to promote cheer.

With that cheer came a greater childlikeness. And there, I believe, is the secret of Gethsemani's hold on so many thousands. There is a winsomeness about her monks very similar to the mysterious attractiveness of a very small child, and a simplicity as captivating as obvious innocence.

Undoubtedly most of the change can be attributed to the world's most loved flower girl, the little Carmelite under whose protection Dom Frederic had placed his novitiate and whose spirit he recommended to all his monks. The laugh enjoyed by all who knew this fact was that the first postulant was a Carmelite lay Brother! Thérèse was showing her favor and even her preference! From that day to this the two novitiates have always been crowded and even greatly overcrowded.

But the paradox lies in this that the most modern of Trappist abbots was Americanizing his monastery by having his men return to what had made the monks of the Middle Ages great.

Yet the truth goes deeper; for, far from being medieval, Frederic Dunne had gone back not to the Middle Ages only, but back through time to the timeless Christ. With his life he was saying that which Christ had said with His lips: "If any man come after me, let him deny himself. . . . Unless you become as little children you shall not enter the Kingdom of Heaven."

And that brought the greatest paradox into relief which was Frederic Dunne himself. This austere Abbot became a veritable magnet for American youth. The mighty influx, which has puzzled so many for years, began under this man, and seems attributable to the fact that ever idealistic youth found a sincerity here that satisfied their demands for truth and justice. Frederic Dunne was one man who lived the Rule he professed, and loved the God-Man with all the love of a manly heart.

CHAPTER FOURTEEN

The Final Form

THE great Cardinal Newman, master though he was of the English language, all but despaired in his late years because of that language's limitations. He confessed at last that human language in all tongues is more than limited; it is even deceptive, inasmuch as we can never fully convey our ideas to another through it. The listener always colors what he hears with his own subjectivity which is a result of his education, environment, and experience. Hence, what we say and what he hears may be different things. Thus when I spoke in the last chapter of Americanizing Gethsemani, many a man on this side of the Atlantic and many more on the other side would think of nothing but mechanical efficiency, mass production, and material prosperity; statistics, timesaving devices, and riches that bring luxury. I meant almost the opposite.

It was true that Dom Frederic had modernized his monastery, if modernity is measured in terms of electricity, central heating, and suitable plumbing. It was also true that Europeans had reason to think in terms of statistics when they saw the sixty-eight of his first year as abbot mount to over four hundred in his last year. And when they heard of all the improvements in buildings, farm equipment, and transportation, they must have worried lest luxury change the austere, grizzled Lady House of old into some sort of fashionable and flighty Modern Miss.

But Dom Corentine Guyader, Abbot of Melleray and Father Immediate to Gethsemani, soon reassured them. He made but one visitation between Dom Frederic's election and Hitler's rush into Poland. Yet he saw enough then to amaze him and yet assure him that all was well, and very well with his daughter house.

Gethsemani had changed completely. Her physical appearance was surprisingly modernized. For a monk with a green thumb and something of a craze for concrete had transformed the old garth separating the monastery from the gatehouse. It used to be a tangle of wild grasses and overgrown trees. It now was a garden of loveliness which not only pleased the eye but actually soothed the spirit. Paint, linoleum, rock wool, and wax had done away with much that was noisy, unsightly, and dusty in the guest department, while new beds and electric lights gave promise of a modicum of convenience and a touch of comfort to prospective retreatants. The church, with ambos in place of the heavy, meaningless bridge, a lengthened choir, and four new altars, looked far more monastic and much more beautiful. The increase in novices had necessitated the enlarging of refectory, dormitory, chapter room, and scriptoria. The yard showed a new all-metal corncrib, a concrete and steel piggery, a completely renovated interior to the cow barn, a chicken run of concrete blocks fashioned to imitate cut stone. High up in the hills a huge dam was being thrown across the mouth of a valley so that a large lake would free Gethsemani forever from the fear of summer droughts and fire hazards. Blueprints were made for a garage, horse barn, new novitiate, and that daring feat of architecture: the hollowing out of a basement under the entire length and breadth of the monastery, so that a full story might be added to her without increasing her height an inch.

These things amazed the visitor; for he well knew the Trappist regime and its limit of hours for manual labor. He could roughly estimate the energy, enterprise, and enthusiasm needed to dream half of what Gethsemani's men had already accomplished. In all his years he had never heard anything in the entire Order to compare with it.

But that was not all that amazed him. There were intellectual accomplishments in the same order and number. One of Dom Frederic's first acts had been to assign one of the older Fathers in the community to the task of writing the life of Dom Obrecht. He wanted it as tribute to the man and as testimony to a definite period in Gethsemani's existence — a period that died with the ever colorful Obrecht. And one of the first permissions Dom Frederic had solicited from the Abbot General was to publish books and booklets on the Order for American consumption. He knew that the Trappist life was not known to Americans. He decided to develop writers. He knew there was much sense in the American slogan: "It pays to advertise." That is why the life of Father Joseph Cassant, a young Trappist priest of the twentieth century, who died in France in the odor of sanctity, was translated into English and published by Gethsemani. The same was done with the short life of Brother Yvo Poussin and that of Sister Louise Tessier. Dom Frederic would acquaint America with every category in the Order: priest, choir monk, lay Brother, and Trappistine. Then came *Cistercian Simplicity* and *The Cistercian Life*. Six publications in a single year spoke of American capital, but also, to those with ears alert, of American love for the Cistercian Order. These were the opening moves in Dom Frederic's Americanization of Gethsemani.

Dom Corentine saw the results in two bulging novitiates where young Americans were falling in love with God in typical American fashion — but what pleased the French Abbot was to see them doing it according to the Rule of St. Benedict and after the stipulations in the *Usages* of Citeaux. He had been in many monasteries in Europe and visited those in the British Isles, but confessed he had seen greater regularity nowhere, and nowhere equal spirit.

But what really startled him was to learn that this regularity was bought at a price no American likes to pay — the price of inefficiency. Dom Corentine smiled when he first heard the complaint. To him there seemed little possibility of inefficiency in a monastery where so much had been accomplished with so little show of hurry and excitement, and in so short a time. But then the facts came out: valuable time was often lost during the work period because of the strictness of the silence upon which Dom Frederic insisted. Often a word or two would have saved valuable time, not to mention volatile tempers, while also assuring a correct execution of the assigned task. But again and again Gethsemani's Lord had said: "Rather a less perfect work than the slightest infraction of the Rule." That word or two was never spoken. Dom Corentine smiled more broadly, but did not suggest any change of the Abbot's dictum.

Other abbots from Europe came to the American house and marveled. They found paradox in many forms, for here was real poverty in a house that was truly prosperous. The clothing of the monks was of the cheapest cotton in the summer, and the winter wool was made to last a decade of years thanks to generous patching. The meals in the Gethsemani refectory upset these visiting prelates physically as well as psychically. And while they found the guest quarters fairly comfortable they saw poverty in the rough-hewn floors, bare plaster walls, homemade desks and benches in the monks' quarters. They lifted questioning eyebrows when they learned that Dom Frederic would not allow his men the use of mechanical pencils or fountain pens; because he thought such unbecoming those who vowed Trappist poverty.

They saw austerity in his regime, great austerity; and learned the secret of its ready acceptance by the monks when they found Dom Frederic himself practicing the greatest austerity. Many of the monks took the frustulum from September until Lent, but never Dom Frederic. He argued that the *Usages* tolerated this morning mouthful; they did not prescribe it. So he would take only the prescriptions of the Rule and give God whatever he possibly could in the way of self-denial. During the summer months whenever a monk lost his hour of midday rest he was commanded to make up for it the next morning. But the Abbot himself could be held by visitors or business not only from the midday rest but even from hours of the night rest; yet the first one in the church every morning was Dom Frederic Mary Dunne.

Enthusiasm is contagious. These European prelates saw the explanation of the palpable enthusiasm of this American community — an enthusiasm that touched everything from erecting a modern steel water tower to the observance of the minutiae for mistakes in choir; they saw the full explanation when they looked at the Abbot. One who knew Dom Frederic and then read Jacques Maritain's analysis of America and Americans, might well have suspected that the French philosopher was pen-picturing Gethsemani's Lord when he writes of "that tendency to undertake great things, to have confidence, to be moved by large idealistic feelings and the desire for the active repose of the soul breathing what is eternal."

Those with eyes sharp enough to see recognized in Dom Frederic's reign the dawning of an epoch. Just as Greece passed her rich cultural achievement on to Rome, so Europe, having completed her role, passes all leadership, not only political, financial, and ideological, but even religious leadership on to America. That is why the monastic renaissance, that spirit of faith and fearlessness which made Europe and fashioned Western civilization, began in the grizzled Lady House hidden behind Kentucky knobs ruled by an American who had the genuine American spirit which wrote God into the great seal of the United States and has the omnipotent Creator as the cornerstone of our Constitutions. Frederic Dunne was more humble than the humblest of America's Founding Fathers, and much more religious. They were seeking

God; he had found Him. His was the true American spirit which Maritain rightly diagnoses as the spirit of the contemplative; for no one is as daring, as generous, as adventuresome, as humble, yet as high in hopes as he who will not only seek God but will dare to look upon His face. The contemplative is one who has taken for his love the Infinite, and for his life that "active repose of the soul breathing what is eternal." To achieve that goal, lead that life, win that love, a generosity which knows no bounds is needed. And at last that type of generosity is being recognized as typically American.

Peace is the Benedictine password. Over Gethsemani's gate of entrance it is written large: "Peace To Those Who Enter Here." But it is written even larger in the lives of the men who dwell therein. Peace, that tranquillity of order, which our world lost with the Protestant Revolt and never regained, will come again only when men do what these monks do: place God as the Alpha and Omega of that order; make Him the Great First and the Only Last. The freedom our century craves and clamors for will be won only when men subject themselves as Dom Frederic had all his monks subject themselves to the yoke which makes them free with the freedom of the sons of God. And there is the climaxing paradox of this long list of paradoxes. It is within the confines of Gethsemani's cloister that Americans found the freedom of all freedoms; and after becoming soldiers of Christ in a war that will end only when they leave this earth, they found peace. The man that showed them the way was one who had fallen at last into his final form — and that was the cruciform.

It can be said of Frederic Dunne that he was Pauline by nature as well as by grace. Fiery and full of feeling by nature as had been Saul of Tarsus, yet, like Paul, Frederic never devoted an ounce of his great energy to anyone save Christ or to anything save the glory of God. His, too, was the Pauline "passionless passion" for the Man on the Cross. Whenever he began to speak now quotations welled up spontaneously from the Epistles. It was not that he had become a scholar, but only that abyss had called to abyss. Paul had set up a ringing resonance in the soul of this twentieth-century American who at last was in love with Jesus Christ as he so often urged all of us to be in love with Him; that is, "with every fiber of our being."

Gethsemani's fifth Abbot had a crystal-clear concept of what a Trappist should be. It was identical with Paul's concept of what every true Christian should be: "a man crucified to the world, and to whom the world was crucified"; a man who "carried Christ in his body" — with the five glowing stigmata in his heart if not on his hands, side, and feet; a man who could and did cry: "For me to live is Christ, and to die is gain."

When asked once by Father Louis which was his favorite Epistle, Dom Frederic answered unhesitatingly: "Oh, that to the Hebrews." In that answer you have more than Frederic Dunne's mind and soul; you have the whole bent of his life and his greatest love. For the Epistle to the Hebrews, the most profoundly dogmatic of all Paul's writings, deals with the priesthood and victimhood of Christ Jesus, and with His all-powerful Mass. And Dom Frederic's love for the Mass was great.

One day in the winter of 1945 he left Our Lady of the Holy Ghost, Gethsemani's first daughter house at Conyers, Georgia, just before noon in order to transact some business in Atlanta, before taking the train back to Gethsemani. When the Superior and Guestmaster tried to persuade him to take some dinner before he left, he gave his usual tiny gesture of deprecation and smiled as he said: "I'll manage a sandwich or something on the train." He had taken collation the night before at five fifteen — six ounces of bread, a tin of barley brew, and three ounces of apple sauce. With customary dispatch he transacted his business in Atlanta, then hurried to the station. But the train was late and carried no diner. Dom Frederic smiled. As he opened his Breviary he offered the slight inconvenience to God along with his Office for his two special intentions: that the new foundation in Georgia have the spirit of Gethsemani, and that the mother house never lose hers. He arrived at the Kentucky monastery just as the morning chapter ended. He was at his desk opening mail and ready to receive the religious before the latter had finished their *frustulum.* He began his Mass at 8:15 a.m. after a fast of thirty-nine hours. At 11:30 that day he took his first meal in forty-eight hours — and thought nothing of it. Or rather he thought it small price to pay for the priceless privilege of re-enacting Calvary for the glory of God and the salvation of men.

A similar thing happened in 1947 after the Plenary General Chapter. He boarded a plane on Shannon Field, Eire, on May 16; he said Mass at Gethsemani May 17 in the early afternoon. What was food for the body when he could have Divine Food for the soul? What was inconvenience to himself, when, by it, he could glorify the Infinite and help the teeming millions on earth?

In a certain sense the Mass — as it should be for every contemplative — was his life. The Rule of St. Benedict insists on perfect unity in the monastic family, warning the abbot again and again to be what he is called — a father; and urging the sons of the family to love their father with a special love. By fulfilling that first injunction Dom Frederic made it not only easy but inevitable for us to observe the second. We were one. But he never felt the union more pointedly than when he stood at the altar on feast days, not only as our high priest, but as father of the family, offering God to God on our behalf. As he so often said, the Cistercian life is a liturgical life. But while he seldom spoke in technical terms about this life, it was evident to those who watched him offer the Holy Sacrifice that he was a liturgist in the best sense of the word: one who is deeply rooted in the very soil of that Sacrifice, tinglingly conscious of his oneness not only with Christ the Head, but with all Christ's members.

Not a rubricist in the derogatory sense of an ardent defender of the minutiae, nevertheless he would hold a special Chapter of Faults for priests every week in which proclamations were limited to violations of the rubrics. And with an earnestness that made him eloquent he would quote Teresa of Ávila week after week, telling how she would give her life for the smallest rubric.

Here among his priests he revealed himself most fully. For here, not only with tears in his voice — and Frederic Dunne was no actor — but often enough with tears in his eyes, he would plead with us to pray for our fellow priests. When Russia and Germany had completed their rape of Poland, the unvarying penance he would give to those of us who had been proclaimed was: "Say the *De Profundis* three times for priests behind the Iron Curtain." And whenever word reached him about a priest who had succumbed to the onslaughts of the world, the flesh, or the devil, he would weep — not so much for the soul of the stray shepherd, as for the Heart of the Good Shepherd. For he knew that in the New Law there is only one Priest and that all of us who have been ordained are but syllables of Him who is the Word.

In his sunset years the beauty and truth of the dogma of the Mystical Body burst upon him with a new brilliance. With the directness of the saintly and the simple he pierced to the doctrine's central core and with St. Thomas saw that the Eucharist is the throbbing heart of the Mystical Christ; with St. Paul he saw that each member has the glorious destiny of "filling up in our flesh what is wanting to his passion, for his Body, which is the Church."

Long years ago Frederic Dunne had conceived his role in life to be that of a victim. The concept came from the very nature of the Trappist's existence; being a penitent he has to be a victim; but it was heightened and clarified by Frederic's appreciation of the fact that every priest is Christ, and consequently must be a sacrificial victim. But now with theologians insisting again on the dogma that had lain dormant for centuries, and our Holy Father issuing one of his most moving encyclicals on the truth, Dom Frederic knew more than a rejuvenation; he knew something like divine commendation and heavenly approbation of his past, present, and future. He now taught his doctrine on victimhood with an insistence that was reminiscent of St. Paul.

And yet joy was always dominant in the song of his life and living. Perhaps he showed himself most clearly on the feast of Corpus Christi. Liturgically attuned to every season and feast of the year, the Abbot would grow tender at Christmas, sorrowful at Passiontide, triumphant at Easter, exultant at Pentecost, but on the feast of Corpus Christi and throughout its octave he was simply radiant with what must have been something in the nature of a rapture. To hear him intone the antiphon for the *Magnificat* on this feast was to hear love become articulate. This was one time a son of St. Benedict actualized the caution of the Rule which says "the mind of the singer should be in perfect harmony with his song."

Enemy though he was to all display, for this feast he would urge us to outdo ourselves. The cloister would be ablaze with the beauty of eight huge floral designs, worked out by the monks over the stone mosaics; each emblematic of the Eucharist. Between the designs would stretch long lanes of evergreen. Dom Frederic would plan for all this a good two weeks in advance. "Make the best and most beautiful design you are capable of making," he would say. "But let there be no rivalry, except a rivalry of love. Let every petal you pluck and place in the design, let every particle of evergreen you prepare, be an act of love for Him in the Sacrament of His Love."

As soon as the long vigils ended — Matins and Lauds would end after 4 a.m. and we had been up since 1 a.m. — Dom Frederic would repair to the workroom to depetal roses and daisies, to strip the burning blue of larkspur from its stem, and place fluffy hydrangeas where the designmakers could most easily handle them. At 9 a.m. he would make the round of the cloister to see how near to completion each had brought his design. And for this one day he would depart from his almost Germanic insistence on absolute punctuality in the ringing of bells, and delay the Mass as much as twenty minutes at times.

To study his face as he carried the monstrance that day and to watch him celebrate the abbatial Mass which closed the procession, was to see a man who believed "with every fiber of his being" that God was in that Host.

Unquestionably this feast with its octave was the high point in the liturgical year for Dom Frederic; for the secret of his strength and his saintliness lay in his crystal-clear concept of his dignity and destiny as priest of the Most High God. It was of the priesthood he had talked to Sister Camillus when there was question of his being sent from the monastery because of ill-health at the turn of the century. It was of the priesthood he had written to his favorite sister, Fannie; and which had her offering her life for him and his ordination. It was for the priesthood he had sacrificed his sleep and actually shattered his nerves when a young monk. It was in the priesthood he found his joy, based his life, and centered all his teaching. But it is the victimhood of the priest that explains his living.

St. Bernard has said something about it being a cause for shame to be "a weak member under a thorn-crowned Head"; and that is as good a summation of Dom Frederic's thought as can be given. He was conscious of his membership in Christ and acutely conscious that his Christ was thorn-crowned. He would not be weak.

On the feast of the Conversion of St. Paul in 1947, one of the novices took notes on the short talk the Abbot gave in Chapter as his explanation of the Rule for that day. They run in part:

We are called to study God. Yes, that is our life. To study Him; to know Him. That is our all. But such knowledge leads to love, and love leads us to wish to bring all souls to Him. Yes, all souls! For I say that any religious whose heart is not large enough to embrace the whole world is not worthy to be called a religious. A priest has his parish; a bishop his diocese; but you and I have the entire world for our care.

And the action to which we are called is that of prayer and penance. Oh, prayer without sacrifice may be heard; but prayer with sacrifice is infallibly answered. So let us try to understand what is almost ununderstandable — our vocation. We are called to be united to God. Who can understand such condescension on His part, such elevation on ours? Who can fathom such a mystery of love? We cannot fully understand the vocation to which we are called for we cannot fully understand God. But this much we can understand: we are called to be victims.

Oh, let us make an unconditional surrender of self to God, and seek to do a little more for Him than is strictly required. Let us say: "Lord, you are enough for me; you and your cross."

The cross in some form or other will always be with us. It may come from our superiors. It may come from our brethren. It may come from our body or our soul. Certainly it will come from ourselves; for our self-love is our greatest cross. But let us bear all crosses cheerfully, and thank God for each; for each is a blessing.

The stones in a river bed are worn smooth by the water and by rubbing against one another. We are made perfect by the constant friction of the events of our daily lives. If we would only abandon ourselves entirely to God, and let Him do with us what He wants, we would make rapid progress in sanctity. He knows what is best for us. He has chosen this superior, these companions, this weather, this affliction of the body, this desolation of soul just for us at this moment. Let us thank Him for it all.

In our relations with others, if we will sacrifice our self-will, our own convenience, our own comfort, and try to serve, we will be happy. If we are always the first to give way to the wishes of others, are quick to acknowledge ourselves in the wrong, or to have committed a fault, we will be at peace, and there will be unity in the community. Patience will not be needed in heaven, but so long as we are on earth we must practice it. Be patient with each other, with ourselves, and with Divine Providence.

These are the little sacrifices, the little crosses which will make us great victims if we accept them cheerfully and bear them gracefully. We may never be called on to make a big sacrifice. Our life is made up of little things; but in itself it is no little thing. We are called here to avert the wrath of God; to be lightning rods. We are called here to arrest the justice of God from falling on a sinful world. We do it by prayer and penance. The spirit of penance and reparation should permeate our whole lives and penetrate our every deed. But let us ever remember that what little penance we do is of no value before God, unless it is done in union with Jesus, who alone can satisfy Divine Justice.

God, in His infinite mercy, has called us here from all parts of the world, from all walks of life, for one purpose: that we may be united most intimately to Jesus in His work of restoration and salvation. We are here to sacrifice ourselves with Christ — *Cum Christo cruci affixus sum!* Yes, we are on the cross; but we are on the cross with Christ — and that makes all the difference. That explains why cheerfulness and joy are the dominant note of our existence. God loves a cheerful giver. All that He wants is our love. No matter what we may accomplish, if it is done without love, it will not be acceptable to God. "My son, give Me thy heart." Surely we can give Him that. We can do that one thing He asks. We can love. He asks us to love Him with a special love. "Peter, lovest thou me more than these?" He asks that of us as He asked it of Peter. And our answer should be the same; for "we can do all things in Him who strengthens us."

Put all our trust in Him. Get rid of that accursed confidence in self. "*Sine Me, nihil potestis facere.*" God has said it. "Nihil" — Nothing, nothing at all. But if we have humility, God cannot resist us.

Don't say: "I can't do it"; for that is un-American.

As you see, the man was not a rhetorician. He spoke ex tempore; and, as he admitted, he gave out just what was in his heart. But we came from Chapter with those basic ideas of the need of humility, diffidence in self but great confidence in God, trust in the power of Grace, and God's anxiety to give us all we need, firmly fixed in our minds, and the conviction that the Trappist life was a life of love for God and neighbor proved by generous self-sacrifice in union with the infinitely generous self-sacrifice of Jesus Christ churning in our hearts.

Many people wonder what is the secret of the Cistercian life, the well-spring of Cistercian living. Dom Frederic is the answer to both; for he was incarnated, pulsating, vibrant faith. He believed — and he made each of us believe — all that is professed as belief in the *Credo* of the Christian. Once we realize that faith, far from being blind, is really vision, the sublimity of the Cistercian life and living ceases to be a mystery. St. Paul has said that "Faith is the *evidence* of things that appear not." It is a gift which gives sight; a gift that endows us with X-ray eyes, enabling us to pierce appearances and *see* the invisible. That is why it can be said that the vitality of one's faith depends on the clarity of one's vision; and that the purpose of Cistercian living is not only to seek God, but to *see* Him. Frederic Dunne gave us the clearest vision possible to human eyes when he focused our gaze on the humanity of Christ Crucified.

His eloquence came from his life more than from his lips; and it was an eloquence that commanded the sincerest form of tribute — imitation.

Like all humans Frederic Dunne was a tissue of seeming contradictions. That last sentence in the brief instruction given above was something of a favorite with him. He used it on practically every one of his sons — and very early in their acquaintanceship. As soon as he detected in anyone the slightest sign of hesitancy to carry out an assignment, he would smile and ask with seeming irrelevance: "What are the last two syllables in the word 'American'?" The newcomer would have to pause a moment before answering, but soon would look up and perhaps with a sheepish grin reply: ". . . i — can." The Abbot's smile would then brighten, his eyes twinkle more rapidly, there would be a brief sign of the cross by a hand with a ring on it, and as the newcomer would kiss the ring he would hear: "Be American."

It was impressive, but it could be deceptive to those who did not know the man intimately. For while his was a virile patriotism, it was untouched by any shadow of nationalism. He would insist that we be conscious of our Americanism when it came to getting things done, but with greatest insistence he would teach that among us "there were neither Jew nor Greek, slave nor freeman . . . but all were one in Christ Jesus" (Gal. 3:28).

Perhaps the most palpable paradox about him was the sparkling radiance of his cheerfulness as he led the most austere of lives.

A fairly long list of his seeming contradictions could be drawn, but it would be pointless since all are reconciled by that vibrant faith of his which really was some sort of vision. For example: cloistered though he was behind Kentucky hills, far removed from the world's teeming millions, he was more conscious of what nations were doing to God and what God was doing to nations than any statesman or international politician. He knew that clinched fists shook toward heaven in hate from more lands than that whose flag flaunts the stupid symbol. And that realization shook him. He would quiver from head to foot as he bared the very heart of sin and showed us its essential evil by pronouncing it puny man's outrageous effort to destroy God. With the thorn-crowned Christ silhouetted against the gloom of Golgotha, who can question his analysis? But what gave him some of Gethsemani's original agony was the realization that for the first time in man's long history of unappreciativeness and infidelity a movement was afoot, and had already captured a country which was really a continent, in which the very brazenness of hell was seen on earth as Communists proposed a faith whose power derived from the monstrous vision of man without God.

Atheistic Communism pains the man of faith not only because of its lack of reverence and respect for God, but because of its total lack of respect and reverence for man. These deluded ones are harming themselves more than they are harming religion; for while striving to be like gods they are falling far short of being anything like men. Dom Frederic grieved for them and for Christ; for he had a double vision: he knew himself to be part of sinful, suffering humanity and longed to be ever a greater part of the suffering Saviour of men.

The world would speak of the Iron Curtain, but Dom Frederic could see only a wooden cross. On it the Mystical Body was writhing in agony. He himself was on that cross with every nerve wrenched and every sinew twisted. As the Red Menace crawled farther over Europe the Abbot wondered if the agony of the Mystical Body had just begun; wondered if the three hours would stretch to seemingly endless aeons as a thousand horrors worse than any yet endured crowded in on the Mystical Christ before the final, triumphant "*Consummatum est.*"

One day as I held out a little holy card on which was depicted the head of the dying Christ I saw tears fill the gray-blue eyes of the Abbot and spill down his lined and sagging cheeks. Then he looked at me and asked the awful question: "Father, what will happen to men during the Sabbath the Mystical Body must lie in the tomb before its Resurrection?"

That question gives you the answer to his own life and the life he would have all under him lead. He knew what the world needed. As far as in him lay he would answer that need with a clarity no one could question. He would show the world — both the Christian and the Communistic world — *Christ. Nudus sequens Christum nudum* ("stripped of all, he would follow the naked Christ") tells all, not only for the Abbot but for all under him during his abbacy.

His instruction, entreaties, all his endeavors now resolved themselves into the one plea that we show the world not only men of God but the God-Man. He was convinced that it was not Christianity that was needed, but the Christ. So he would have us show men the poor Christ — for most men are poor; the humble Christ — for not many men are mighty; the simple, hard-working Christ — the Galilean whose hands became calloused from work and whose limbs grew weary from labor — for men must earn their bread by the sweat of their brows. He would have us show the sin-sodden world and the countless humans so laden with lusts the Christ who was all-pure. He would have us be the Solitary of the desert and the lone Man of the mountaintops that prayer and praise might be lifted to the Father all the day long. But more, he would be, and he would have us be the Christ who suffers — for he well knew that life for many is nothing but a throb of misery and a pang of pain. It was the Victim and even the victimized Christ he would have us be — for he was convinced that if any century needed a Saviour it was ours.

That is why his final form was what he tried to give us as our only form — the shape of Christ on the cross or the Cruciform.

CHAPTER FIFTEEN

Caritas Christi Urget Nos

ÈRE LOUIS PERROY has plumbed a depth of Divine Providence when in his *Ascent of Mt. Calvary* he tells us that "God is jealous of the image He imprints on the souls of His chosen ones." That truth explains much that is otherwise inexplicable in the lives of saints and the saintly from Adam and Eve to Maria Goretti and Frederic Mary Dunne.

By the time Gethsemani's Lord was seventy he could have written a chapter very like the famous Chapter 11 of St. Paul's Second Epistle to the Corinthians, wherein he tells all he suffered for the sake of his apostolate. The resemblances between Dom Frederic and St. Paul extended to surprising limits. It is reported that the Apostle of the Gentiles was not much to look at physically. He was short of stature, bleary-eyed, bald-headed, and had a pronounced paunch. Much the same could be said of Dom Frederic. Years in the printery had so strained his eyes that in later life they were weak and often watery. Most of his hair had gone long before he was removed from the priorship. And a strange abdominal growth gave him a most peculiar paunch. Then, to quote Dr. Michael Joseph Henry: "X-ray examination showed . . . he had extensive arthritis in and about the right shoulder."

I can tell you it was so extensive that the Abbot could never lift his right hand any height without excessive pain, and it caused him to carry his head continually far in front of its natural position.

Sister Camillus had kept after him about his duodenal ulcer until, in 1912, he allowed Dr. August Schachner to operate. But in 1945 the Abbot told me he had not known a natural or a normal functioning of the alimentary tract in all of forty years. Now came heart trouble. Dr. Henry gives the professional diagnosis as "marked sclerosis of the aorta"; but that technical term tells us nothing of the pain that shot across the Abbot's chest from time to time, of the dyspnea which so often had him gasping, of the dizziness and the dancing black spots before his eyes. . . . Yes, he suffered, suffered intensely from his body; and how aptly he could have borrowed from Paul and concluded his summary with "Besides these outer things, there is my daily pressing anxiety, the care of all the Churches" (2 Cor. 11:28).

By that phrase he would have meant more than Gethsemani and her stepdaughter house, Our Lady of the Valley, in Rhode Island. He would have meant even more than the foundation he was planning for Georgia and the future foundations he foresaw as inevitable because of the steady influx of postulants to the Kentucky mother house and the constant stream of applications from the boys who were pushing the Nazis back to Germany and sweeping the Pacific clear of the Japs. He would have meant the anxiety that was pressing on his heart for the Cistercian houses in the countries torn by the war. He had exhausted every possible approach in his efforts to reach the Trappists in Central Europe who had suffered so outrageously under Hitler, while the plight of the Trappistines in Japan hung over his heart. This solicitude came not only from his keen consciousness of his oneness with every member of the Cistercian Order, but more precisely because of his sharp sensitiveness to the sufferings of Christ.

When Catholics were persecuted in Poland Dom Frederic knew a physical as well as a mental anguish. When the Reds martyred thirteen Trappists in Spain, Gethsemani's Lord gloried in their having died for Christ, but because he lived in Christ he felt and shared in some degree their death agonies. It was not that he was psychic, but only that he was a mystic with the sound, sane, sober, sensible mysticism of the Mystical Body of Christ. That fact is revelatory. It shows just how jealous God the Father and God the Holy Ghost are of the image of God the Son stamped on the souls of their chosen ones. It was a jealousy that had the Holy Ghost perfecting by the Gifts of Wisdom, Knowledge, and Understanding the virtue of faith He had implanted in the soul of Frederic Arthur Dunne at Baptism.

John of St. Thomas has explained this marvel of divine jealousy by saying that "although Faith goes straight to God in His Reality, it shows us Him afar off and, as it were, in shadows and enigmas. When perfected by the Gift of Understanding, however, it penetrates, even here on earth, into the profundity of God and removes partly those shadows. When further perfected by the Gift of Wisdom and various forms of the *sensus Christi,* which are further expressions of the same precious Gift, we can, in a certain sense, feel, touch, see and taste God in Himself."

Not many of us appreciate that wondrous endowment called "the gift of faith." Few realize that it gives us a possession of God. Too many of us envy the Blessed in heaven without ever reflecting on the fact that our possession of God by faith is just as real as theirs by vision. The sight of God is different, but not the reality of His dwelling in our hearts; for the truth of the matter is that if we but soften the brightness of the mysterious picture of the life of glory, we get a very accurate picture of our life of grace. It is the same reality that lies at the root of the heavenly life and the supernatural life on earth. It is true, of course, that above we will possess it unveiled and without the possibility of losing it, while here below we have it clouded, and the unhappy possibility of losing it is ever present. But apart from the difference between faith and vision, the possession is just as actual. God dwells in our hearts just as really as He dwells in the hearts of the Blessed, and we love Him with a love that will not change after our entry into heaven. "Charity never dies," says St. Paul. And that is why I have so often said that heaven begins on earth or it will never begin at all; for the just man, the saint on earth, performs the same triumphant acts of knowing and loving through which he will possess God for all eternity in heaven. Such is the profound reality of the supernatural life on earth, and is seen best in that *sensus Christi,* that Christ-consciousness, John of St. Thomas talks about and which Abbot Dunne manifested so clearly in his later life.

Every soul in the state of grace knows and possesses God. But, as St. Augustine has remarked, in some this knowledge is of an indiscriminate kind, a lifeless sort of thing; while in others it is vital, vibrant, and, as it were, experimental. Therein he has expressed the difference between the man who takes his talent and wraps it in a napkin and the faithful servants who so work with their endowment that they double it. Granted that faith is a gift, it nevertheless remains true we, by our co-operation, can and should enhance it. Our knowledge of God is too often a cold, speculative, abstract thing, which produces only sterile ideas. Whereas what we want and can have is the living, throbbing knowledge Dom Frederic had, a knowledge that reaches out and touches Reality.

I am not speaking of flashes of feeling or surges of sentiment. I am not referring to those moments of ecstasy which come to every religious from time to time; moments in which God is actually seen to be our All. In such moments we realize clearly that the Creator is the whole secret of our existence; that we really belong to God; that, in very truth, we, as individuals, have a work to do for the Divinity which is our specific life's work. These are sublime moments which come to every religious from time to time. But they are only moments and, more often than not, they are emotional moments.

What I am speaking of is deeper, better, more commonplace, and much more pleasing to God. It is the virile, vital, ardent faith which gives one that *sensus Christi* which enables us not only to "see His Blood upon the rose, His Cross in every tree," but to have the sparkle in every human eye say the same thing to us as does the flicker of the sanctuary lamp, telling us God is here.

That was the *sensus Christi* Frederic Dunne had. Now for one who was in no sense a profound or professional theologian and who had made his studies from books compiled by men who were so hypersensitive to the effects of the Protestant Revolt that they stressed in their treatises *De Ecclesia* the divine organization rather than the divine organism; the authority inherent in the hierarchy rather than the life of God implanted in the baptized; the primacy of Peter and the infallibility of the pope rather than the indwelling of the Holy Ghost as the soul of the Mystical Body of Christ and the sublime dignity of mortals being His members; for such a one, therefore, to have as keen a Christ-consciousness as had the Abbot speaks eloquently of his life of prayer. It was this which brought to his mind an illumination that was far from natural and to his heart a quickening that could come only from the Holy Ghost. It tells us also how jealous God was of this soul and how that jealousy spurred the Spirit on to work in that soul. It gives us also the key to something which often mystifies: the radiant joy of the saintly.

We find these chosen ones literally steeped in sufferings physical, mental, interior, and exterior. Yet we always find them joyous and radiating that joyousness. The secret lies in this *sensus Christi* which is the culmination and quintessence of faith; a faith which gives knowledge; a knowledge that begets love; and a love which creates joy. It is this joyful love and love-filled joy that explains the activities of the saints and the saintly; for they, with St. Paul, can sum their lives up in the words: *"Caritas Christi urget nos."*

I can never forget the morning I saw this "consciousness" in operation and had to marvel at its practicality and down-to-earthness. The Abbot was sending quite a few CARE packages across the seas. A young secretary hurried in with the question: "To whom are these packages going, Reverend Father?" He was looking, of course, for names and addresses. He got more than he was looking for when the ever alert Abbot, who was struck by the way the youngster had worded his question, allowed his heart to speak and gave the true but surprising answer: "They are going to Jesus Christ."

Undoubtedly Abbot Dunne was a contemplative.

That statement is going to be challenged by those who have been brought up only on modern commentaries of John of the Cross and who know something of the ceaseless activity of Dom Frederic Mary Dunne. How could anyone so Martha-like, so continually busy about so many things, be also Mary? He began with sixty-eight souls — for each of which he knew himself responsible to God Almighty. He saw that number grow until at his Golden Jubilee of entrance, he was responsible to God for one hundred and forty-five souls. What a continual outpouring of self such a charge entails! How could he be a contemplative?

Add to this his monopoly of all the offices necessitating contact with the outside world. Watch him hurry down to Georgia to look over sites for his first foundation. Then see him arrange every detail of the preparations and supervise the packing of everything from patches for clothing to the gold vessels for the altar and even the altars themselves. Once that foundation is made, follow him out to Utah, watch him change into a hunting outfit to talk real estate with Mormons; go with him on three such trips and finally feel the impact on his mind and heart when $100,000 is named as the purchase price for the William C. Parke Ranch, an eighteen hundred acre estate, hidden high in the Rockies, eighteen miles east of Ogden and two miles from the tiny town of Huntsville. Plunge with him into the thousand details of preparing all the necessities for this foundation; then realize that almost immediately he had to go through the same distracting experience for his third foundation on the Luce Plantation at Mepkin, South Carolina, and was deep in negotiations for a fourth foundation in Upper New York when he died; then you may admit that his love for Christ was goading him on, but you will ask how he could ever be a contemplative.

And if you could sit at his elbow as he slit his mail and sped through it finding therein everything from intricate moral cases demanding almost immediate solution to contracts for buildings in Georgia and Utah, for books in New York, Chicago, and Milwaukee; applications for admission from all over the world. If you could stay and listen to the continual stream of interruptions from the phone and the door and hear him offer consolation to everyone and advice to most, you would wonder even more why I say that he was a contemplative.

But had you read something of Teresa of Ávila or reflected a bit on the life of St. Paul, you would not be so surprised. Better still had you seen as the English woman, Caryll Houselander, has seen that "Christ is man's contemplative" and drawn all the logical consequences from that truth which she so rightly labels as "almost blinding in its tragic glory," you would understand. God looked at man and loved him and became like him, taking on Himself the shape and color of man's sins; that shape being the shape of the cross, and that color, the stripes of His blood. Thus does this young woman tell the whole story of what is contemplation and what are its consequences. When one gazes so steadily and with such love at another that he becomes like that other, you have a contemplative. That is what happened to Frederic Mary Dunne. All unwittingly Miss Houselander has depicted Dom Frederic as she expertly paints a contemplative as "standing not before a painted Cross, but before blankness, himself cruciform; his arms extended, his hands empty, his naked feet still, his heart broken open for His Lord's sorrows. . . ." Intuition has led this woman to the truth that the real contemplative "becomes like the Crucified on whom he looks always with the dark eyes of Faith; for man cannot help becoming like one on whom he gazes steadily forever."

What intrigues me more than Miss Houselander's intuition is the pen picture she drew so perfectly of Dom Frederic as she went on with her description of the true contemplative saying: "He is stripped of everything. He is empty-handed; because arms stretched out wide enough to embrace the Crucified reach out to a width that embraces the world, and hug nothing to self because the hands which open to receive the nails must let go their hold on everything else."

How perfectly that "embrace of the world" and that "hugging nothing to self" portray Gethsemani's Abbot! He had seen that it is only the selfless man that God can use and he had resolved to be useful to God. His very occupations, which so many falsely imagine would have precluded all possibility of his becoming a contemplative, were the very things that saved him from all delusions about genuine sanctity and actually brought him to the perfection of the contemplative life; for that perfection is found in intense faith generating a love which is *ardor*.

It was the Cistercian, William of St. Thierry, who said: "Your vocation is to be united with God . . . to possess Him in the union of perfect love." Dom Frederic fulfilled that vocation, for very early in life he realized with St. Thérèse that sanctity lies not in the prayer of quiet nor even in the quiet of prayer so much as in fraternal charity; not in mystical experiences, but in union with the will of God. But he knew if he was to be a saint he would have to be a contemplative saint; and I believe it was God the Holy Ghost who, in jealousy, gifted him exceptionally and led him to the truth St. Augustine has expressed so perfectly and pithily when he says a contemplative is one who "lives in the Word." *"Vivere in Verbo"* are the Saint's exact words.

The resolve "to live in the Word" turned Saul of Tarsus into that torch of truth we call the "Apostle of the Gentiles"; it changed Augustine, the self-indulgent rhetorician from Tagaste, into the self-denying Bishop of Hippo and the Church's Doctor of Grace; it made the ever active American Frederic M. Dunne into a true Trappist and a full-blown Cistercian contemplative. For it is Etienne Gilson who has described the latter for us when he says "the Cistercian Contemplative is a lover who is so deeply in love that he forgets himself entirely as he devotes all his energies to the Beloved." Frederic Dunne was always on the go, but never without his invisible Companion; always preoccupied, but never oblivious of his ever present Beloved; always busy about many necessary things, but never without constant leisure for the one thing necessary. He had literally countless works in life, but only one lifework: and that was the continual contemplation of the God who continually contemplates man.

Hence his life became cruciform; his living became Christ; his every heartbeat nothing but a further "filling up of those things that are wanting to the Passion." And he knew the joy which prompted the Curé d'Ars to make the startling statement that "Even if there were no Heaven or hereafter, it were Heaven enough to serve God here on earth."

Merciless is the only word that describes Dom Frederic's attitude toward his body in his later years; but merriment is as good a word as any to describe the atmosphere in which he moved and the dominant tone of his soul.

He knew his physical condition, especially the action and reaction of his heart, better than any physician. He realized that mountain heights and rarified atmosphere would never be any part of a specialist's prescription for him at his age and in his condition, yet he hurried to Utah and the mountains with all the enthusiasm of a boy on an outing. Again and again he boarded trains for the West, heedless of his heart's ache, mindful only of that heart's love for Christ.

After the news of his first foundation in Georgia had broken to the world, offers of land and invitations from bishops came in from all over the country. To some of us many looked really enticing, but Dom Frederic, dominated by the same principle that had him foregoing gifts in Florida and California to make a purchase of a plantation in Georgia for his first foundation, had eyes only for the most Christ-desolate spot in the land. When the Bishop of Salt Lake City sent his invitation, the Abbot of Gethsemani knew his searching was ended. I wonder if he had an inkling of all this spot would take out of him before he had converted it into an oasis for God and the soul of man. I'm inclined to think he did, and that is why he so often mumbled *Caritas Christi urget nos* — "The love of Christ goads me on."

Daily, his constant cry of "So much to do, and so little time in which to do it" took on new meaning. He became something of a commuter between Salt Lake City and Gethsemani as he searched for the ideal spot where he would build his third Powerhouse of Prayer.

During this shuttling a thought-provoking revelation was made. I believe that most of us could go to Salt Lake City and return with pity perhaps for the beliefs of the Mormons and some degree of marvel at their material successes in the land and the striking architecture of their temple. Dom Frederic returned with an observation that not only reveals his soul, but searches ours: "That land seems possessed by the devil." Because so God-conscious, Dom Frederic was also keenly devil-conscious — a phenomenon not rare among the saints. How often I saw it manifested.

When a postulant who seemed rightly and even richly endowed

for the Trappist life suddenly left, I was curious enough to ask the Abbot what had happened. "The devil, Father. Just the devil," was his only reply. When feast days approached or the time for the annual retreat neared, we always heard the exhortation from our Abbot to "Be on your guard. The devil will be more active now than ever."

Moderns, and especially modern Americans, fail to give the devil his due. But not so Dom Frederic. Most people would see nothing but ignorance, bigotry, and spite in some of the actions perpetrated in and around Conyers shortly after the Trappists had arrived in Georgia, but Abbot Dunne had keener vision. He said: "The devil does not like our new foundation." If the history of man, from the fall of Adam and Eve to the rise of Communism, tells us anything, it tells that the devil has no love at all for anything good. So it was natural for him to exert his preternatural powers against this all-out effort on the Abbot's part to establish another Silent City of God on this ever noisy and quite pagan continent.

I suspect now it was this devil-consciousness that contributed to Dom Frederic's extraordinary patience with and tolerance of what we would call human contrariness and out and out cussedness. He saw deeper and realized that more than man was making the particular mess and more than human perversity was at work in the human before him. It was an insight all superiors need and no confessor should be without. It was an insight that could aid the nervous millions in our neurotic age and bring some semblance of peace to shattered souls. If, like Dom Frederic, we gave the devil his due, we would come to a much clearer understanding of the much misunderstood complexity which is a human soul — the battleground where, as Shakespeare says, God and the devil fight.

Those who might marvel at this devil-consciousness in a man so patently in love with God, fail to appreciate the possessiveness of all love and the jealousy in every lover of every possible rival. Because they love so fully, saints are fully aware of Satan. That is why Gethsemani's fifth Abbot was so alive to the maneuvering of Lucifer and his minions.

He was keenly concerned about what was happening to Christ in Europe, Asia, Africa, Australia, and the two Americas, but never more concerned than about what was happening to Christ in his own monks. That is why, despite the almost overwhelming growth of Gethsemani's community, he still maintained practically every office which entailed contact with the outside world. These few letters will give you an idea of some of the details he carried in his head lest any of his sons be bothered with them.

Herman Erhart, president of the General Exterminating Company of Louisville, had been visiting Gethsemani since he was a boy of ten; for his father, an architect from Alsace, was an intimate friend to Edmond Obrecht. When Dom Frederic became abbot, this intimacy of father and son did not lessen, for the new Abbot had many projects for which the elder Erhart could draw plans, and many favors the younger could do, as is revealed by such a letter as the following:

May 18, 1938

Reverend and dear Father Frederic:

Following the instructions in your letter received this morning, I have contacted the Kentucky Stone Company from whom the crushed limestone was ordered and am advised by them that the order was forwarded immediately by them to their plant in Irvington, Kentucky, from where it has been or will be shipped at once. They said they would check the order and let me know their findings. I also contacted Montgomery Ward Company and was advised by them that the total amount due on your order, including freight to Gethsemani, was $36.67, and that if you would send a check made out to Montgomery Ward Mail Order House in Chicago and mark it "Attention of Mr. Dowdle, Catalogue Manager," it might and probably would facilitate the shipment of your order.

I have located a coffee roaster, description of which follows: It is a number 221 Royal, guaranteed in good working order. The bean drum measures 46½ inches in circumference by 22 inches in length; approximately the size of a ten gallon drum, which I feel would be large enough for your purposes. The agitator operates by electricity, but the heat is derived from gas or gasoline burners, which you will have to furnish and install; however, I do not think this is a very serious matter. Let me know if this seems like it will meet with your approval, and then we will go into the matter of the cost.

How is the dam coming along? I was disappointed you did not mention it in your letter. Mr. Turnheim 'phoned and I told him about the spillways. He seemed to want very much to have one in the center of the wall and expressed a desire to run down next Monday. I do not know if this will suit me, but in the meantime you can tell me if it will suit you. My father may want to come along on the next visit also.

Mr. Vance called today and asked about the relative level of the water head (when the dam is full) as compared to the elevation the pump will be on down at the Monastery. It is necessary for him to know this in order to figure the friction against the size of the pipe. If you will please let me have this by return mail, I will appreciate it.

I am glad the bricks arrived O.K. and hope that they came up to your expectations.

I had a call from a friend today who wants to know where he can buy, locally, the cheese that you make. I have tried to remember the name of the dealer you mentioned, but have been unable to do so. Will you kindly let me know by return mail so that I can give him the information Saturday.

With best personal wishes to you and yours, I am

Sincerely your friend,
Herman.

From the same source comes a breathless note which indicates the pace Dom Frederic set and held.

Dear Rev. Fr.:   Dec. 6, 1939

It was with considerable chagrin that I noted on my return

to the office this afternoon that the sash had never been picked up by the truck company. I have just notified them not to come for it since I intend to send it by the L and N. I am forced to believe that your attitude toward the truck companies is the correct one. I am putting the sash in my car and taking it to the Station myself so I will be sure it gets out this evening.

I called Stanley this morning and told him that since I was not going down this week-end, I would like for him to take along the Crozier Crook, as well as some apples, as you requested, and he assured me this would be done.

I am sorry about the delay on the sash, although I am in no way responsible for it. I assure you it is the last time I will depend on the truck company for rural delivery.

Yours in haste,
Herman.

P.S. Just returned from the Freight Station and am enclosing the Bill of Lading.

In lighter vein, but with equal speed and pointed insistence the Abbot once wrote to a J. Everett Hagan, a long-standing friend of the monastery who was employed in the New Haven, Kentucky, office of the Southern Bell Telephone and Telegraph Company:

Dear Mr. Hagan:

We are again isolated from the world; but this time, too much so! We have a fine telephone system, but cannot call anyone — not even the Exchange!

The only thing that is absolutely reliable about it is the monthly bills. These never fail, even if everything else does.

I was in New Haven [Kentucky] a couple of days ago with a distinguished visitor, and his remarks about the condition of the telephone poles and wire between the two points were anything but complimentary. I wonder when something to improve the appearance of both is to be done.

In the meantime please restore communications between our telephone and the Exchange as soon as possible; for it is usually when this is out of order that we need it most.

Yesterday we were called, and only a very little noise of the bell was heard. Later on we could not call you. Today again we were just able to distinguish a signal from you, but although we have tried many times to call you, we have been unable to establish contact. Please help us out at once — if not sooner!

Very truly yours,

The Abbot

Just to show that literally everything in the monastery was under the care of the Abbot, I cite from two letters sent in 1942 by the president of the Gans Chemical and Supply Company. The first runs:

Dear Father Frederic:

I received your letter this morning regarding your washer, and have turned your inquiry over to Mr. Herndon Mercke of the Jefferson Woodworking Company of this city, who will quote you on a rebuilt washer.

You need have no hesitancy in doing business with this firm, and it is my personal opinion that it would be to your best advantage to purchase a rebuilt machine rather than to try to shop around for a used washer.

In fact, it is almost impossible to obtain anything in the line of used equipment for a laundry today.

With sincere thanks for the best wishes sent me at Easter, and assuring you of my willingness to be of service to you at all times, I remain

Very truly yours,

Albert J. Gans.

The second says in part:

. . . I found the cuttings at the office when I returned this morning and want to thank you for them.

With this letter I am sending my personal check in the amount of nineteen dollars ($19.00) covering the case of eggs you sent in last week, and also the lard and other things which I secured myself at Gethsemani.

Under separate cover I am sending you a Burpee Catalogue, and between pages 8 and 9 you will find two packages of Celtuce seed. This is the seed I spoke to you about some time ago, and the directions are on the package as well as on page 8 of the Catalogue.

Would appreciate your giving this new vegetable a trial in your garden, and letting me know how it turns out.

In the package with the Catalogue and seeds, I have also put a sample of the black iron metal from which the molds can be made.

I am sorry I could not go ahead with the molds without putting you to all this trouble, but I feel certain that you understand what conditions are today.

Thanking you for all your many kindnesses to me, I remain

Very truly yours,

Albert J. Gans

The same type of correspondence was being carried on with men in many other cities in the country.

When he first took office, Dom Frederic had but one secretary, and he was so "amply sufficient" that he was also given the task of keeping the books. By the time the Utah foundation was made, the Abbot had three men working on the books and five different secretaries — no one of whom was ever fully caught up on his work. His ordering of Christmas cards tells the story pointedly. In 1935, his first year as abbot, he had three hundred made, and found by New Year's that he had overestimated his need. In 1945 he ordered fifteen hundred and before the end of December was telling his secretary that for the following year he was to secure at least two thousand — and that number did not prove quite sufficient.

Despite the enlarged secretariate, the Abbot himself could be heard tapping his typewriter immediately after the night Office, which ended daily about 4 a.m. And this is a sample of the letters that came from his own hand. It is to a Sister of Charity of Halifax, who had a brother in the monastery.

Nov. 2, 1939

My dear Sister: —

It was with pleasure that I heard from you again. . . .

In the first place I beg you to thank the good Sister who is sending us the stipends, and tell her that the requested Masses were promptly arranged for, and are probably already said or about to be said. We always treat such good donors as friends and benefactors, and as such they are included in our prayers.

One expression in your letter was most gratifying, namely this: "I want the Sisters to be real religious." This requires no comment. True religious are saving the world today; let us take every precaution to be in that heavenly Salvage Corps. The commotions on earth will pass; history will continue to repeat itself. But Eternity is so long. This reflection is ever ancient and even new; we can never ponder and ruminate enough on such truths of our Religion.

We are still hard at work on our new novitiate building. Postulants are ever applying, but no one of them ever thought of asking: Have you room for me? There will be room for forty novices soon, I hope.

Your brother is quite busy. He is never without a heap of papers on his desk and seems too busy to worry about the world or anything in the world. Trappist atmosphere has this sort of anaesthetic effect: it deadens the sensibility to things and doings outside the enclosure walls, with the one exception — of praying for them.

Please remember me to your dear Mother and all the family. Begging God to bless you and your work. . . .

One that is a bit more informal, yet ever maintaining that happy combination of the human and divine is this one of August 8, 1941, to the same Sister:

My dear Sister Mary Clare: —

I wish to begin a little note, but it will be a first class miracle if it is finished as promptly as I would wish, and first it is to offer you every good wish and the promise of my poor prayers for a happy Feast Day for you.

Many thanks for the offerings forwarded for the Novena. God grant that you were filled with many graces throughout your holy retreat; for our intentions included this as well as the recovery of your good Sister.

We are as busy as usual with the thousand and one things that join to make up our day: harvesting, repairing buildings, retreats, etc., etc., added, of course, to the monastic duties of Rule. You mention something of the cares devolving on you from the management of 38 Sisters; sympathize also with one who must be responsible for 135!

Your good brother has begun to say the Masses from August 6th to the 15th; I am sure God's graces are being offered you abundantly. I am happy to add that your brother's health is good; that he is as busy as ever; and that he is delighted with the news of the family.

I was privileged to assist at the Eucharistic Congress in St. Paul and found it an immense stimulant to Faith. In fact, the entire affair was one grand Act of Faith in the Real Presence. But I was very glad to be at home again. The place for a monk is in his own monastery!

Asking for a special share in your fervent prayers, and begging the good God to bless you, your work, and all your intentions, I am

Faithfully yours in SS Corde Jesu,
Fr. M. Frederic, o.c.s.o.

Examples of such personal touches and genuine kindnesses, so characteristic of the man, could be multiplied almost endlessly. One other which comes to mind at the moment was told me by Albert Gans of the Gans Chemical and Supply Company. One summer day when delivering some goods Dom Frederic had asked him to obtain, he brought his tiny niece Sally along with him. Though only eight at the time, and no bigger than a good-sized doll, Sally was a lady and could not enter the cloister. So Abbot Dunne left his ever crowded desk and went out to the gate to talk to Mr. Gans.

Having just returned from Our Lady of the Trinity in Utah, the Abbot was full of his subject and talked enthusiastically about the location, describing the mountains quite graphically. Little Sally, who was listening to it all, suddenly broke in with "Oh! The Rockies. How I'd love some rocks from there to show Sister at School. She talked about those mountains last week."

That was all that was said by the little girl; yet, when the Abbot returned some three months later from another trip to Utah, he called Mr. Gans and told him to be sure to bring Sally with him the next time he came out, for he had brought some rocks from the Rockies for her!

It was such incidents that caused Doctor J. Raymond Boone, who had taken care of all the dental work at the abbey for thirty-five years, to exclaim: "I've known a lot of religious in my life — Brothers, Sisters, monks, and priests — but never have I come across another like Frederic Dunne. He is the most human saint one could imagine!" And this humanity was felt not only by those within the monastery, but even by outsiders.

One example lies before me in a carbon of a letter addressed to Mary Maginnis, a Louisville girl who had a brother in the Gethsemani community. Mary had just joined the WAVES, I believe, and had been ordered to Boston, Massachusetts:

May 21, 1942

Dear Mary:

I am sorry to have missed you when you were here with your dear Grandmother and your good brother the other day. I could not get away at the time. When I called up Brother a bit later he told me you had just left. The good God so willed it, no doubt.

Now I learn from your brother in the Community here that you are going East, and that you have no friends or relations there. I would like, therefore, to suggest a couple of names, good people who will be able to help you secure proper accommodations and friends. I take the liberty of recommending you to [here he gives the names of the two]. They have a brother in our Community, and are well known to me. As you also have a brother with us, I am sure they will take pleasure in recommending to you those things a young girl needs in a strange city.

I will send to both of them a copy of this letter, so that you will not take them by surprise.

Begging God to bless you and your trip East, I am

Sincerely in SSmo Corde Jesu,

fr. Frederic, o.c.s.o

Abbot.

Small wonder so many hundreds boasted of having the Abbot of Gethsemani as personal friend. There was more than natural sociability and human kindness behind all his kindness and sociability. It was that *sensus Christi* that had him seeing Christ everywhere and in everyone. It was the *Caritas Christi* which was having the same effect on him as on St. Paul . . . *"urget nos!"*

CHAPTER SIXTEEN

His One Work

L ATE one night at the end of January in 1948, Captain James Kinnarney, retired president of the Kinnarney Detective Agency, received a wire from St. Louis asking him to be at the Union Station in Louisville when the night train from Missouri pulled in the following morning. It was signed simply "Father Frederic." That was enough for the Captain. He had known Frederic Dunne from the days when the young boy from Florida was vice-president of the school on the hill called Gethsemani College. The years had brought a deepening of affection and a heightening of esteem. There was practically nothing the Captain would not do for Gethsemani's Lord. This request to be at the Union Station was considered an honor by the Captain, but it bespoke some change in the Abbot's original plan, and that puzzled Kinnarney.

As the detective stared at the wire his mind went back over the years to the day he first met Frederic Dunne. The Kinnarney twins, his sons, had been at the monks' boarding school. They did not like it. So almost daily they would send pathetic letters home to their mother begging to be taken home since they were not getting enough to eat. Mrs. Kinnarney was touched. But the detective in the Captain came to the fore. One morning he suddenly invited his wife on an outing. They boarded an early train and were at Gethsemani College by dinnertime. They were invited to sit into table with their sons. As dish after dish, heaped high with good substantial food was laid before them, a merry twinkle stole into the Captain's eyes. Hardly a word was spoken during that meal, but every now and then one of the twins would lift a furtive eye toward his father and then turn his gaze back to his plate and grin sheepishly. The Captain rode home that evening with his wife alone as company. No more pathetic letters were received by the mother. But what had impressed the Captain more than the heaped-up dishes of health-giving food was the affable and alert young Vice-President. Years of police work had sharpened the Captains eyes for character. He recognized something intangible, yet obviously exceptional in the young Father Frederic Dunne.

He smiled now as he thought of the sheepish looks of his sons that day, but then his expression changed as he recalled how worried he had been as the two boys grew to manhood and went their separate ways in life. He felt sure that he owed it to the prayers of Frederic M. Dunne that each of the twins had a priest of God by his side as he was dying and went to meet God fortified by the Sacraments. Captain Kinnarney knew he could never be grateful enough to God for that, nor could he ever fully manifest his appreciation to Frederic Dunne.

As he held the telegram he ran down the years with Frederic Dunne. He found them filled with pleasant memories. A slight smile of satisfaction lifted the corners of his lips as he recalled the look he started in the Abbot's eyes the day he handed him a check large enough to pay Mercer Harbin for his Honey Creek Plantation outside Conyers, Georgia, where Frederic Dunne was to make the first foundation of Trappists from an American house. That was genuine joy to the Captain. He smiled more broadly as he thought of the way the Abbot had caught his breath the day the Captain, after listening to the Abbot's account of Utah and the price demanded for the Parke Ranch, had quietly said:

"I believe I can take care of those Mormons for you, Reverend Father." When the Abbot tried to protest the old Captain had silenced him with "Shh! This is not a donation I am making; it's an investment. You have to pray for your benefactors, don't you? Well, all the money in the world won't be enough to give you if you win for me and Mame and all the rest of mine what you won for the two boys. Reverend Father, there is only one thing I want in life, and that is a happy, holy death. You can get it for me."

The Captain was eighty-two years old that spring, but had more energy than a man of sixty. He looked at the telegram again, shook his head, and told himself he had made a very wise investment even as he had greatly helped a man he loved more and more each day that he lived.

The following morning the Captain was at the depot before the sun had burned away the haze that so often hangs over Louisville on a winter's morning. When the L. and N. train came in ten minutes late, the Captain stood at the gate and watched the stream of passengers coming toward him. He spotted two Roman collars but no Abbot Dunne. He suddenly began chewing his unlit cigar and wondered at the strange tension that was seizing him. The stream was thinning now. He grew more alert. He saw that the porters had practically cleaned away the line-up of bags, but midway up the platform he thought he recognized the little black bag the Abbot always carried. Before he had covered half the distance he saw the Abbot bending over to fetch it himself. Kinnarney not only took the bag from the Abbot's hand, but supported the ashen-faced Abbot with his arm.

"O.K. Reverend Father. Easy does it," he said, and guided the prelate down the platform toward the gate. "The car's parked out in front. The starter's an old friend of mine."

"You have friends all over, haven't you Captain?" said the Abbot in an attempt at a pleasantry.

"There's only One I want, Reverend Father. And He lives above. He's the only One who really counts." The Captain was darting an eye every now and then at the Abbot as he led him through the teeming areaway toward the side door and his parked car. What he saw frightened him. Pain was written deeply on every feature. The whole countenance was ashen-gray and this foreboding color was heightened by the purple of the lips. When the Abbot made no further comment the Captain went on: "Didn't sleep so well last night, did you?"

As the Abbot climbed into the car, he laid his hand on his breast in evident distress. The Captain slammed the door behind him, hurried around to the driver's seat, and pressed the starter. It was only after they were away from the curb that the Abbot answered. "I did not sleep at all last night, Captain."

"Rocky road?"

"No. . . . But yesterday at the Consecration of the Bishop of Belleville I had a little experience. I think it would be wise for us to stop at St. Joseph Infirmary for a few minutes on the way out."

Very little more was said that morning as the Captain threaded his way through dense downtown traffic. It irritated him somewhat to find it running heavy all the way out to Eastern Parkway, and even on to the hospital itself.

"We'll go in to Sister James Marian. She'll get Doctor Abell or Doctor Henry for me."

The Captain knew now that the Abbot must be a very sick man. For him to make such a concession as stopping at the infirmary was tantamount to saying he was deathly ill. All the way out from the station the Captain had been thinking of the plea he had made in public before the entire community at the celebration of the Abbot's golden jubilee of entrance into the Order. Being called on for a few words, he had stepped up to the microphone and begged the Abbot in the name of the community and all his friends to be kind enough to them to take it a bit more easily, to spare himself. For a split second the Captain feared he might have overstepped the bounds of propriety, but the applause which burst spontaneously from all sides and was sustained for several minutes, told him that no matter what propriety said he had spoken the community's mind.

It had done no good. The Abbot had only smiled that morning and gone right on driving himself mercilessly. It was only four months after that plea that the Abbot, while on his way to Louisville, had been in an auto crash which gave him a five-inch fracture of the skull, a cut over the eye which necessitated six or seven stitches, and in which the Abbot himself felt sure some broken glass had been left, while his whole right side from shoulder to hip was black and blue from the violent manner he had been thrown against the door. For a time it was feared both his arm and some ribs had been broken. That he had suffered a brain concussion was obvious. But what had he done about it? Allowed a country doctor to stitch his face and bind his wound, then insisted on being driven back to the monastery, forty miles away, where he immediately plunged into his usual round of work despite his bandaged head and aching body. A few months later a neglected cold turned into pneumonia, and the congested lungs did not help the ailing heart. Yet, despite all complications, when the Prior brought Communion to his room each morning, the frightfully sick Abbot would throw back the covers, pull his feverish body out of bed, to kneel on the bare floor to receive his God. In less than two weeks he had thrown off the sickness and was at his desk again working full time.

Kinnarney shook his head and chewed his unlit cigar as memory after memory crowded in on him. He recalled the morning he had met the seventy-three-year-old Abbot on his return from one of his many trips to Utah and heard about the hemorrhage he had suffered from the rarefied atmosphere of the Rockies.

"Why don't you let someone else go there for you?" the Captain had asked in a complaining tone.

"If anyone has to bleed for that foundation, I'm the man," had been the laughing response.

The Captain had spoken to medical friends and learned how dangerous it was for a man in the Abbot's condition to be going to Utah. He had passed the information on to the Abbot as tactfully as he could only to be put off with: "God will take care of us, Captain. And don't forget *'sine sanguinis effusione, non fit remissio.'*"

"Whatever that means," had been Kinnarney's response.

"It means I've got to keep on going west until things are settled, and that you are to stop worrying about me."

As he now carried the little black bag up to the desk on the corridor known as "First East," Captain Kinnarney was planning. If he could persuade Sister James Marian to get the Abbot to bed, he would see that he stayed there for some time.

He did not have to use any persuasion. The alert little nun took one look at the Abbot's face and lips, led him to a private room, told him the house doctor would be right over for an examination and she would leave word at the front office to have Dr. Irving Abell or Dr. Michael Joseph Henry drop down the minute either arrived. She then nodded to the bed and said: "I'll be back as soon as you're in bed."

She closed the door softly, then turned to find the Captain waiting for her. "Sister," he whispered in his best conspirator's tone, "as soon as he gets in bed I'm going to steal his clothes. That's the only way we'll keep him here, and he needs a rest."

The little nun smiled. This old ex-detective always lifted her spirits with his obvious loyalty and manifest love for his friends. "Let us see what the doctors say, Captain. I'm sure they will order a rest."

"He never pays attention to doctors, Sister. Help me now to

perform a larceny. When the doctors are fussing about him, you open the doors in such a way that I can slip into the clothes closet unseen. I'll take all the consequences."

Both Doctor Abell and Doctor Henry were in the Abbot's room before the house doctor had completed so much as a cursory examination. They asked very few questions, but before long the electrocardiographing machine was rolled in, the Abbot's wrists, ankles, and chest greased, and the metal tabs attached. Soon he was being wheeled to the radiological department for an X ray of his heart. Shortly after noon the two doctors were in the room again, and in his ever quiet voice Doctor Abell was telling the Abbot that he would see him in the morning, that he was to take things very quietly, and get as much rest as possible. What neither doctor told him was that the electrocardiogram looked worse than a seismogram after a long and violent earthquake, and that the enlarged X ray showed a pronounced sclerosis of the aorta. And what the Abbot did not know was that by the time the doctors had left his room his clothes were in town at a cleaner's who had been told there was no rush and that he was not to yield them up to anyone save James W. Kinnarney.

Among them — the doctors, Sister James Marian, and Captain Jim — they managed to keep the Abbot in bed for almost five full days. But there was to be a profession at Gethsemani the second week in February, so the Abbot commanded the Captain to get his suit from the cleaners or there would be a scene. The doctors had not officially discharged him, but from past experience they knew that the most they could do was give the best medical advice possible, then pray some of it would be followed. Absolute quiet was their persistent prescription. The Abbot took it all smilingly.

Perhaps he meant to follow some of that advice, but he was hardly back at the monastery when things began to happen which had him not only seeing the hand of God but quite clearly hearing His voice. The community at Gethsemani was larger than it had been when he made his two foundations, and applications for admission increased daily. Now, Bishop Emmet Michael Walsh of Charleston, South Carolina, after repeatedly inviting the Abbot to come to his diocese to look over the state for a possible location for his third foundation, suddenly sent word that he had an estate which would satisfy every Cistercian requirement, and it was offered as a gift. Remembering what Georgia had cost Captain Kinnarney and the staggering price demanded for Utah, the Abbot blinked at the Bishop's message and silently blessed God. That communication ended all quiet for him.

In March, 1948, he was in South Carolina, talking to the Bishop and visiting Mepkin Plantation, the Luce estate, thirty-five miles north of Charleston. What he saw and heard was enough to precipitate a real cardiac crisis. Over seven thousand acres of land, most of it virgin forest, surrounded the loveliest home he had seen in years, set in a veritable fairyland Nature had formed from water, trees, and trailing moss. He found himself farther from the nearest small town than he was in his beloved Gethsemani. He saw limitless possibilities in the site for a community to support itself by real manual labor as it lived far from the haunts of men as St. Benedict prescribed, and gave ceaseless glory to God as Citeaux ever aimed to do. He returned to Gethsemani all aglow and gave such an account to the Chapter that the vote to accept it was all but unanimous.

In April he was in Charleston again to talk with Claire Boothe and her husband Henry Luce, who had flown down from New York to meet the Abbot and discuss the donation.

Despite the excitement over the proposed foundation and the ever engrossing work at the mother house, the Abbot was not allowed to forget the condition of his heart. For every morning as he bent over to lace his shoes, he would find his ankles swollen; often during the day he would have stabbing pains across his chest and the arm to wrist syndrome; and more than once we found him bleeding profusely from the nose. This had some of us fearing a cerebral hemorrhage.

But on he went.

In May he was in Utah to make the canonical visitation, which took him all of a week. In June he was in Rhode Island for the visitation of the Valley. From there he went to Upper New York to view an estate a certain Mr. Richard Worrell was anxious to give the Abbot for a fourth foundation. Frederic Dunne went over every inch of the property and even paced off the attic, showing Mr. Worrell how he could convert it into a dormitory for two dozen Trappist monks. Despite the heat of the season and the enticement of the Adirondacks, the Abbot would allow himself only one day for this business. He hurried back to Gethsemani to plunge into preparations for the centennial celebration of the New World's Protoabbey, and to take care of the ever mounting details of his house and her daughter houses.

July went in a fever of harvesting, building, buying new farm equipment, endless negotiations about the two foundations actually made and the two that were in prospect, and plans for a flight to Europe to attend the General Chapter of the Cistercian Order.

Sunday, August 1, found him with every day of the month accounted for; but before Wednesday's dawn he had made his final accounting to God of all the days of his seventy-four years.

It was heart trouble, as the doctor who acted as coroner, said; but it was not the trouble of the heart he thought. It was not exactly because that heart was overburdened with cares that would tax the strongest human heart, that it had stopped; but rather because it had overflowed with a love for the Divine. It was the heart trouble of the saints.

That is the final solution of the mystery of his life which was presented by his mysterious death.

Because that is the solution, I have mentioned few of his innumerable friends, given next to nothing of his mountainous correspondence, written little of his material accomplishments in the thirteen years of his abbacy as I have drawn up this memoir of his days.

In the little more than decade of years that he reigned, there was little inside or outside the monastery that remained as it was when he received the miter. Under Dom Edmond Obrecht Gethsemani was little more than a name connected with a very colorful character. It was really the Abbot of Gethsemani who was known the world over, and not Gethsemani. But under Dom Frederic Mary Dunne, the opposite occurred: the abbey became known to millions who never even heard the name of her Abbot. By the publications he sponsored, the Cistercian Spirit was at last recognized and appreciated in America and elsewhere for what it really is: not love of penance, but penitential love; not stern asceticism so much as true mysticism; not escape from life, but the capture of real life and living; not a distortion of Christianity, but an all-out dedication of every power of body and soul to the perfect imitation of Him who said He was the Way, the Truth, and the Life. As Etienne Gilson put it: "this is a recovery, not a discovery; a life of an elite who maintain the full spirit of the Gospel in a world unable to bear it; a life of joy which expands and perfects all the faculties of the soul in the contemplation and praise of God."

Frederic Dunne made "Gethsemani" and "Trappist" household words not only in America, but elsewhere; and he did it in such a way that while the words still maintained much of their mystery, they spoke clearly of the world's great twin realities: sin and the sinless Son of God — love of self and sacrificial selfless love.

But even this great achievement was not his life's work; it was, like all the others, only another great work of his life. From earliest years in the monastery he knew he had only one life's work to do; as he matured under the expert guidance of the Holy Ghost what that work was became ever clearer.

He would be the first to chide me were I to list as the accomplishments of his abbacy the four foundations he sponsored — two of which he actually made, and two which he prepared for in the immediate future; the phenomenal rise in personnel from sixty-eight when he was blessed and given a crozier to over two hundred and sixty when his body received its final blessing; the transformation of the abbey's yard from ramshackle huts and houses into modern steel and concrete buildings for poultry, pigs, and a prize herd of Holsteins; the modernization and mechanization of the farm which doubled the harvest and rendered the community more and more independent and self-sustaining; his renovation and remodeling of the massive monastery itself and its far-flung fields. No, he would not bear with me were I to speak of these as the work of his abbotship; for just as he knew he had only one life's work, so he knew he had only one work to do as abbot.

There was much of the medieval knight about this modern monk. He was a Galahad questing the Grail with all the white fire of a determination that would never cool. He had unsheathed his sword that August afternoon in 1894 when he crossed the old wooden cloister to enter Gethsemani's novitiate and had deliberately flung away its scabbard. He became a crusader whose one crusade was to conquer self and spend his life on Calvary helping the Man on the Cross complete His Passion and save the world.

That was the work of his life and his life's work. He did it; but he would never approve of my telling the world about it were I to call it *his* work. He might permit me some few words were I to do as I have tried to do: show it to have been the work of God, especially of God the Holy Ghost, whom he so often called "the forgotten Person of the Blessed Trinity." He would never allow me to say he had climbed the ladder of humility to arrive at that love which is found at its summit, the love which casts out fear; but he might not interrupt me were I to say that the Holy Spirit led him up the seven steps of sanctity and had him continually confronting the Christ.

Whether he would allow it or not, that is the truth; and that continual confrontation brought about a configuration. But not without what I have hinted at all along — his heroic co-operation. Frederic Dunne had not only heeded the Master's invitation to follow Him, he had achieved what St. Bernard said is the purpose of that following: he had overtaken Christ. And nowhere is this shown more clearly than in the tiny smoking compartment of the *James Longstreet* as it stood idle outside Knoxville behind the panting engine that seemed anxious to be on its way with the *Flamingo* to the deeper south.

To die far from his beloved monastery and his many loving monks; to die stripped of the black and white of the habit he had worn so lovingly and loyally for over half a century; to die on the leathern couch of a modern Pullman instead of on the straw and ashes of the medieval monks; to die without the oil of Extreme Unction or the Wheat and Wine of the Eucharistic Viaticum; to die alone, though the father of over two hundred and fifty sons; to die alone as the heat haze of a sweltering dawn hung over a strange city was to take the last white turn on the road less traveled by and meet the Christ — for it was to die a death like that of Jesus: alone, in desolation and darkness, in a silence that was eerie, with nothing but a drop of gall on one's lips.

It was the last purification made by a God jealous of the image of Christ in a sterling soul. It was a death, however, precious in the sight of the Lord, and hence, one that was met in the presence of the Lord of Life and the Mother of Mercy surrounded by adoring Cherubim and Seraphim. That little smoking compartment was crowded as Dom Frederic Dunne's great heart broke from a love no human heart could hold. His life's work was done — he had put on Christ.